In Pursuit of Performance

Johns Hopkins Studies in Governance and Public Management
Kenneth J. Meier and Laurence J. O'Toole Jr., Series Editors

In Pursuit of Performance

*Management Systems in
State and Local Government*

EDITED BY PATRICIA W. INGRAHAM

The Johns Hopkins University Press

Baltimore

The Johns Hopkins University Press
2715 North Charles Street
Baltimore, Maryland 21218-4363
www.press.jhu.edu

Library of Congress Cataloging-in-Publication Data

In pursuit of performance : management systems in state and local government /
edited by Patricia W. Ingraham.
    p.   cm.—(Johns Hopkins studies in governance and public management)
    Includes bibliographical references and index.
    ISBN-13: 978-0-8018-8568-6 (hardcover : alk. paper)
    ISBN-10: 0-8018-8568-X (hardcover : alk. paper)
    1. Government productivity—United States. 2. Management information systems—
United States. 3. United States—Politics and government. I. Ingraham, Patricia W.
II. Government Performance Project (U.S.)
    JK468.P75157 2007
    352.3'82130973—dc22   2006022816

A catalog record for this book is available from the British Library.

Contents

Preface

The data and other information reported in this book were collected by the Government Performance Project in the years it was located at the Maxwell School of Citizenship and Public Affairs, Syracuse University. The project was funded by The Pew Charitable Trusts. The current iteration of the Government Performance Project, which now focuses only on state governments, is located at the Pew Research Center in Washington, D.C.

This book describes as clearly as possible the processes used by the Maxwell project and its experts. Two points need to be emphasized, however. The first is that the assessment processes described here were not carefully controlled academic exercises. The Government Performance Project was a joint activity in which academics and our methods were paired with teams of journalists (from *Governing* magazine) and their methods. We made concerted efforts to ensure that empirical rigor was the rule of the day, but in the final analysis, parts of the process were subjective. To provide crisp and succinct explanations and accounts of all the processes would entail detailing each step in a five-year process, for each level of government and for each member of the project team (at several points in the project, that number approached 100). Neither our records nor the focus of this book permit that. In addition, the journalistic method of analysis is far different from that used by academics. We sought consensus with our journalist partners consistently and attained it most of the time. The reality is, however, that the processes were not tidy, and a full description would probably read more like a diary than an objective academic exercise. Given the subjective nature of some of the processes, the precision that some external observers undoubtedly desire is simply not possible. Furthermore, this book focuses on lessons learned rather than more narrowly on methods employed. The descriptions we do provide are as precise and careful as we can make them, given the nature of the endeavor.

The second point deserves some emphasis: this edited volume is about lessons learned from the Government Performance Project, but that is only part of the story. We focus on the ways in which state and local governments have approached management systems, how the various configurations of those systems look, and how governments have—or have not—made use of management systems as a tool in building capacity for long-term performance. The book examines each of the levels of government studied over the years that the GPP was housed at the Maxwell School. It also examines the extent to which the models and methods of analysis applied in the GPP may have utility for governments not included in the GPP surveys. Each of the management systems—financial management, human resource management, information technology management, capital and infrastructure management, and managing for results—is examined in some detail by the faculty experts responsible for the GPP work.

Because there has been such an extensive interest in the GPP in both the United States and abroad, the book discusses criteria-based assessment and its various applications to management systems in a way that can be useful for those considering assessment of their own governments. The cost and time involved in the GPP process make it unlikely that the exact methods will be replicated, but a broad understanding of the principles of practical application of criteria-based assessment remains useful. Furthermore, the data collected by the GPP are a rich source of descriptive information. Because the GPP surveyed all fifty state governments twice, as well as the largest city and county governments, in this book we are able to provide more extensive description of management in state and local governments than has ever before been available.

Because of the large numbers of governments studied, the book is also able to provide a useful analysis of the differences in ways governments perceive and pursue management and management systems as policy tools for improving performance. The book moves beyond previous work in describing "successful" governments—that is, governments with high capacity and therefore high performance potential—in ways that permit their comparison with those governments at the other end of the scale.

The chapters that follow are intended to inform a broad base of readers about lessons learned from one extensive effort to study management—viewing management not as an isolated technical activity but as a critical capacity without which effective performance is unlikely to occur. Again, although the scope and depth of the initial Government Performance Project will most likely not be replicated by any government or institution, the lessons learned are often transferable. The continuing interest in the broad area of developing management capacity for state and local governments—only heightened by events such as hurricane Katrina—suggests a well developed audience for these lessons.

Over the years, many people contributed to the success of the GPP. All of the authors in this book were expert analysts in the project who performed the original analyses and made significant contributions throughout the process. Many others who contributed are noted in the first GPP book from the Johns Hopkins University Press, *Government Performance: Why Management Matters* (with Philip G. Joyce and Amy Kneedler Donahue). For the present volume, special thanks are extended to Jen Cook, Maria Fernanda Ariceta, Jordie Hannum, and Tyler Overstreet for their invaluable assistance. The staff of the Alan K. Campbell Public Affairs Institute, Bethany Walawender and Kelley Coleman, provided excellent assistance at every step.

The editor and authors sincerely hope that the material we provide here will serve to better inform government managers and executives, as well as the analysts and students who study them, about the basic architecture and content of key management systems. We also hope that the examples presented here provide replicable models of success—and paths to it. Above all, our goal is to illustrate again how and why good management matters to good government and better performance.

In Pursuit of Performance

CHAPTER 1

Studying State and Local Government Management Systems
Why We Need to Do It

PATRICIA W. INGRAHAM

State and local governments in the United States are, in many ways, the bedrock of American democracy. They deliver most of the services citizens see every day: garbage collection, road maintenance, bus and other transportation services, libraries, and police and fire protection. They play a critical role in the lives of American youth. They provide widely available health and mental health care. They directly provide for the elderly who can no longer care for themselves. Thomas Jefferson argued that in the American system local governments would be most effective and accountable because they are closest to the people.

Today, state and local governments do remain closest to the people, but they have also become enmeshed in laws and rules made by other levels of government and the courts. Because they are the end of the line for intergovernmental funding—which is increasingly complex—they are frequently confronted with mandates to deliver services that strain both financial and human resources. This is true in the cases of Medicaid, education, and homeland security, to name just a few.

There are many reasons for the often unhappy relationships that have resulted. The United States is one of the few advanced nations in the world whose national government creates service delivery mandates for other levels of government without providing adequate funding to ensure the capacity for such delivery. The dramatic policy debates about health care, national security, or environmental policy, for example—policies with enormous implications for state and local governments—do not happen in Sacramento, Albany, or Bismarck. They take place in Washington, D.C. The outcomes of the debates, however—the nitty-gritty of service delivery—are most evident in state, city, and county governments. For their part, state governments often create additional laws governing personnel, financial management, and other daily management activities. Civil service laws are one example.

In this already complex web, unpredictable revenue streams and increasing demands for services are also important influences. Since the terrorist attacks of September 2001, state and local governments have incorporated a frontline role in national security into their daily activities. State-approved driver's licenses, for example, have become a first line of defense in identifying suspicious persons. The need for greater care and scrutiny in the approval of these licenses is evident, as is the need for additional resources to support the more intensive activity. More recently, Hurricane Katrina demonstrated the critical role that state and local governments play in terms that are now indelibly impressed on the nation.

When cities, counties, and states do a good job of delivering services under these conditions, it is rarely noted. Citizens *expect* their garbage to be picked up, fire service to be readily available, and potholes to be repaired. Service delivery is supposed to be routine. The energy it takes for such routines to be done well is often overlooked. Managing multiple service contracts, hiring and retaining quality employees, treating citizens equitably and well while retaining control of budgets and costs and finding creative solutions to complicated and increasingly intergovernmental problems are serious challenges. State and local governments meet them on a daily basis.

At the same time, the roles played by state and local governments in policy design and implementation continue to be important. The consistent stream of "new federalism" ideas from Washington and elsewhere argue that the governments closest to citizens need to be more involved in public policy, but that is often more rhetoric than reality in the follow-through. State and local governments argue that federal policy makers fail to understand the enormous burdens placed on lower levels of government by federal mandates and rules and the constrained policy choices that often result. While both arguments are robust, they are rarely engaged in the same arena.

The dance between state and national governments, and the appropriate balance of power between them, may appear to be a modern phenomenon. It is, of course, as old as the constitutional debates. The nagging nature of the underlying questions, however, is fundamental to democracy. A deep-seated distrust of the ability—or willingness—of states to act equitably and competently has repeatedly spurred federal assumption of power and responsibilities. The inability of the national government to deliver all that it promises without the assistance of state and local governments rebalances and constantly energizes the debate.

In the context of this broad sweep of theory and values, it is important not to lose sight of important characteristics of state and local governments. First is the obvious reality of the enormous variation among them: they are homes to state and local politics, priorities, and economic and social capabilities. Political priorities in Minnesota are not the same as those in California. Politics and political priorities in North Carolina's Mecklenburg County are different from those in Monroe County, New York. The landscapes on which federal, state, and local priorities interact are shaped by multiple—and sometimes unpredictable—forces, and the outcomes of national policies are firmly nested in these variations.

The variations, in turn, are related to the government's ability to deliver services effectively. It is this quality—the capacity to manage resources effectively in pursuit of performance—that is explored in this book. The extent to which state, city, and county governments are able to muster their management resources well frames and underpins the reality of everyday service delivery. Its significance lies, in fact, in its mundane nature.

Governmental capacity can be defined and described in many ways. It is, quite clearly, the basic ability of governments to fulfill the responsibilities of democratic governance. It is the ability to use public resources wisely and to target them to desired objectives. It is the ability to manage programs and people effectively. And it is the ability to evaluate or assess whether goals are being met. All of these capacities link to performance in some way. Without question, they are present in different configurations and to different degrees in state and local governments. Some municipalities have developed the capacity well. Others have struggled. In 1993, for example, the National Commission on the State and Local Public Service noted "a growing consensus among both citizens and public officials that state and local institutions of government need to drastically improve their capacity and performance if we are to meet the challenges of our rapidly changing economic and social systems."[1]

The struggle to maintain financial stability is enormous. The National Association of State Budget Officers sounded a note of alarm in 2002: "Nearly every state is in fiscal crisis. Amid a slowing national economy, state revenues have shrunk at the same time that spending pressures are mounting."[2] The same pressures are felt at the county and city level. County executives across New York noted in 2003 that the continued rise in mandated health care costs would demand substantial tax increases every year for the foreseeable future. In 2006 the Pew Charitable Trusts reported that, despite revenue exceeding forecasts in forty-two states in 2005, "money is still tight and the overarching challenge for officials in most states is to meet competing demands for spending."[3] Even in cases where it is substantial, therefore, management capacity will be pushed to its limits in the next decades.

The Significance of State and Local Management

State governments have been called laboratories of democracy, but the term could be applied to local governments as well. There are about eighty-seven thousand state and local governments in the United States.[4] These include cities, counties, school districts, townships, villages, and water and sewer districts, to name just a few. Jurisdictions commonly overlap; a municipal water district may include a large part of a county, a city, several towns, and a village, all of which have distinct political authorities and budgets. Critical activities such as economic development frequently cannot be undertaken without mutual cooperation and formal agreements. Some jurisdictions are forbidden by state law from providing certain services, which are reserved for other units. Counties in New York, for example, cannot be housing providers. As Ann O'Bowman and Richard Kearney observe, the explosive growth of special single-service districts is one outcome of these restrictions.[5] The existence of such districts, while permitting a broader range of activities and flexibilities, adds another layer of complexity to the task of managing government.

State and local governments are also notable for the diverse governance arrangements they represent. Arrangements for levels of top elected officials' authority (strong mayor versus weak mayor, commission, or professionally managed governments, for example; or gubernatorial authority to appoint top officials versus popular election of other top officials), length and frequency of legislative sessions (the Nebraska legislature, for example, meets only every two years), the role of appointed professional managers (city and county manager governments, for example, versus strong mayor or county executive governments), the size of the legislative body, and other differences mark the panoply of state and local government units. There is significant discussion and debate about which form or forms are most effective, but for purposes of this book it is enough to note that the diversity is substantial.

Despite this diversity, important challenges facing state and local governments are common. Health care provides one important example. For the past two decades, rising health care costs have been identified as a significant problem for every level of government and every sector of society. Summarizing the findings of the National Commission on the State and Local Public Service a decade ago, Frank Thompson observed that "no other policy sector has been such a potent source of fiscal stress at the state and local levels."[6] He details the broad range and complexity of state and local involvement in this policy area:

> [States] license physicians and other health care workers to practice.... They determine whether a hospital can add to its physical plant.... [They] greatly affect the supply, nature, and geographic distribution of human resources, facilities, and equipment in this sector.... States also mandate certain practices by private health insurance companies, encourage, or even require, employers to provide health insurance to their workers[, and] regulate what hospitals can charge for their services.... States and localities also function as providers and insurers of medical and nursing home care, directly delivering care through public hospitals, health departments, and clinics. Through Medicaid and other programs, states pay providers to serve certain categories of people.... The above description of "health care" does not include other services closely related to public health—safe water and environmental protection and regulation, for example.[7]

There is no better indication of the importance of services provided by state and local governments than the response to the terrorist bombings of September 11, 2001. The demands on fire, police, medical, and other emergency management were massive. The levels of coordination that were required demonstrated in frightening detail the fragile web of connections in the services and supports that make life or death differences for citizens. In 2005, Katrina reiterated these lessons.

Management Capacity and Performance

Performance—or, more accurately, improved performance—has been the underlying objective of most government reforms of the past several decades. As a goal that is readily understandable by citizens and elected officials, performance is hard to beat. It suggests more attention to cost, urges movement toward a focus on alternative strategies of service delivery, asks whether there is duplication and redundancy in government activities, and emphasizes improved transparency in government operations. Fundamentally, however, the bottom line of performance reform is the bottom line. Performance reforms have frequently been accompanied by budget cuts, downsizing, and substantial reorganization of government structures and agencies. Effectiveness—or success—has been viewed in terms of dollars saved and positions cut.

This book takes a different perspective. It reports on the findings for state and local governments from the Government Performance Project, a six-year analysis of management systems at all levels of government.[8] The working assumptions about performance in the GPP are as follows:

- Improved performance does not happen on demand. Performance is not likely to occur in the absence of fundamental organizational capacity. The creation of this capacity in government is long term and is based on institutionally based systems and activities. One important component of this capacity is management, which, in this analysis, requires strength and capability in five critical management systems: financial management, capital and infrastructure management, human resource management, information technology management, and managing for results.
- There will be variations in capacity across the systems, within one government, and across governments.
- Critical attributes of these management systems can be described, measured, and compared. (See figure A.1, in appendix A to this volume, for the schematic of the assumptions.)

There are important caveats. The GPP analysis did not measure performance per se; rather, it analyzed and measured one component of performance's foundation—management systems. Although the analysis argued that management systems are a platform for broader performance, it did not consider all of the critical elements of governmental performance; nor did it measure policy outcomes. In the end, then, the GPP provided the ability to distinguish between well-managed governments and governments that needed improvement, but this is clearly only one important variable in assessing government performance. The five management systems studied—financial management, capital and infrastructure management, human resource management, information technology management, and managing for results—are core management functions found at all levels of government. They were chosen after extensive consultations with government managers, academics specializing in public management, and other experts in the field. Managing money, people, and structural assets is a fundamental responsibility of governments large and small. Information technology management, though a more recent addition to managerial activities, is now crucial to effective planning, evaluation, and decision making. And, at a time when performance-based government is increasingly the norm, managing-for-results systems are becoming critical links between resources and results.

Although the chapters that follow discuss high-capacity or well-managed governments, the reader should not interpret this as a focus on who did the best with the most resources. Rather, the authors describe how governments made management choices, how those choices looked, and how well governments did with available resources. The GPP revealed wide variation in this regard, both across management systems and across levels of government. Indeed, some governments were quite unconcerned with any systems other than financial management. One official, speaking of managing for results, observed that "when times were good, nobody cared, and when times were bad, it didn't matter anyway." As Sally Coleman Selden and Willow Jacobson demonstrate in chapter 4, human resource management was problematic for many state and local governments, owing to extensive procedural constraints, difficulties in workforce planning, or problems with integrating technology adequately into human resources systems. They also provide evidence of rapidly shifting strategies in this management area, however, as managers and elected officials work to adapt to changing demands. B. J. Reed, Lyn Holley, and Donna Dufner's analysis of information technology systems in chapter 5 notes that effective governments have become so only by devising ways around political and budgetary cycles. In that regard, Yilin Hou observes in chapter 2 that many state and local governments continue to experience difficulties in fully embracing multiyear budget plans and in providing adequate funds to deal with many levels of emergency.

Politics and the political setting of the management systems are also not the specific focus of the chapters in this book. Of course, politics matters everywhere. Governors, mayors, and county executives change frequently. The politics and political climate of some states, cities, and counties explain a good part of the highly unionized structures within which management systems—notably, human resource management systems—operate.[9] And budget cycles and the politics they imply cannot be ignored.

The omission of specifically political analysis, therefore, is not intended to suggest that politics does not matter to management. Rather, it is a choice based on limits on resources, potential access, and the likely quality of the information obtained.

For some of the same reasons, the analysis did not specifically examine leadership. Not surprisingly, studying leadership is often interpreted as an intensely political activity. Again in the interest of retaining a focus on management and on working within resource and time limitations, a specific focus on leadership was not a part of the Government Performance Project. Nevertheless, as chapter 7 demonstrates, leadership emerged as a significant influence. Based on document analysis, content analysis, and comparisons between high- and low-capacity governments, the presence and quality of leadership proved to be important factors. Obvious leadership was present in high-capacity settings and was much less evident or absent in lower-capacity governments. It is important to note, however, that because the GPP did not specifically measure leadership, conclusions about its role in building capacity are the results of comparative analyses completed after initial reports on the project were published.

The Government Performance Project analysis was conducted over the period from 1996 to 2003. The first year (1996) involved a pilot study that examined four federal agencies, four states, four counties, and four cities. Those results were confidential and were used solely for instrument testing and improvement and for the creation of the initial GPP Survey (1997). In subsequent years, the fifty state governments were surveyed twice, and the thirty-five largest cities (by revenue) were surveyed once; forty large counties (distributed geographically) were surveyed in the final year (2001) of the survey activity. The final formal year (2003) of participation by Syracuse University's Maxwell School of Citizenship and Public Affairs was devoted to academic analysis and reporting as well as preparation of descriptive statistics from survey results.[10] Additional analysis has been done since that time.

Methodology

How were the results reported in the following chapters obtained? The GPP devised criteria for each of the systems based on literature reviews, expert advising, and effective practice analysis. The criteria for each of the systems are noted in the chapters that describe the systems (see also appendix B to this volume for a complete listing). Here, only the pros and cons of criteria-based assessment are described.

Criteria-Based Assessment

Criteria-based assessments are widely used in both public and private organizations. They are different from—and should not be confused with—best-practice analysis. Best-practice work prescribes specific solutions, actions, and reforms, often from a small set of observations. Criteria-based assessments describe conditions or parameters against which potential performance and capacity can be gauged. Such assessments also allow for the consideration of specific settings and environmental conditions—for example, economic constraints. Well-recognized applications of criteria-based assessments include the criteria used by the Baldrige Award in the United States and the European Foundation for Quality Management in western Europe. Popular balanced-scorecard analyses are also fundamentally criteria based.[11] In all of these cases, bases for comparison—across organizations or governments, across units within one organization, or for one organization at different points in time—are created through sets of clearly stated and widely accepted descriptions of desirable conditions against which the performance, capacity, or behavior of an entity may be examined. Criteria are created from experiential and expert analysis as well as from examination of governments or organizations judged to have been highly effective over time. It is not assumed that there is only one path to achieving the conditions described by each criterion: the assumption is that each government or organization will pursue a strategy most in keeping with its own political and economic environment. In other words, implicit in the assessment is the extent to which governments use wisely and well the resources available to them.

The Government Performance Project analyzed large numbers of governments. Criteria-based analysis made it possible to draw comparisons across these governments and to pursue difference analyses, such as comparing high- and low-capacity governments. These distinctions were useful in analyzing the various pathways to capacity building used by different governments. Each government capitalized on particular environmental strengths or capabilities—or on the strength of an already well-developed management system—to chart its own course. Obviously, those governments determined to have the highest management capacity and the best potential for performance were successful in building capacity in all or most of the systems studied.

Applying the Criteria

Information about management systems came from three primary sources: surveys, documents, and interviews. The academic analysis depended primarily on the written surveys and on documentary analysis, including content analysis. Extensive validation—follow-up interviews, cross documentary checking, and consideration of other reports and analyses when possible—provided additional information. Interviews by journalist partners provided a third information source and check. As the following chapters demonstrate, however, the kinds of information obtained varied from system to system. Some of the analyses—those related to financial management, for example—had the benefit of numbers, statistics, and other hard data. Others—managing for results being the clearest example—were more dependent on qualitative analysis and on analysis of strategic documents.

Grading

The summative assessments of each of the management systems in each of the governments studied were grades from A to F. Because the GPP was a partnership between the Maxwell School and *Governing* magazine, these grades were initially published in the magazine. They reflect the academic-journalist collaboration. Elements of that collaboration included Maxwell ratings based on academic analysis, extensive joint discussion of preliminary conclusions, follow-up contact with the governments for additional information, and collaborative grading sessions. The grades reported in the tables in appendix C to this volume are the product of those sessions. The statistics reported in the following chapters, however, reflect the in-depth analyses that were the critical components of the academic conclusions, including survey results, cross-documentary validation, and second interviews of managers by project staff, for validation and clarification. Although there was agreement between the academic experts and the journalists in well over 90 percent of the cases overall, careful readers will note that there is not a perfect match between the academic results and a small number of final grades. This is the result of the collaborative grading process and the occasional need to align the different analytical perspectives. In the end, the multidimensional perspective permitted a fuller understanding of the governments analyzed but required balancing information sources in some cases.

The criteria were clarified by further specification and learning as the project progressed. An annual practice of feedback sessions to which all participating governments were invited, called Learning Conferences in the project, permitted clarification, fine-tuning, and adjustment of criteria. Because a substantial part of the analysis relied on lengthy surveys completed by employees of the governments analyzed, questions and suggestions about the criteria were consistently offered by those employees as well. Perhaps the most important point highlighted in the first five years of criteria utilization was that the criteria were not absolute. They were statements against which governments could be assessed, but they were also standards that allowed consideration of particular contexts, circumstances, and challenges.

An additional caveat: in the chapters that follow, the most frequent source of information about what governments did and how they did it was the governments themselves. Many observers are critical of the quality of information provided by such self-evaluation. However, in addition to the already extensive information obtained from the surveys, governments' self-evaluations were checked and cross-checked a number of times and from a variety of sources. The people interviewed by the journalists, for example, were not the same ones who completed the surveys. Supporting documents, Web sites, and so on also provided information from a variety of sources. And, as the authors of the following chapters— the area experts—analyzed the information provided, their expertise and ability to compare information from different governments provided a final check.

The downside of criteria utilization should also be noted. Appropriate use of criteria application and analysis is an enormously complex and time-consuming process. The amount of information required and collected is sometimes overwhelming. Yet if multiple perspectives are to be considered and documented, and if the circumstances of individual governments are to be fully considered, several kinds of information and sources of data are necessary. The Government Performance Project had adequate support for the endeavor from The Pew Charitable Trusts. Certainly not all research— or all governments—could enjoy that privilege. This suggests careful front-end selection of which criteria, and perhaps which management systems, are of the greatest significance to the research or to the government seeking to analyze its own capacity.

Using Criteria-Based Assessment to Draw Lessons

The findings of the Government Performance Project described alternative paths to building management capability. During the first five years of the project and since, many governments relied on the lessons and examples of the GPP as a kind of management handbook. Interestingly, those governments assessed as having the highest capacity for management were often the most voracious consumers of lessons learned. Thus, while governments such as Phoenix and Virginia were serving as learning examples for other governments, they were also pursuing ways in which to do better themselves.

There are also important lessons to be learned from the large numbers of mid-level or B-grade governments, because each of them attained that level by demonstrating particular capacity in at least one system. The reasons that single systems—most often budget and financial management systems—were emphasized depended on a number of factors and demonstrated a variety of perspectives on the need for building core management strengths. Some governments viewed strong initial capacity in one or two systems, for example, as drivers toward greater long-term strength in others. Other governments simply did not believe that high capacity in all five systems was necessary to effective government—or was possible, with limited resources.

The grades, therefore, masked substantial variation across governments. Furthermore, the GPP decision to use the governments themselves as the units of analysis masked substantial variation within those governments. This qualifier applied most clearly to highly decentralized governments. Perhaps the starkest example is that Georgia, having abolished its state civil service by the second round of state analyses, had great difficulty in explaining its interesting case in single-unit terms (although it should also be noted that in a 2005 analysis, conducted under the second phase of the GPP, Georgia received one of the highest grades for its human resources system).

The foregoing comments should be viewed as qualifications, not indictments. Overall, the Government Performance Project collected the most comprehensive information about the management of state and local governments ever assembled. The chapters that follow detail five years of that experience in city, county, and state governments. They richly describe the nature of critical management issues in these governments. They also provide excellent insight into how public managers and leaders conduct the daily business of government. The chapters demonstrate that most governments do recognize the link between building management capacity and improving long-term performance and actively work to pursue that capacity—in a word, they know that management matters.

NOTES

1. See Frank J. Thompson, ed., *A Crisis in the Public Service: Managing State and Local Government* (San Francisco: Jossey-Bass, 1993).

2. *The Fiscal Survey of States* (Washington, DC: National Association of State Budget Officers, 2002) p. vii.

3. Pew Charitable Trusts, "State of the States Report, 2006," www.pewtrusts. org/pdf/stateof states report 2006.pdf (accessed February 9, 2006).

4. Ibid., 4.

5. Ann O'Bowman and Richard C. Kearney, *State and Local Government*, 6th ed. (Geneva, IL: Houghton Mifflin, 2005).

6. Thompson, *Crisis*, 31.

7. Ibid., 30–31.

8. The GPP is discussed in the following references: "Government Performance Project State Survey" (A. K. Campbell Public Affairs Institute, Maxwell School of Citizenship and Public Affairs, Syracuse University, data collection 1998, publication 1999; data collection 2000, publication 2001), www.maxwell.syr.edu/ gpp/grade/state_2001/stategrades2001.asp; "Government Performance Project State Survey" (A. K. Campbell Public Affairs Institute, Maxwell School of Citizenship and Public Affairs, Syracuse University, data collection 2001, publication 2002), www.maxwell.syr.edu/gpp/grade/county_2002/grades.asp; "Government Performance Project State Survey" (Syracuse, NY: A. K. Campbell Public Affairs Institute, Maxwell School of Citizenship and Public Affairs, Syracuse University, data collection 1999, publication 2000), www.maxwell.syr.edu/gpp/statistics/ 2000%20City%20MRF%2011.06.02.htm.asp#Mix%20of%20Planning/.

9. For additional evidence, see the final report of the New Jersey Initiative (Syracuse, NY: A. K. Campbell Public Affairs Institute, Maxwell School of Citizenship and Public Affairs, Syracuse University, 2003). The study was funded by The Pew Charitable Trusts and the State of New Jersey.

10. Many articles and book chapters from the students and faculty experts appeared over the course of the analysis, as well. For a listing, see the GPP Web site at www.maxwell.syr.edu/gpp/. In addition to this book, the academic reports include the GPP final report, *Managing for Performance: Management Systems in State and Local Government* (Syracuse, NY: A. K. Campbell Public Affairs Institute, Maxwell School of Citizenship and Public Affairs, Syracuse University, 2003); and Patricia Ingraham, Philip G. Joyce, and Amy Kneedler Donahue, *Government Performance: How Management Matters* (Baltimore: Johns Hopkins University Press, 2003). Brief summaries of each government analyzed and grades for each of

the management systems, as well as an overall grade, were published annually in *Governing* magazine.

11. See Patricia W. Ingraham and Donald P. Moynihan "Creating-Criteria Based Capacity Measures for a Comparative Setting," *International Journal of Public Administration* 9, no. 2 (2006): Robert S. Kaplan and David P. Norton, *The Balanced Scorecard: Translating Strategy into Action* (Watertown, MA: Harvard Business School Press, 1996).

CHAPTER 2

Putting Money Where the Need Is

Managing the Finances of State and Local Governments

YILIN HOU

The Government Performance Project proposition that there is a link between management capacity and managerial performance clearly applies to financial management. Survey results from state and local governments provide solid evidence of the validity of the model; further assessment of the grades given offers explicit insight into the nature of the linkages. Both lead to the overall conclusion that management of government finances should be viewed not as freestanding but as rooted in institutional settings and established traditions.

This chapter reviews the financial management analyses of the GPP. It begins by defining capacity and *performance* as they relate to financial management and then explores the significance of financial management in governmental management systems. The rest of the chapter is a condensed summary of key findings from four rounds of GPP surveys, citing the state of Utah as an example to illustrate the link between strong capacity and high performance. The chapter concludes with overarching lessons and suggestions for improvement in future research endeavors.

Capacity and Performance in Financial Management

Financial management is a dynamic process. Its outcomes are subject to the influence of many external factors that are outside the control of policy makers and managers. In this setting, performance can be random and outcomes unintended. The creation of capacity, on the other hand, is a purposive process. Capacity changes, generally as designed, through a gradual set of activities, permitting self-correction along the way. In this sense, assessment of capacity is potentially more accurate than measurement of direct performance.

Although a high positive correlation can be assumed between capacity and performance, translating capacity into performance takes time. This lag time allows exploration—even prediction—of the direction of the performance vector. A theorized time series trend of the capacity and performance of a government's financial management displays a smoothly fluctuating curve, with performance following capacity. If the financial management capacity of a government is found to be high, measures of performance should rise over time if lower than the median before the assessment or above the median if the high capacity has been in place for some time. For a government with a lower level of capacity at the time of assessment, it can be assumed that performance may be turning sour if it used to be a high performer or that its performance may be already in the poor range if the low capacity has lasted for some time.

To capture management capacity, the GPP financial management surveys targeted capacity indicators in four major domains of governmental financial management: a multiyear perspective on budgeting, mechanisms that preserve stability and fiscal health, the availability of information, and control over financial operations.[1] These branched into seventeen specific management areas, with one criterion for each area.[2] For example, the criterion for domain 1, "Multiyear perspective on budgeting," is "Government makes meaningful estimates of its current revenue and expenditures." Possible capacity indicators for this area include the following: "It is a legal requirement that the government entity conducts revenue/expenditure estimates" and "Revenue/expenditure estimation is a responsibility shared by the executive and legislative branches." In a high-capacity government, these two indicators are mandates of law. In a low-capacity government, they may be mere "practices," to be used at the discretion of incumbent officials or may be nonexistent.

Financial Management as a Foundation of Government Functions

Government cannot function without financial management. Raising revenue through taxation and then spending tax dollars to provide public goods is the basic rationale for critical functions for all governments. The significance of financial management is evident in many ways. The finance department and the budget office are among the most important agencies in all states, for example, their heads having direct access to the governor. At local levels, however small the entity, finance is an indispensable office;

in many municipal governments the business administrator (or manager) is heavily involved in budgeting and spending decisions.

Among professional staff, financial managers are often the best educated, the most professionally qualified, and the most experienced of all officials in state and local governments. Financial managers are among those with the longest tenure, who know the entity inside out and who often serve as institutional memory. Public financial management is the function on which voters and taxpayers focus most of their critical attention and for which legislators have created the most laws and regulations. Finance laws are among the "thickest" and densest in state governments. Revenue and expenditure are also the most heatedly debated items between the executive and legislative branches. Indeed, in some cases, voters have chosen to elect an independent comptroller or auditor as an extra check on both the executive and legislative branches.

Finance is also the public function with the most numerous professional standards issued by organizations like the Governmental Accounting Standards Board, the National Association of State Budget Officers, and the Government Finance Officers Association. Although these standards often appear as "recommended best practices" rather than obligatory regulations, governments are under pressure from the general public to adopt the recommendations for higher transparency, accountability, and ultimately better performance.

Finally, financial management is often the first among government departments to employ new technology. Computerization was applied in the finance function before others, and the most investment from the Y2K "campaign" went into finance-related management areas. Overall, heavy investment in technology has provided financial management with more integrated accounting and reporting systems. Finance is also the first department in most governments to learn from the market. Group procurement and contracting out are already established practices in many governments, for example. As Dennis Strachota and John Peterson note, "The public sector and the private sector share many of the techniques and financial disciplines, more so than ever before."[3] Perhaps most importantly however, the public sector now places much more emphasis on financial planning and control because in a sense all management decisions have financial implications.[4] Management decisions are now made in a more coordinated manner than in the past, with financial managers in direct charge of the control process.[5] The significance of the financial system, in short, cannot be overstated.

Findings from the Government Performance Project

This section summarizes findings from key areas of the financial management section of the GPP survey. In the survey instrument, assessment criteria fell into four domains, each of which covered three to six management areas, in conformity with actual financial operation so that it would be easier for respondents in the governments to follow. Assessment of financial management was conducted with a different grouping of the criteria. The major change was the merging of the original domain 3, "Sufficient financial information is available to policy makers, managers, and citizens," into domain 4, "Government has appropriate control over financial operations"; in addition, a few management areas were moved across domains. The newly grouped criteria are as follows:

Domain 1, "Multiyear perspective on budgeting," covers four areas:

1. timely budget adoption
2. structural balance between recurring revenues and expenditures
3. accurate estimation of revenue and expenditure; and
4. gauging future fiscal impact of financial decisions

Domain 2, "Fiscal health and stability," branches into three categories:

1. effective use of countercyclical fiscal devices
2. responsible management of debt
3. proper management of investments

Domain 3, "Spending control and financial reporting," covers four areas:

1. appropriations control
2. cost analysis
3. auditing
4. financial reporting

A multiyear perspective is the strategic focus of effective financial management, a precondition for fiscal health and stability. Spending control and financial reporting are concrete moves in daily operation to implement the multiyear perspective for fiscal health and stability. Thus these three domains are complementary, forming an organic whole of financial management capacity. Governments that excel in all three domains are high performers.

Multiyear Perspective on Budgeting

The four management areas in domain 1 collectively build toward the multiyear budgeting perspective. Adopting budgets on time prepares a government for the next fiscal year, whereas late adoption necessarily has adverse consequences. Maintaining proper balance between revenues and expenditures, though seemingly an annual issue, exerts a lasting impact on long-term operation. Accurate estimation and forecasts and gauging impacts of current decisions on future fiscal health underpin strategic planning.

Timely Budget Adoption

The budget is the financial plan and operation guide for a government. However, the budgeting process is highly politicized and involves many players and levels of coordination. Bargaining and compromise between the executive and legislative branches, as well as among competing interest groups, are hallmarks of the process. The ability to pass a budget on time for the new fiscal year is an important indicator of the political environment of financial operations.

Survey results show that timely adoption was not a problem for most entities: nearly 90 percent of states and cities adopted their fiscal year 1999 and 2000 budgets on time. There were notorious exceptions: New York State did not pass a budget on time in twenty years. The rate of timely adoption was lower at the county level than for states and cities: from fiscal year 1997 to 2001, it varied between 69 and 80 percent.[6] The survey responses did not reveal the causes of delay among the remaining governments surveyed or whether the delays at the three levels were comparable in nature. Although local politics may be a factor that contributed to late adoption of the counties' budgets, state politics is by no means easier (many scholars would claim it is messier). Furthermore, if we speculate that intergovernmental revenues (from the federal and state governments) may have complicated the process for counties, cities should have been in the same situation. Future research must explore the links between structural constraints, political environments, increasing demand, and other influences on capacity for timely budget adoption. The consequences of this failure also clearly deserve additional attention.

Structural Balance between Revenues and Expenditures

Balancing the annual budget is a legal requirement at the state and local levels. But the task of balancing is easier said than done. Among the fifty states, only nineteen struck a balance between their current revenues and current expenditures; another seventeen states' budgets balanced using carryover surpluses. Local governments, on the other hand, achieved balance uniformly and consistently: for fiscal years 1996 through 1998, the cities on average not only balanced their annual budgets but ended each year with a positive margin both in their general funds (average 1.57% and median 0.88%) and total operating funds (average 2.39%, median 1.81%). The counties on the whole came out with even larger general fund surpluses than the cities. (It is important to note that the time of observation was during the economic prosperity of the late 1990s.)

Revenue and Expenditure Estimation

Adopting budgets on time and maintaining structural balance both require accurate estimates about the volume of revenues and expenditures for the coming year and for future years.[7] Estimates should be conducted each year and updated regularly within the fiscal year. Forty-two states conduct budget estimates covering two or more years. The same number of states update their estimates for the current year two or more times.

Again, there are problems; accurate estimates do not come easily. They can be developed only by well-trained, experienced professionals with the help of advanced computing equipment, using data on many aspects of the society accumulated over time. Budget estimation is a resource-intensive enterprise. Every percentage point increase in estimation accuracy is achieved with millions of investment dollars. Nonetheless, this process is an important contributor to financial management capacity.[8]

From table 2.1, the following inferences can be made. First, for fiscal years 1996 through 1999, the fifty-state average accuracy for both revenue and expenditure of the general fund and total operating fund is fairly high. If we take a 5 percent error rate as the benchmark, the average accuracy was better than the benchmark. Second, all of the average and median rates for revenues are positive and those for expenditures are negative. This consistent pattern of positive rates for revenue and negative rates for expenditure estimates pinpoints states' widely adopted practice of fiscal conservatism or "protective" estimates, that is, underestimating revenues and overestimating expenditures so that annual financial operations are more likely to end with surpluses.

The error rate of general fund revenue (3.5%) is higher than that of total operating fund revenue (2.79%), indicating that conservatism in revenue estimation is more clustered in the general fund than in the total operat-

Table 2.1. Accuracy of State Revenue and Expenditure Estimates (percentage) (*N* = 50)

	1996	1997	1998	1999	Four-year average
General fund revenue					
Average	4.20	3.83	4.75	3.07	3.59
Median	1.14	2.77	3.41	1.60	2.49
Lowest	−8.10	−7.62	−12.61	−12.39	−11.03
Highest	65.63	67.68	64.95	65.67	65.70
Total operating fund revenue					
Average	1.75	3.35	3.94	1.64	2.79
Median	1.90	1.02	1.04	0.97	0.83
Lowest	−11.43	−15.73	−12.77	−12.91	−10.20
Highest	29.46	77.64	80.24	41.73	47.23
General fund expenditure					
Average	−2.03	−1.27	−2.09	−1.33	−1.67
Median	−1.35	−0.97	−1.52	−0.47	−1.17
Lowest	−23.02	−28.38	−28.61	−29.14	−27.25
Highest	14.50	26.30	15.35	13.42	16.62
Total operating fund expenditure					
Average	−4.12	−2.63	−3.56	−4.33	−3.60
Median	−2.05	−1.58	−2.61	−1.64	−2.20
Lowest	−41.89	−43.27	−43.90	−40.80	−42.23
Highest	26.40	29.31	32.70	15.58	24.22

Note: Data are for fiscal years. Federal funds are included. Revenue estimation accuracy = (actual revenue − estimated revenue) / estimated revenue. Expenditure estimation accuracy = (actual expenditure − estimated expenditure) / estimated expenditure.

ing fund. On the other hand, the error rate of general fund expenditure is smaller than that of total operating expenditure, implying that the total expenditure was overestimated more often. Finally, in most cases, the absolute value of the average in both revenue and expenditure estimates is larger than that of the median, indicating that revenue estimation is positively skewed and expenditure estimation is negatively skewed. In a nutshell, some states exercised extreme fiscal conservatism.[9]

The thirty-five large cities presented more accurate average rates with their estimates than did the states (table 2.2). The error rates of revenue

Table 2.2. Accuracy of City Revenue and Expenditure Estimates (percentage) (*N* = 35)

	1996	1997	1998	1999	Four-year average
General fund expenditure					
Average	2.75	2.32	2.63	3.77	2.87
Median	2.15	1.57	2.81	5.98	3.13
Lowest	−3.87	−1.48	−38.79	−7.19	−12.83
Highest	15.35	7.20	19.41	9.33	12.82
Total operating fund expenditure					
Average	3.33	1.97	5.07	2.99	3.34
Median	2.71	3.05	3.33	3.97	3.26
Lowest	−10.87	−20.25	−12.18	−14.84	−14.53
Highest	20.20	12.27	25.79	18.65	19.23
General fund expenditure					
Average	0.54	0.24	0.17	0.77	0.43
Median	0.38	0.02	−0.09	−1.00	−0.17
Lowest	−13.99	−3.65	−5.93	−5.98	−7.38
Highest	14.61	5.86	6.24	11.85	9.64
Total operating fund expenditure					
Average	1.89	2.31	1.96	−0.83	1.33
Median	2.07	0.56	0.73	1.85	1.30
Lowest	−20.43	−7.14	−12.81	−30.12	−17.62
Highest	23.49	23.12	25.81	15.76	22.05

Note: Federal funds are included.

estimation range from 2.8 to 3.4 percent and the error rates of expenditure estimation float only between negative 0.4 percent and 1.3 percent. Both ranges are much smaller than the 5 percent benchmark. Such high accuracy leaves little room for intended fiscal conservatism. The cities' revenue estimation error rates may be intentional, but these figures are not large when compared with states' error rates, because that small margin is barely enough for working capital needs. The positive sign on expenditure figures implies that the cities spent more than they had planned, which is against intuition and also contrary to evidence in the existing literature.[10] Perhaps the cities exercise "conservatism" in estimation of revenue but not of expenditure. Finally, the cities do not show much difference between the estimates for their general fund and total operating fund.

The percentage of counties that conduct and update their revenue and expenditure estimates exceeds that of states and cities. Among the forty counties, thirty-eight estimate for at least the coming year and one out-year, thirty-five forecast two out-years, and thirty-six update their estimates within the fiscal year quarterly or semiannually. The accuracy of estimation, however, displays features different from those of the states and cities (table 2.3). First, estimation accuracy of the general fund revenue is much higher (that is, the error rate is lower): the annual average and the four-year all-county averages fall below 2 percent. This "excellent" accuracy, however, is difficult to interpret. A detailed discussion is beyond the scope here. The error rate of general fund expenditure estimation, on the other hand, both annual and four-year averages, exceeds the 5 percent benchmark.

Second, the highly accurate revenue estimation leaves little room for the practice of fiscal conservatism in estimation. The off-the-mark accuracy of expenditure estimation, on the negative side only, serves as the major means of "protection." In this light, the higher error rate perhaps

Table 2.3. Accuracy of County Revenue and Expenditure Estimates (percentage) ($N = 40$)

	1996	1997	1998	1999	Four-year average
General fund revenue					
Average	−0.65	0.39	0.22	1.35	0.33
Median	0.46	1.63	1.13	1.71	1.23
Lowest	−28.46	−26.26	−26.78	−12.09	−23.40
Highest	11.17	9.64	9.44	11.97	10.55
General fund expenditure					
Average	−6.52	−7.78	−7.22	−6.76	−7.07
Median	−4.62	−6.93	−4.96	−5.19	−5.42
Lowest	−32.61	−31.71	−31.50	−24.24	−30.02
Highest	6.07	7.04	16.35	3.48	8.23

Source: Data from counties' comprehensive annual financial reports.
Note: Federal funds are included. Accuracy = (actual expenditure − estimated expenditure) / estimated expenditure.

no longer represents an error. It is intended. Third, in both revenue and expenditure estimation, distribution of the statistics is negatively skewed. For revenue, this indicates more cases of actual revenue lower than the expected amounts; for expenditure, however, more counties spent less than planned for, confirming our observation that these county governments rely on the differential of estimated and actual expenditures to accumulate positive year-end surpluses.

Gauging the Future Fiscal Impact of Financial Decisions

All management decisions bring financial impacts. Assessing all major decisions and preparing for their possible financial consequences, therefore, is not only essential to improving the accuracy of estimation and budgeting but is also a necessary step toward achieving a multiyear perspective. Like estimating revenue and expenditure, gauging financial consequences is also a labor-intensive activity; but unlike estimation, which is conducted at most a few times a year, tracking important management decisions is an ongoing activity. To smaller governments, the strain on expertise and resources might turn out to be daunting.

Almost all states assess impacts of state legislation, the main method used being the fiscal note and the length of assessment extending to more than one year. Only thirty-five states assess the impacts of federal legislation.[11] Forty-four states assess out-year impacts on pensions, but only twenty-seven assess impacts on vacations. At the local level, only twenty of the cities and roughly half the counties surveyed have a formalized process for assessing the impacts of all local legislation;[12] the number that assess pension and accrued vacation liabilities is even lower.

Summary of Findings

The rate of timely budget adoption is highest with the states; it drops for cities, and is lowest for counties. Counties and cities do better than states in maintaining the structural balance between revenues and expenditures. On the whole, all surveyed governments achieved high accuracy rates on revenue and expenditure estimation. I interpret their high accuracy rates as fiscal conservatism or protective estimation. For states, this conservatism is more prevalent in estimates of general fund revenue and total operating fund expenditure. Some states go to extremes in self-protection: the thirty-five cities achieved higher accuracy rates than the states, leaving little room for a presumption of fiscal conservatism. In relative terms this is more obvious in revenue than expenditure estimation. The counties' accuracy rate on revenue estimation also surpassed that of states. Counties' error rate on expenditure forecasts, however, was higher than the states error rate. Such "errors" reflect the counties' fiscal conservatism.

Although almost all states assess the financial impacts of state legislation, only 70 percent of them assess those of federal legislation. The proportion drops to 60 percent for the cities and 50 percent for the counties. This fact indicates that the surveyed governments still have a lot of work to do toward fully embracing the multiyear perspective on budgeting.

Fiscal Health and Stability

Countercyclical Fiscal Devices

While fiscal health has always been the due responsibility of every government, large and small, maintaining fiscal stability is often considered an exclusively federal responsibility.[13] Theorists have forwarded contrasting propositions. Edward Gramlich, for example, believes that state and even local governments may have a role to play.[14] Quite a few countercyclical fiscal devices exist for needy times; two major ones are the budget stabilization fund (BSF), popularly called the rainy-day fund, and general fund balances. The former became widespread in the 1980s; the latter has historically been used as reserves.

Since the mid-1980s, researchers have uncovered empirical evidence at the state and large city levels about the effects of the BSF.[15] More recent research indicates that countercyclical fiscal policy exists at the subnational level and that the BSF was effective at the state level in the last two decades of the twentieth century.[16] Survey results show that by the end of 1999, forty-five states had legislation enabling a budget stabilization fund. At the time of the survey, Alabama was considering implementing a BSF pending legislative action, and Illinois's legislature had passed BSF legislation, pending the governor's signature.[17] The proportion of local governments with BSFs is much lower, only seventeen cities and sixteen counties among those surveyed. What has caused the delay of BSF legislation at the city and county levels is beyond our knowledge with currently available data. Perhaps the local governments are going through an exploration process similar to that in the states before the 1980s. The 2001 recession may become a trigger for governments of large cities and counties to adopt the BSF, as was the case with the states after the early-1980s recessions.

Among governments that have a budget stabilization fund, the states kept a relatively higher BSF balance: the average level for fiscal year 1999 was 4.84 percent (median 3.26%) of general fund expenditure. Among these states, the balance ranged from 4 to 9 percent in twenty-seven states and from 2 to 4 percent in nine states. The balance maintained by the cities was much lower: below 2 percent in about half of the cities, between 2 and 6 percent in the rest. Counties' BSF balances do not lend themselves to comparison owing to the small number of funds that are real BSFs.

General fund balance is defined here as the balance of the general fund at the end of each fiscal year that can be appropriated in the next fiscal year or used to cover any unexpected expenses. A review of general fund balance as a percentage of general fund expenditure in the surveyed governments reveals different patterns at the three levels: for both the annual and the three-year average of the median, highest, and average balances, the states ranked the lowest, the cities higher than the states, and the counties the highest (table 2.4). Interestingly, this order is exactly opposite that of governments that have adopted the BSF at these three levels. A prelimi-

Table 2.4. General Fund Balance as Share of General Fund Expenditure (percentage)

	1996	1997	1998	Three-year average
States (*N* = 50)				
Average	2.33	2.57	4.23	3.04
Median	2.61	2.64	3.58	2.94
Lowest	−55.74	−56.55	−69.58	−60.62
Highest	25.10	23.85	26.52	25.15
Counties (*N* = 39)				
Average	10.82	11.56	13.41	11.93
Median	5.89	6.78	8.08	6.92
Lowest	−1.23	0.00	−5.35	−2.19
Highest	48.19	55.02	49.74	50.98
Cities (*N* = 35)				
Average	7.00	6.81	8.28	7.36
Median	5.19	4.84	7.12	5.72
Lowest	−11.03	−8.17	0.00	−6.40
Highest	28.87	28.16	29.27	28.77

Source: Data from comprehensive annual financial reports of these governments.
Note: Federal funds are included. Figures are actual amounts at the end of each fiscal year. Positive figures represent general fund surplus and negative ones denote general fund deficit.

nary conclusion from the summary statistics is that the states rely mostly on the BSF as a countercyclical fiscal device for self-protection against revenue downfalls, whereas the counties depend almost solely on the general fund balance as fiscal reserves. The cities present a case in the middle—they maintain some reserves in the BSF and also a relatively large amount in the general fund.

Why do the states and counties utilize different devices? A probable reason, when the politics of spending is taken into account, is that at the state level, legislators often employ pork barreling to favor their electorates, thus forming spending pressure that goes against fiscal reserves during good years. On the other hand, since the tax revolt movement of the late 1970s, taxpayers have tended to restrict the taxing power of state governments that are in a sense farther away from their direct provider of vital services, thus forming the political pressure that fights against taxation to favor refunds during booms. Therefore, state governments need the legally mandated BSF to "protect" their reserves against spending pressure, while county governments, which do not face this dilemma, can be comfortable with the general fund balance as reserves. The cities again represent the middle case.

Table 2.5 presents the distribution of general fund balance in various ranges, from deficit to more than 20 percent of general fund expenditure. This distribution further illustrates the difference between the three levels. A striking difference is the percentage of each level in deficit: the general

Table 2.5. Distribution of Average General Fund Balance as Share of General Fund Expenditure, 1996–1998 (percentage)

	States		Counties		Cities	
	N	%	*N*	%	*N*	%
Deficit	11	22	1	3	2	6
0–2	10	20	7	18	8	23
2–5	10	20	8	21	5	14
5–7	2	4	5	13	4	11
7–10	6	12	3	8	6	17
10–15	4	8	5	13	6	17
15–20	5	10	2	5	2	6
>20	2	4	8	21	2	6
N	50	100	39	100	35	100

fund was in deficit in 22 percent of states, in contrast to just 6 percent of cities and 3 percent of counties. As striking is the percentage in the range of large surpluses (over 20%)—only 4 percent of states and 6 percent of cities but 21 percent of counties. The cities stand out in the middle range: their percentages in the 5 to 10 percent and 10 to 20 percent categories are higher than those for the states or the counties. How should we interpret these results? Obviously, there is not one perfect policy that fits all levels of government. Different devices better serve different levels. Thus in assessing the performance of state, city, and county governments, appropriate measures should be applied.

Debt Management

As J. E. Peterson and Thomas McLauphlin have noted, borrowing "is one of the most potent and profound activities undertaken in government finance."[18] On one hand, debt is raised out of necessity, when currently available resources are limited but superseded by the demand for services. On the other hand, borrowing with a promise to return in the future promotes intergenerational equity: construction of infrastructure benefits future as well as current residents, and it is therefore not equitable to burden current taxpayers with all the financing for such construction. As obligations in the future, debts are targets of tight regulation and strict public scrutiny at the state and especially local levels (by state governments). This is evident in debt limitations in state statutes that date back to the mid-1800s and the expenditure limitations imposed on governments from the tax revolt movements in the late 1970s and early 1980s. Debt management is a broad area. State and local government debts vary in scope, methods, and instruments used. The GPP surveys covered a fraction of the area that the survey designers considered the common core of the most important information. Table 2.6 summarizes debt management policies and practices at the three levels.

Debt Policy. Establishment of a debt policy is the first and most important step in debt management. A "good" debt policy, according to the Government Finance Officers Association (GFOA), covers all aspects (twenty-four in all) of debt management; thus the presence or absence of debt policy is a strong indication of the quality of debt management in a government. Debt policy is divided into three categories: informal, formal or administrative, and adopted. An informal policy is in many cases unwritten; managers simply follow the "understood" practices without documentary guidance. Informal policy is better than no policy at all but lacks the

Table 2.6. Summary of Debt Management Policies and Practices

	States		Cities		Counties	
	N	%	*N*	%	*N*	%
Debt policy						
None	1	2	1	30	0	0
Informal	6	12	12	34	10	25
Formal or administrative	14	28	11	31	7	18
Adopted	29	58	7	20	19	48
Inadequate information for judgment	0	0	4	11	4	10
Formal oversight body						
Yes	38	76	8	23	21	53
No	12	24	23	66	15	37
Inadequate information for judgment	0	0	4	11	4	10
Debt capacity management						
Comprehensive	n.a.	n.a.	6	17	15	38
Simple	n.a.	n.a.	17	49	13	33
No	n.a.	n.a.	5	14	7	18
Inadequate information for judgment	n.a.	n.a.	7	20	5	13
Method of sale						
Competitive	n.a.	n.a.	n.a.	n.a.	31	78
Negotiated	n.a.	n.a.	n.a.	n.a.	3	8
Inadequate information for judgment	n.a.	n.a.	n.a.	n.a.	6	15
Limitations on maturity						
None	8	16	n.a.	n.a.	5	13
End of fiscal year	1	2	n.a.	n.a.	n.a.	n.a.
Greater or = 20 years	18	36	n.a.	n.a.	n.a.	n.a.
Less than 20 years	13	26	n.a.	n.a.	12	30
Varies	5	10	n.a.	n.a.	n.a.	n.a.
Life of Facility	5	10	n.a.	n.a.	18	45
Use independent advisers						
Yes	41	82	n.a.	n.a.	n.a.	n.a.
No	9	18	n.a.	n.a.	n.a.	n.a.

bondage of written rules. A formal policy is written as a set of rules or ordinances that have not been officially approved by the legislative body. In some cases, formal policy is an administrative regulation drafted by the executive branch. The best and strictest is a policy that has been adopted by the legislative body and thus is part of the legal requirement.

Among the three levels, the states have the highest percentage of adopted policies (58%), followed by the counties (48%); falling far behind are the cities (20%), which also have the highest percentage of formal or administrative policies (31%). The order is reversed in the percentage of governments using informal policies; among those without policies, cities come first and counties last.

How should these differences be interpreted? First, states are under the strongest legal constraints in debt management, by tradition and necessity.[19] This means that each state should have instituted an adopted debt policy. Absence of such policy indicates a serious loophole in management capacity. Second, the local levels differ from the states, with far fewer adopted policies. A puzzle remains: under the same federal system and subject to the state law stipulations, why should there be such systematic differences between county and city governments?[20] The implication for management capacity assessment at these two levels is probably simple: an adopted debt policy is best but a formal or administrative policy may suffice.

Formal Oversight Body. The prominence of debt management in government finance establishes the necessity for oversight, even when the government has an adopted or formal debt policy. *Formal oversight body* refers to an organ created specifically for the purpose of advising, supervising, and reviewing the operation of debt management, ideally including members from the executive branch (chief financial officer, chief elected official), the legislative body (the finance committee), professionals (experts from the private sector or academia), and citizenry. By such a definition, the city council, county council, or a loose meeting of executive officers and legislators are not an oversight body.[21] A formal oversight body must be a fully functional expert group with real authority to supervise management and review performance reports. Such an independent committee can best enforce the legal requirements and serve the community.

Under this strict definition, thirty-eight states have a formal oversight body, indicating that existence of this body is a widely adopted capacity builder. The other twelve states have something they call "oversight body," although these do not fit the GPP's definition. Fifty-three percent of the counties have formal oversight bodies. Because this percentage is higher than that of counties with adopted debt policies, it is clear that some counties with formal debt policies also have formal oversight bodies. Although only 23 percent of the cities surveyed have formal oversight bodies, that is again a higher proportion than cities with adopted debt policies. These data indicate that some entities with no adopted debt policies employ the formal oversight body mechanism.

Debt Capacity Model. Debt capacity model refers to the method used in calculating and thereby effectively controlling the ratio of debt to vital finance indicators so that the total amount of debt is kept within safe limits. Debt capacity models can be comprehensive or simple. Comprehensive models use elaborate formulas and many relevant data variables from inside and outside the government; they also have higher requirements for computing equipment, software, and expertise. Owing to the level of resources and commitment these models entail, comprehensive models tend to be used at higher levels of governments. Simple models use some formula and data variables but on the whole are simpler in methodology and narrower in coverage. They are more often employed at lower levels or when a government does not commit a lot of resources to the endeavor.

In this regard, the counties seem to have done better than the cities. Whereas 38 percent of counties use comprehensive models, only 17 percent of cities do so. The percentage for both counties and cities is lower than those employing adopted debt policies. Thirty-three percent of counties and 49 percent of cities use simple models. These statistics lead to two inferences. First, use of comprehensive debt models is associated with adopted debt policies. Higher percentages of adopted policies may lead to wider use of comprehensive models. Second, that a fairly high percentage of county and city governments use simple debt capacity models indicates that at local levels a simple model should be regarded as sufficient for their needs. In general, a higher percentage of counties than cities employ stronger capacity measures like the adopted debt policy, formal oversight body, and comprehensive debt models. This consistent comparative superiority indicates that counties are somehow in a better management position than the cities. The reasons behind the superiority, however, cry for an explanation.

Method of Sale. Methods of bond sale are either competitive (with several bidders) or negotiated (with only one bidder). Research has provided evidence that competitive sale helps reduce the cost of debt issuance. Negotiated sale, on the other hand, is often the only choice when the issue is small. The county survey shows that nearly 80 percent choose to use competitive sale, indicating that this method has become the most widely accepted mechanism at the local levels. It is also reasonable to argue that competitive sale may be the primary method used in state and big city governments, and that these governments consider competitive sale a useful practice to improve management capacity.

Limitations on Debt Maturity. The states and counties turn out to be similar with respect to their limitations on debt maturity.[22] Nearly half (46% of states and 45% of counties) allow debt maturity of twenty or more years, or as long as the life of the facility financed with the debt;[23] a dozen of each (26% of states and 30% of counties) allow maturity of less than twenty years. Such close similarity on debt maturity limitation is not surprising considering that all limitations originate from state finance laws. Following this line of thought, the cities should not be far away from these categories of maturity limitations.

Use of Independent Advisers. Another widespread practice in debt management is the use of independent advisers from the private sector. The advisers are hired to offer a third opinion, more expertise, and objectivity. Forty-one states hire advisers, indicating that it is a valued practice among states. City and county surveys did not ask this question, but an educated guess would be that they also use advisers owing to the relative size of these entities. Therefore, that the use of independent advisers improves government management capacity can be inferred.

Investment Management

Investment is another important function of state and local government financial managers. Regardless of whether it is a cash-flow borrower with its general fund and whether it issues general obligation bonds, a government has long-term assets in other funds as well as short-term operating balances that need to be invested for the best return on them. Long-term investment is a full function at the state level, though not necessarily so at local levels, especially if the local government is small. Investment management policies of state and county governments are summarized in table 2.7.[24] Discussion here focuses on long-term investment.

Long-Term Investment Policy. The presence of an established policy for long-term investment is the basis for management capacity. Observations fall into four categories: no policy, informal, administrative, and adopted policies. *No policy* indicates a government does not have long-term investment as a full function in its financial management. *Informal policy* refers to cases in which investment is guided by past practices rather than written rules. *Administrative policy* can be called formal, for these policies are

Table 2.7. Summary of Investment Management Policies

	States (N = 50)		Counties (N = 40)	
	N	%	N	%
Long-term investment policy				
None	2	4	0	0
Informal	7	14	1	3
Administrative	22	44	5	13
Adopted	19	38	20	50
How value of portfolio is determined				
Mark to market	37	74	21	53
Other	13	26	4	10
Strategies to maximize return				
No apparent efforts	6	12	1	3
Some strategy but not elaborate	22	44	15	38
Use of equities, professional advice, or prudent man rule	22	44	8	20
Schedule of portfolio valuation assessment				
Annually	9	18	2	5
Quarterly	2	4	0	0
Monthly	24	48	2	5
Weekly or daily	15	30	21	53
Decision makers of asset allocation				
Elected officials (treasurer)	19	38	3	8
Appointed officials (CFO)	7	14		
State law sets parameters			13	33
Independent advisory board (state) or professional staff (county)	24	48	18	45
Oversight body monitoring				
No	36	72		
Yes	14	28	7	18
Required report of portfolio performance				
(Less than) annually	10	20	5	13
Semiannually	8	16	0	0
Quarterly	14	28	6	15
Monthly or more often	18	36	15	38
To whom is information reported				
None	9	18		
Executive branch only	17	34	7	18
Both branches	24	48	19	48

Source: Data from state and county surveys.
Note: Almost half of the forty counties do not have a real investment function; the calculations, however, still use forty as the denominator.

coded into rules or other administrative manuals. *Adopted policy* is the highest order, written into state statutes.

With two exceptions, all states reported some kind of long-term investment policy, of which twenty-two are in administrative regulations and nineteen in statutes.[25] Although many counties do not engage in long-term investment, all that have this function use either adopted (twenty counties) or administrative policies (five counties). This is not surprising in that most local finance affairs are regulated by the state finance law.

"Mark to the market" (adjusting the valuation of investment to reflect current market values) is the dominant method used in determining the value of portfolios at both the state and local levels. The schedule of portfolio value assessment in 78 percent of state governments and in 58 percent of county governments is monthly or shorter; only a few do it semiannually or annually. This is an obvious advantage of a developed financial market and wide application of the Internet. In addition, almost 90 percent of state governments and 58 percent of county governments employ strategies to maximize the return on their investment. Interestingly, among the strategies used, the role of "prudent man" is still listed, indicating that personal experience and expertise continue to matter.

Asset Allocation. Investment decisions with regard to asset allocation are in most cases professional: in nineteen states the decision maker is the elected treasurer, who in today's environment is usually a person who knows finance and has experience in financial management; in another seven states decisions are made by an appointed official who is usually the chief finance officer or finance director, a person with a lot of expertise and experience. Most noteworthy are the twenty-four states in which the decision maker is an independent investment advisory board that is usually composed of government finance officials, investment experts from the private sector, and the general public. At the county level, about half of the discretionary decisions are made by professional staff—people with qualifications and experience in financial management. A sizable portion of decisions are not discretionary. They are preset in state finance laws, further evidence that investment management of local governments is highly regulated by the state.

Formal Oversight Body. Like the oversight body on debt management, formal oversight body is defined here as an organ composed of members with finance expertise from not only the government itself (both branches) but also the private sector and the general public. In striking contrast to debt management, for which thirty-eight states have a formal oversight body, thirty-six states have no formal oversight body for their investment activities. In a similar fashion, only seven counties have an investment oversight body.[26] This is probably illustrative of the fact that state and local legislative bodies as well as the general public do not scrutinize investment management as closely as debt management. Why is it so? Current literature does not offer much insight.

A revenue-expenditure analysis may help explain this phenomenon. Debt is on the revenue side of government finance, and investment is on the expenditure side. Debt represents a long-term burden on taxpayers, so the public scrutinizes debt management. Investment, on the other hand, is management of money that is already in the government's hand, over which taxpayers can exert less direct influence; they care less about investment than about debts. People with financial knowledge would cry that this does not make sense because assets and short-term balances are still public money. But the reality is "out of hand, out of direct control," and so the citizens simply do not cast an examining eye. Legislators mostly follow the electorate. If voters do not care, why should they? A more detailed and powerful explanation should no doubt go much further than this simplistic story. As a consequence, though thirty-two states require quarterly or shorter reporting of investment performance (this percentage is higher than at the county level), eight states require only semiannual reporting and ten mere annual reporting. In only twenty-four states are reports of investment performance submitted to both the legislative and executive branches; in seventeen states such reports are submitted only to the executive branch, and in nine states the reports are not submitted to either of the two branches in particular. This is a problematic situation.

Summary of Findings

More than 90 percent of states have a legally required budget stabilization fund; the percentage for cities and counties is less than half. (Perhaps it will take some economic bumps for more local governments to adopt a reserve fund.) In like manner, while states' average BSF balance in 1999 was around 5 percent of the general fund expenditure, the balance at local levels was much lower. General fund balance, the other major countercyclical device, presents a different picture. Counties have the highest balances and states the lowest, with cities in the middle. Obviously, state and local governments employ different countercyclical devices to keep their fiscal reserves.

An adopted debt policy is associated with a formal oversight mechanism but an administrative debt policy is not. More counties than cities use comprehensive debt capacity models. Perhaps a simple debt capacity model is sufficient for local governments. More counties than cities seem to use top management measures. States and counties share similar percentages of debt maturity limitations. Use of independent debt advisers seems to be a widely adopted practice at both state and local levels. Competitive sale is the major method of debt issuance and is a capacity-building practice.

At the state level, long-term investment policies are mostly adopted or administrative. At the county level the ratio of adopted or administrative policies is even higher because local governments are regulated by the states. Decision making regarding asset allocation is mostly done by people with expertise and experience. At the county level, most decisions are determined by preset parameters in state finance law. The general public and legislative bodies do not seem to pay much attention to investment management; nor do most governments have a formal oversight body for investment activities. Thirty-six percent of states require only semiannual or annual reporting of investment performance. In 34 percent of states, the reports are submitted only to the executive, and in 18 percent, to neither the legislative nor the executive branch.

Spending Control and Financial Reporting

Checks and control, an old theme in public finance, are the mechanisms employed between the executive and the legislative branches and between upper and lower levels within the executive branch, to make sure that public money is spent in the manner and within the specified amount that has been assigned. The past two decades have seen a trend toward increasing the discretionary power of frontline managers to improve the efficiency and effectiveness of government programs. My interest here is in how the old theme and the new trend have interacted. Reporting of the results of financial operation to taxpayers, investors, and other interested parties is a natural extension of the internal checks and control.

Appropriations Control

The appropriations act passed by a government's legislature offers detailed information about how specific the spending authorization has been. Provisions in the appropriations act or the finance law indicate the levels of authority of the chief elected official and frontline managers to divert funds. Table 2.8 summarizes appropriations control in the states.

Table 2.8. Appropriations Control in the States

	N	%
Level of appropriation		
Agency: one level	18	40
Department: two levels	11	24
Program: three levels	8	18
Object classification: four levels	8	18
Line item: five levels	0	0
Governor's ability to move funds		
Unlimited or no discretionary authority	7	14
Very high threshold (too much flexibility)	18	36
With threshold requiring legislative approval	25	50
Managers' ability to move funds among departments		
Inability to move funds, or no external approval	7	14
Very high threshold	21	42
With threshold requiring external approval	22	44
Managers' ability to move funds among programs		
Inability to transfer or no internal or external control	9	18
Very high threshold or no external approval	25	50
With threshold requiring approval	16	32
Managers' ability to move funds among object classifications		
Prohibited or absence of all checks	5	10
Lack of dollar amount or internal/external approval	24	48
With threshold requiring internal and external approval	21	42
Managers' ability to move funds among line items		
Prohibited, no, or excessive checks	9	18
Lack of dollar amount or internal approval	13	26
With threshold requiring internal approval	28	56
Agency's ability to retain savings		
No	20	40
Yes	30	60

Note: Owing to incomplete responses from some states, the number of states in each category does not always add to fifty.

The extent of legislative control is indicated by the level of specification in the appropriations act: five-level appropriations go directly to the line-item level, leaving no room for managerial flexibility, whereas one-level appropriations allocate money to the agency, granting a huge amount of discretion to managers. Survey results show that no states still use five-level appropriations and eighteen states grant managerial discretion by adopting one-level appropriations, which indicates a drastic change from strict legislative control in the past. More than half of the states try to strike some balance between legislative control and managerial flexibility by adopting two- to four-level appropriations.

According to the statistics, the governor, as top executive officer, enjoys adequate flexibility in making spending decisions so as to better implement his or her policies. In eighteen states governors are granted a lot of discretion—they can legally move large amounts of funds without legislative approval. In half of the states, gubernatorial authority in moving funds is set at a moderate level, requiring legislative approval, to balance control and flexibility. In seven states, the governor either has no limit as to the amount of appropriations he or she can move or cannot change appropriations at all. Gubernatorial discretion, on the whole, is fairly visible.[27]

The amount of discretion granted to managers is more germane to the present discussion; it is managers who operate government functions on a daily basis. Whether it is moving funds across departments, programs, object classifications, or line items, the proportion of states that prohibit altering appropriation amounts is below 20 percent in all four cases (14, 18, 10 and 18 percent, respectively). Between 32 and 56 percent of states set a threshold that requires internal (from superiors within department or agency) or external (top executive or legislature) approval.[28]

In each of these cases (except moving across line items), about half of the states allow high thresholds or do not specify requiring approval. If high thresholds are set on top of reasonable thresholds, such an "overdose" of discretion may be abused. Because of these measures, 60 percent of states now allow agencies to retain part of their savings from appropriations, which is an effective incentive to encourage efficiency and discourage wasteful year-end spending sprees. In general, states seem to have moved farther toward managerial discretion.

Cost Accounting

Cost information is very helpful as a planning and budgeting tool and as a performance measure. Cost accounting is useful in obtaining detailed information about the unit costs of each activity and in allocating indirect costs. Although a relatively new technique and still in its early stages of application in state and local governments, cost accounting is becoming more prevalent. It should be used as a capacity indicator in performance assessment. However, conducting cost accounting is resource, manpower, and equipment intensive and often also requires extensive data collection. These limits have restricted its wider application.

Among the three levels of government, the widest use of cost accounting is found at the state level: eleven states reported using activity-based cost accounting in most of their agencies; twenty-two states use it only in some agencies; three states reported no use; and the rest did not respond to this question, which is a strong indication of no use (see table 2.9). The practice is more widely used in allocating indirect costs: twenty-three states reported

Table 2.9. Cost Accounting in the States

	N	%
Use activity-based cost accounting		
None	3	6
Some agencies	22	44
Most agencies	11	22
Allocate indirect costs		
None	1	2
According to federal grant requirements	5	10
Some agencies	19	38
Most agencies	23	46
Allocate unit costs		
None	3	6
Some agencies	31	62
Most agencies	12	24
Use cost analysis		
None	1	2
For setting user fees: one category	9	18
For making decisions about contracting out: two categories	7	14
For management research: three categories	33	66

Note: Owing to incomplete response from some states, numbers in each area do not always add to fifty. In GPP surveys, "agency" refers to the level of unit that reports directly to governor.

its use in most agencies, nineteen states in some agencies, and another five use it as required by federal grants. Forty-three states, by far the highest percentage, reported using this technique to allocate unit costs. More specified purposes of conducting cost analysis include setting user fees, making contracting-out decisions, and management research.

Auditing

Since each government must by law compile financial statements for use by taxpayers, investors, and other interested parties, auditing has always been an important part of governmental financial management. In using the financial reports, the concerned parties like to have a third opinion about the reliability of the statements governments make; auditing thereby becomes necessary.[29] In recent decades, auditing has begun to extend beyond the conventional "reliability check" function to become a means by which governments improve performance.

Summary statistics presented in table 2.10 show that 47 state governments conduct internal audits: twelve by independently elected auditors, twenty-seven by auditors appointed by the legislature, and the other eight by auditing offices in the executive branch. In addition, thirty states hire independent auditors in the private sector. Overall, auditing independent of the executive branch is commonplace. This can be taken as a capacity builder. States' responses regarding the capacity of auditing to improve the performance and effectiveness of relevant government authorities were mostly positive or very positive, a sign that auditing has been used by the government in improving performance.

Financial Reporting

Financial reporting has long been subject to legal stipulation and professional standardization. The finance laws of most states provide detailed rules regarding the manner, frequency, and transparency of financial statements by state as well as local governments. The Government Finance Officers Association launched an Excellence in Financial Reporting Award program, which sets standards for the content (basic information, balance sheets, notes to the sheets, and supplementary statistics), deadline of publication (within six months after the end of each fiscal year), and, more significantly, user-friendliness of the report. All levels of government are encouraged to apply for the award if they adopt the generally accepted accounting principles and publish comprehensive annual financial reports. Our research found that winning this award is a good proxy for timely

Table 2.10. Auditing in the States

	N	%
Conduct internal audits		
None	3	6
By elected auditor	12	24
By an executive office	8	16
By legislative appointee	27	54
Use independent auditor		
Yes	30	60
None	20	40
Audits cover financial compliance and control mechanism		
Agree	15	30
Strongly agree	34	68
Audits cover financial performance measures		
Neutral	9	18
Agree	24	48
Strongly agree	9	18
Audits cover program performance		
Neutral	6	12
Agree	24	48
Strongly agree	11	22
Audits provide useful information		
Agree	22	44
Strongly agree	24	48
Audits help improve effectiveness of responsible authorities		
Neutral	7	14
Agree	22	44
Strongly agree	15	30

provision of accurate and reliable financial information to the general public.

Information from the GFOA indicates that many state, city, and county governments covered in the GPP surveys have won the Excellence in Financial Reporting Award, some for many consecutive years. Counties have done especially well in financial reporting—of the forty counties in our survey, thirty-seven (92.5%) counties won the award for their comprehensive annual financial reports for the 1997–98 fiscal year, and thirty-eight (95%) for the 1998–99 fiscal year.[30]

To better communicate financial information to citizens, many state governments have gone an extra step by compiling and publishing a more user-friendly report, either *Annual Citizens' Report,* as in Texas, or *Quarterly Cash Report,* as in California. Such reports are free of finance and accounting jargon, concise in content, and readily available in book form or online (PDF file). In addition, most of our surveyed governments have made their budgets and financial reports available online for on-screen viewing or downloading and printing. These measures have made the communication of financial information much faster, more direct, and thereby more immediate to citizens. Therefore, these measures can be taken as strong indicators of governmental financial management capacity.

There are two caveats. First, receipt of the GFOA award is founded on adoption of the generally accepted accounting principles and compilation of a comprehensive annual financial report. Although almost all states now follow these practices, some states prohibit their local governments from these same practices.[31] New Jersey, for example, allows only its municipalities to compile annual financial statements on a modified cash basis.[32] Second, because they require extra resources, online financial reports have so far not been widely affordable in small governments. Thus these measures may not be as applicable in small local governments.

Summary of Findings

Appropriations have shifted dramatically from focusing on control toward granting managerial flexibility. Both the governor and managers in state governments can move funds under a reasonably high threshold without external approval. Against this background, it seems that proper control should remain a measure of capacity. Although indirect costs are widely allocated within the states, in general, activity-based cost accounting needs to be strengthened. Among the surveyed governments, auditing has gone beyond control to improving performance; and winning the GFOA award is generally an indication of competent financial reporting.

Utah: A High Performer in Financial Management

An example illustrates how strong management capacity is linked to high performance. Utah stood out as the best among the fifty states in the year

2000 GPP survey. What carried Utah to this stature was its strong capacity in financial management.

Multiyear Perspective on Budgeting

Utah's executive and legislative branches work cooperatively to guarantee a smooth budgetary process. From 1997 through 1999, Utah adopted its budget by the end of each March, three months before the start date of its new fiscal year, July 1.[33]

Strong fiscal discipline is Utah's second feature. The state government maintained a strong current year structural balance of revenues over expenditures. From fiscal year 1996 through 1999, it kept sizable current-year budgetary-basis balances. The four-year average balance was near 5 percent, which is the widely adopted benchmark and higher than the 3.2 percent average among all fifty states. Utah's fiscal discipline is also embedded in management details. First, for more than ten years, the state never had to take any unusual actions to retroactively balance its budget.[34] Second, when tobacco settlement revenue came in, instead of putting it into the general fund the state deposited half of it into a restricted account for substance abuse prevention programs and cancer research and put the other half into an endowment fund. Third, when the general fund has surpluses at the end of a fiscal year, 25 percent is transferred into the budget stabilization fund, in accordance with a legal requirement, and most of the rest is used to fund miscellaneous one-time projects in the next year. Finally, the state's finance law plays a strong role: it fixes the major operating funds (like the general fund, the school fund, the transportation fund, and restricted funds) at appropriated levels, and it prohibits state agencies from spending more federal funds or dedicated credits than they collect during any fiscal year.

Utah cultivates a strong capacity in revenue forecasting through a consensus process with the legislature that results in high accuracy. Its Revenue Assumptions Committee, composed of members from the Governor's Office of Planning and Budget, the state Tax Commission, academics, state agencies, Salt Lake City, the Legislative Fiscal Analysts Office, and private consultants, builds the data and theoretical (modeling) basis for revenue forecasts. The planning and budget office employs elaborate models to forecast revenues (the Tax Commission runs its own forecast models). The two organs then meet to achieve consensus.

The revenue estimates serve as a cap to spending. In addition, Utah has a legal spending limit that is tied to the growth in population, inflation, and personal income. The revenue and expenditure estimates are updated three times a year: once in October to serve as working estimates in the governor's budget process; a second time in late November, to be used in governor's final recommendations; and a third time in mid-February, as the final legislative estimates for the appropriations act. The Revenue Assumptions Committee meets once more in late May. Forecasts are made two years into the future. Five- to ten-year projections are made as needed.

Estimates of general fund revenues and expenditures achieved high accuracy, with rates that exceeded the fifty-state average and the field excellence benchmark of 2 percent (table 2.11). Estimates and forecasts are released to news media and posted on the state's Web site to provide up-to-date financial information to all interested parties. To gauge the fiscal impact of financial decisions, Utah annually estimates liabilities on pension, accrued vacation, and sick leave. The Governor's Office of Planning and Budget and the Legislative Fiscal Analyst's Office both track federal legislative and budget actions and estimate their potential impact on state finance. Fiscal notes are used to assess the impact of state legislation for a minimum of two years into the future.

Strong Capacity to Defend Fiscal Health and Stability

To avoid financial embarrassment from unexpected occurrences, Utah exercises fiscal conservatism by keeping its expenditures well below its revenues (both in terms of generally accepted accounting principles). From 1995 through 1999, its actual annual balance ranged from 22 to 28 percent, while the fifty-state average was between 6 and 9 percent.[35] In the common understanding of financial management, a 5 percent balance is good. Although 1995 to 1999 were years of record prosperity, a balance in excess of 20 percent is still very high.[36] On the other hand, Utah does have a legally

Table 2.11. Accuracy of Utah's General Fund Estimates, 1996–1999

	1996	1997	1998	1999	Four-year average	Fifty-state average
Revenue	0.48	1.60	1.72	1.81	1.40	3.57
Expenditure	−0.41	2.63	−1.76	−0.85	−0.10	−1.62

Note: Federal funds are included.

required budget stabilization fund, whose annual balances are shown in table 2.12.[37] A quarter of year-end general fund surpluses are automatically transferred into this fund until it reaches the cap—8 percent of general fund appropriations, which is in the high range of state budget stabilization fund caps. The BSF balance ratios are not high but may suffice in the conservative financial management context of Utah.

Utah's adopted debt policy is also conservative, with a low debt limit (1.5 percent of taxable property value), the objective being to "keep the debt ratios in the low to moderate categories." A formal oversight body is in place to ensure that "the state has sufficient debt capacity." General obligation bonds are limited to twenty years, but in practice the general obligation bonds for buildings are issued with maturities of six years, which is much like pay-as-you-go financing, further evidence of the state's prudent use of annual surpluses.

With an adopted policy and a sizable long-term portfolio, Utah is prudently active in investment activities, which are conducted by the Office of the State Treasurer (an elected official) and reviewed monthly by the Money Management Council.[38] Asset allocation is based on opinions of hired consultants; performance is reported quarterly to an advisory committee. Detailed parameters are provided for in the Money Management Act, which includes, among other things, a list of qualified instruments, credit quality, maximum maturity, diversity, and equity caps.

Table 2.12. Counter-cyclical Fiscal Devices in Use in Utah, 1995–1999

	1995	1996	1997	1998	1999	Five-year average	Fifty-state average
General fund balance[a]	28.36	27.65	27.27	28.48	22.06	26.76	7.82
Unreserved undesignated balance[b]	0.84	0.02	0.12	0.44	0.01	0.29	2.84
Budget stabilization fund[c]	3.61	3.67	3.81	4.15	4.09	3.87	4.39

[a]General fund balance is the balance of revenue over expenditure divided by expenditure.
[b]The ratios are the general fund unreserved undesignated balance over general fund expenditure.
[c]The ratios are the actual year-end balance of BSF over general fund expenditure.

Operational Control and Financial Reporting

Utah appropriates for three levels, from agency down to department and program, balancing control with managerial flexibility. There are no limits to the governor's power to transfer funds; managers, however, must get permission from the governor to transfer funds across departments or programs.[39] Agencies can retain part of the savings from appropriations. In this sense, Utah's financial management combines control with managerial flexibility.

Nonetheless, control remains tight. For a wide array of reasons, most departments in most agencies apply activity-based cost accounting and allocate indirect costs (on top of federal requirements); unit costs are allocated in some departments of some agencies. Auditing is conducted at several levels: agency internal audits, legislative audits by an auditor general appointed by the legislature, the elected state auditor, and independent auditors hired by the state. From 1985 to 2001, Utah won the GFOA award for excellence in financial reporting for seventeen years in a row.

Four years of GPP assessment shows that high-performing governments share most features of strong management capacity, confirming the project's assumption that capacity drives performance. High performers at the city and county levels present different features from the states, mainly owing to the smaller size and limited availability of resources and expertise necessary for some of the capacity indicators.

Conclusion

A panorama of financial management in the surveyed state and local governments reveals some overarching lessons that may serve as themes in government performance measurement. First, a longer-term perspective on budgeting (or planning) is a key to stronger management capacity and better performance. Every initiative aimed at curing old problems or introducing reforms starts with planning, which has been embraced by all entities. Success in improving performance is achieved by adopting longer-term planning; failure is often largely the result of negligence of this longer-term perspective. Examples are numerous. The city of Austin, Texas, greatly improved its accuracy of revenue and expenditure estimation by tying short-term budgeting to long-term forecasts. Budgeting and planning are no longer isolated activities. Budgets have become strategic documents into which all planning ultimately falls. Budgeting and planning are best integrated into strategic plans for the entire government as well as for individual agencies. This is budgeting for the future, for development, for revitalization, and for performance. The city of Milwaukee, the state of Washington, and the Commonwealth of Virginia are good examples. Gone are the days when government financial management was merely a matter of balancing the annual budget by filling up revenue holes with whatever one-time resources are available. Public financial management thrives on longer-term planning. Absent this base, management capacity cannot grow strong and performance remains below public expectation.

Second, strong fiscal discipline is more than ever an essential requirement in public financial management. It is a requirement for governments at all levels, for both the executive and the legislative branches, and for all component units within government as well. Their substantive role in the national economy and in the provision of vital public services requires that state and local governments be active in maintaining fiscal health and fiscal stability. For this purpose, adoption of formal countercyclical devices with adequate reserves is a must; formal policies for debt and investment management with fully functional oversight bodies should be adopted and implemented.

Third, checks and controls as themes for public financial management are viewed positively and are done in ways and manners that go beyond mere control to improving capacity and boosting performance. Thus striking a balance between control and managerial flexibility is a new task for researchers and practitioners: how can the balance be institutionalized, and how can a good balance in financial operations be implemented? Perhaps when the balance is achieved, new ways to check the balance is necessary. Above all, survey results and assessment grades from four rounds of the GPP financial management section testify to the validity of the capacity model for government performance measurement. High performers in the GPP assessment are evidence that governments with strong management capacity are more likely to generate high managerial performance; entities that lag in performance lack in capacity.

The Government Performance Project provided support for a long-held proposition: as a foundation of governmental operations and a centerpiece among management systems, financial management should be a strong indicator of the overall performance of a government. A government with low capacity in financial management cannot be expected to present high overall performance, whereas to achieve high overall performance a government must possess high capacity in financial management.

In all four years of assessments, financial management was consistently the strongest among the five governmental management subsystems: the financial management grade was in most cases higher than the grades of the other four systems and higher than the overall grade (see table 2.13).[40] Further evidence comes from the correlation between the financial management grades and the overall grades. The four-year mean correlation between the two is 0.80, the highest among the systems. Also noteworthy is the high correlation between the grades for managing-for-results and financial management, as illustrated in table 2.14. This relation supports the proposition that further development in governmental financial management is required to enhance longer-term planning. It is planning in the longer-term perspective that links financial management with managing for results.

The Government Performance Project was a tremendous endeavor that offered opportunities to observe many facets of financial management functions at the state and local levels. The materials and data obtained are

Table 2.13. Average Scores of Management Systems

	States				Four-year
	1998	2000	Cities	Counties	average
Financial management	8.60	8.58	9.14	8.43	8.69
Capital management	8.16	8.20	8.67	7.50	8.13
Overall	7.60	7.96	7.97	7.50	7.76
Information technology	6.70	7.96	7.17	7.81	7.41
Human resources	7.56	7.88	6.94	6.90	7.32
Managing for results	6.80	7.40	7.86	7.10	7.29

Table 2.14. Correlation between Financial Management and Other Area Grades

	States				
	1998	2000	Cities	Counties	Mean
Managing for results	0.69	0.65	0.68	0.72	0.69
Capital management	0.71	0.57	0.57	0.64	0.62
Human resource management	0.51	0.45	0.60	0.61	0.54
Information technology management	0.63	0.45	0.37	0.57	0.51

yet to be fully excavated. This chapter serves as a summary of findings from the assessment; it also offers clues for future endeavors and presents puzzles that need thorough exploration.

As comprehensive and well-planned as the GPP financial management surveys were, in hindsight room for improvement existed should anyone decide to launch a new project of this scale. Three recommendations are prominent. The first is to examine the financial management system in each surveyed government: location of the budget office and the finance department, access of directors of such organs to the chief elected official, and how they function. These entail detailed case studies to generate reliable answers.

Next, if collected systematically, detailed information on the education, qualifications, training, and length of service of financial managers will shed more light on the function of the financial management system. However well the system is designed for higher capacity, it is ultimately the human factor that accounts for the actual function and performance of the system. Unfortunately, research so far can offer little information about this important factor.

Finally, indicators and measures used for grading management capacity may need to be different for the states, counties, and cities. After all, state governments possess quite different features from local levels; city and county governments perform different roles in terms of service delivery.[41] As with debt policy, an adopted policy is best for the states, but a formal policy may suffice at the city and county levels. Such differences among the levels of government may not have been unique to debt management but rather common and valid in many other areas, as well.

APPENDIX

Financial Management Assessment Procedures and Methodology

For reliable and objective assessment results and consistency between different rounds of assessment for the same level of government, assessment procedures were standardized. The procedures introduced below are an example used in one round of the actual assessment.

Working Criteria and Weight

The first step in standardization was to assign significance levels and weights to criteria and subcriteria, as reflected in appendix table 2.A.1. In this process some subcriteria were combined to be more operable for the level of government being

Table 2.A.1. Grading Benchmarks

Grade	Absolute standard	Real score	Interval
A	≥ 85	85	15
A−	<85 ≥ 75	75	10
B+	<75 ≥ 68	68	8
B	<68 ≥ 60	60	8
B−	<60 ≥ 55	55	5
C+	<55 ≥ 50	50	5
C	<50 ≥ 45	45	5
C−	<45 ≥ 41	41	4
D+	<41 ≥ 38	38	3
D	<38 ≥ 35	35	3
F	<35	0	3

assessed. As shown in the table, the total number of points, corresponding to the weights, is 100.

Calculation of Scores

The second step was to design a detailed codebook for use by data analysts to convert qualitative and quantitative management information into numerical values that are taken as raw scores for each subcriterion. Raw scores were normalized on a scale of 0 to 1. Normalized scores were then converted into real scores by multiplying a factor obtained by dividing the weights given to each subcriterion by the number of variables used in assessing that subcriterion. Finally, the real scores were summed. The seventeen subcriteria, with their levels and weights, are presented in table 2.A.2.

For example, twenty-one variables were used to assess investment and cash management (subcriterion 2e). Every piece of information related to these variables was assigned a numerical value (the range varies from 0 to 2, 3, or 5 among variables) according to the codebook. Next, the values were normalized. A variable given a raw score of 4 on a scale of 0 to 5 became 0.8 ($\frac{4}{5}$) after normalization. The normalized scores of all twenty-one variables were then summed. The multiplying factor was obtained by dividing the weight for this subcriterion (10) by the number of variables (21): $\frac{10}{21} = 0.48$. The normalized sum multiplied by the factor is the real score for investment and cash management. The sum of the real scores for each subcriterion served as the final score.

Grades by Absolute Standard

With the maximum possible score being 100, the scoring range was divided into eleven intervals that correspond to various letter grades as shown in table 2.A.1.

Table 2.A.2 Financial Management Assessment Criteria, Significance Level and Weights

	Criterion	Significance level	Weight (total = 100)	Notes
1	Multiyear perspective on budgeting		22	
1a	Meaningful current revenue and expenditure estimates	1	12	Merge with 1b
1b	Meaningful revenue and expenditure forecasts	1		Merge into 1a
1c	Gauge of fiscal impact of financial decisions	2	10	Merge with 2c
2	Mechanisms that preserve stability and fiscal health		40	
2a	Budget that reflects structural balance between ongoing revenues and expenditures.	1	10	
2b	Effective use of counter-cyclical or contingency planning devices	1	10	Merge with 4c
2c	Appropriately manages long-term liabilities, including pensions	4		Merge into 1c
2d	Appropriately used and managed debt	1	10	
2e	Investment and cash management practices that appropriately balance return and solvency	1	10	
3	Sufficient financial information for policy makers, managers, and citizens		18	
3a	Accurate, reliable, and thorough financial reports	3	6	Merge with 3c and 3d
3b	Useful financial data for government managers	5	2	
3c	Budgetary and financial data for citizens			
3d	Timely financial reports			
3e	Gauge of cost of delivering programs or services	3	6	
3f	Budget that is adopted on time	4	4	
4	Appropriate control over financial operations		20	
4a	Balance between control over expenditures and managerial flexibility	1	10	
4b	Effectively managed procurement, including contracts for delivery of goods and services	2	10	
4c	Recovery plans and programs that support business continuation after a disaster	5		Merge into 2b

The use of the 100-point scale, instead of the median or average of final scores, as the basis of grading ensures an absolute standard, one that does not change from one year's assessment to another's. In this way, governments are compared along a fixed scale, not a floating one. Such a process allows more comparability across years of assessment cycles.[42]

Data Sources

The most important data source was the comprehensive GPP financial management survey, with closed- and open-ended questions covering qualitative and quantitative aspects of all significant financial management areas. Each year's survey questions remained approximately the same as in previous years with minor adjustments to suit the level (state, city, or county) of governments. Terms used in the survey were strictly defined at the front of the survey as well as in the questions in which they occurred to assist respondents in understanding what information is being requested.

Another data source was the published official documents that served as checks against survey responses. Particularly important among these documents were comprehensive annual financial reports and budgets. Statements of revenue, expenditure, assets, and liabilities all receive strict examination. Notes to the statements, transmittal letters, audit opinions, and explanations offered in these documents provide excellent insight into financial management. A third important source includes management policies, finance laws, and regulations adopted by the government. The presence of meticulously designed, well-formulated, and well-implemented policies and regulations was taken as a strong indication of sound management capacity.

To ensure fairness to governments situated in different phases of the economic cycle (boom or recession), researchers took an extra step to identify and track the trend in financial management of the state, city, or county. For this purpose, researchers examined comprehensive annual financial reports for five (state and city) to nine years (county) before the year of assessment.

Research Team and Coding Reliability

The financial management research team at the Maxwell School was composed of a faculty specialist, one senior research associate serving as the coordinator, and several research assistants. The faculty specialist was the leader of the team, responsible for the design and implementation of all evaluation tools and the overall evaluation operations.

The research associate and research assistants served as analysts, each coding a portion of the assessed governments or some of the financial management areas of all the governments. After initial coding, the data were double-checked by switching governments or areas among the analysts and by doing statistical analysis of the preliminary raw scores. Coder bias was corrected through discussion between coders, and remaining issues were resolved by the faculty specialist, using his professional judgment. Systematic bias was corrected by adjustment to the scoring tools and through statistical manipulation.

Each analyst then took responsibility for two or three subareas of financial management, such as debt management and investment management, for all governments under assessment. The purpose of this step was to identify patterns that emerged in years before the assessment. Scores were calculated and real scores converted into grades through an automated process, separate from coding, performed by data analysts to ensure the utmost objectivity.

NOTES

1. From the pilot survey in 1997 through the county survey in 2001, the survey instrument for financial management went through several revisions for better and more accurate assessment by using more closed-ended questions; consistency remained through the several revisions.

2. The major domains are the four overarching criteria of assessment, and the areas are the seventeen subcriteria used in the survey instrument. Although the criteria were also revised in the course of the GPP study, mainly through regrouping of the subcriteria, the framework remained unchanged. For details, see appendix B to this volume.

3. Dennis Strachota and John Peterson, introduction to *Local Government Finance: Concepts and Practices,* ed. John Peterson and Dennis Strachota (Chicago: Government Finance Officers Association, 1991), pp. 1–8.

4. E. F. Brigham, *Financial Management: Theory and Practice,* 3d ed. (New York: CBS College Publishing, 1982).

5. J. L. Esser, in the foreword to *Local Government Finance: Concepts and Practices,* ed. John Peterson and Dennis Strachota (Chicago: Government Finance Officers Association, 1991), p. vii, notes similar issues when talking about changes in the operating environment of state and local financial management since the mid-1980s. He points out five changes: The federal government reduced the level of assistance to state and local governments. Accordingly, states expanded their role in domestic policy. Practices of governmental financial management became increasingly shaped by professional standards. Information technology has grown to play an increasing role. And governments now make more use of the financial markets.

6. Five counties did not provide a response to this question. The timely adoption rates for these five years are 69 percent for 1997, 71 percent for 1998, 77 percent for 1999, 80 percent for 2000, and 74 percent for 2001.

7. In the GPP financial management survey, the term *estimation* refers to predictions for the coming fiscal year, and *forecasts* to predictions for futures years. The word *projection* is used more generally. Since even the forecasts are but a few years into the immediate future, this chapter uses the three terms interchangeably, for convenience of discussion.

8. Figures in the estimation accuracy tables (tables 2.1 to 2.3) are calculated by subtracting the actual amount from the estimated amount and then dividing by the estimates. Positive ratios for revenue indicate that actual revenue is larger than estimated; negative ones mean that actual revenue is smaller than estimated. Negative ratios for expenditure indicate that actual expenditure is smaller than estimated; positive ratios mean that actual expenditure exceeds revenue. Smaller absolute values indicate higher accuracy rates.

9. The true story would be more complex because financial managers are oriented toward higher accuracy to raise their professional reputation, whereas elected officials may face political pressure from large surpluses. Reasons for such high "error rates" deserve separate treatment.

10. Whether this is, at least partly, a result of the urban nature of the cities in contrast to the states and counties is beyond what the author can offer a reasonable interpretation for with the current amount of information, but it is open to further investigation.

11. Thirteen states use methods other than the fiscal note.

12. Only twenty-one cities provided usable responses to this question, making the percentages distorted. But it is likely that those that did not provide clear responses probably did not have a formalized procedure for the assessment.

13. R. A. Musgrave, *The Theory of Public Finance* (New York: McGraw-Hill, 1959); Wallace Oates, *Fiscal Federalism* (New York: Harcourt Brace Jovanovich, 1972); R. A. Musgrave and P. B. Musgrave, *Public Finance in Theory and Practice,* 5th ed. (New York: McGraw-Hill, 1989).

14. E. M. Gramlich, "Subnational Fiscal Policy," in *Perspectives on Local Public Finance and Public Policy,* vol. 3, ed. J. M. Quigley (Greenwich, CT: JAI Press, 1987), pp. 3–27.

15. Richard Pollock and J. P. Suyderhoud, "The Role of Rainy Day Funds in Achieving Fiscal Stability," *National Tax Journal* 43, no. 4 (1986): 485–97; R. S. Sobel and R. G. Holcombe, "The Impact of State Rainy Day Funds in Easing State Fiscal Crises during the 1990–1991 Recession," *Public Budgeting and Finance* 16, no. 3 (1996): 28–48.

16. Yilin Hou, "What Stabilizes State General Fund Spending during Downturns?" *Public Budgeting and Finance* 23, no. 3 (2003): 64–91.

17. Having BSF legislation does not mean having a real budget stabilization fund. For example, a state may have no BSF balance at all for some (even many) years; some states may have merely a within-the-fiscal-year device that is not, strictly speaking, a budget stabilization fund.

18. J. E. Peterson and Thomas McLauphlin, "Debt Policies and Procedures," in *Local Government Finance: Concepts and Practices,* ed. John Peterson and Dennis Strachota (Chicago: Government Finance Officers Association, 1991), pp. 263–92, quotation on p. 263.

19. States have much more in the way of resources and power to issue debt than do local governments, so the regulation is more necessary than at the local levels.

20. Obviously, the question of why more of the cities use the informal rather than formal and adopted debt policies deserves a separate, more detailed study.

21. Some survey respondents referred to their councils as oversight bodies.

22. The city survey did not include this part of the debt question.

23. Ten percent of states allow a maturity of the facility life, 36 percent allow twenty or more years; the two percentages combined amount to 46 percent.

24. Owing to differences in the survey instrument, the statistics of city investment policies are not compatible with those of states and counties.

25. The exceptions are Hawaii and South Dakota. Both states, however, have pension funds and administrative rules for short-term investment.

26. Ten counties reported having an oversight body composed exclusively of members from the executive branch. This is not, according to our definition, an oversight body. Another six counties have auditing personnel in the organ but no public involvement, again falling out of our definition of oversight body.

27. Gubernatorial discretion in the budgetary process is more forcibly visible in the line-item veto power of the governor in many states.

28. This threshold varies depending on the size of the state. But on the whole, it is high enough for adequate managerial discretion.

29. S. J. Gauthier, "Auditing," in *Local Government Finance: Concepts and Practices,* ed. John Peterson and Dennis Strachota (Chicago: Government Finance Officers Association, 1991), pp. 221–40.

30. The GFOA also presents an Excellence in Budget Presentation award, which was won by seventeen counties for their 1997–98 fiscal-year budgets and by twenty counties for their 1998–99 budgets. These awards are based on the compiling of the report, not the quality of the overall financial management.

31. Kansas has compiled and published its comprehensive annual financial reports only since 1999. New Mexico still has not adopted this practice; its financial statement remains the *Annual Financial Report,* compiled on the budgetary basis of accounting.

32. The rationale for this stipulation, according to a key official of the New Jersey Department of Local Affairs, is that the cash basis is a more accurate reflection of the financial status of the local governments. A similar claim was cited by Kansas officials before 1999 for not adopting the comprehensive annual financial reports format.

33. The survey question on budget adoption covered only 1997 though 1999, though information on prior years can be obtained from state documents. The Utah legislature convenes for forty-five calendar days in the first quarter of each year. According to Utah's response to a 2000 GPP survey question, the state budget "is always passed before the session ends."

34. In general, such unusual actions use nonrecurring revenues to cover recurring expenditures, such as sale of assets, nonroutine transfers from other funds into the general fund, reduction of pension contributions, delay of bill payments, and short-term borrowing for operational uses.

35. Actual annual balance is calculated as general fund revenue minus expenditure divided by expenditure. All are actual figures, in conformity with generally accepted accounting principles.

36. Utah's low ratios of unreserved undesignated balance of the general fund may give observers a wrong impression: How could the more than 20 percent general fund balance end up with such low (much lower than the fifty-state average) ratios of the unreserved undesignated balance? Utah reserves or designates much of its year-end balances for following years' one-time expenses, thereby eliminating some "unexpected" items and their expenses in the coming year.

37. Utah's BSF, called a budgetary reserve account, is enabled by section 63, chapter 38, of the *Utah Code Annotated.*

38. The portfolio is about 10 percent of the own-source actual total operating fund expenditures in 1999. With a 4.54 percent annual return rate, investment interest is 0.44 percent of estimated own-source total operating fund expenditures for fiscal year 2000.

39. Utah's governor also has line-item veto power.

40. In the first round of state surveys and in the city and county surveys, the financial management grades given to three entities were lower than their overall grades. This number rose to seven in the second round of the state surveys.

41. In the context of the GPP, for which both the thirty-five cities and the forty counties were selected based on the size of their revenues, some counties overlap with the thirty-five metropolitan areas; even so, the distinction in service delivery between the cities and counties remains true.

42. Absolute standards are the working rule; in actual assessment, however, adjustments of the grade may have to be made for serious state, city, and county issues or problems that are outside the evaluation system but must be taken into consideration. Examples are cases of corruption and scandals or lack of key components of financial management systems.

CHAPTER 3

Underpinning Government

Capital and Infrastructure Management in State and Local Government

CAROL EBDON

Service demands and the level of government spending on capital projects necessitate a good capital management system. In the 2000 fiscal year, direct expenditures on capital outlays by state and local governments amounted to $217 billion, or $771.31 per capita.[1] Over the past two decades, several reports have concluded that governments' capital spending has not kept pace with infrastructure needs and that maintenance of capital assets has been inadequate.[2] In its "2001 Report Card for America's Infrastructure," the American Society of Civil Engineers gave an average grade of D+ across the areas it studied and estimated five-year investment needs at $1.3 trillion.[3] Recent changes in accounting standards that will require governments to report additional information relating to inventory, costs, and the condition of infrastructure are further evidence of the importance of capital management.

Capital management differs greatly across government jurisdictions, in everything from how they define a capital asset to the type of planning they do to the capital-financing methods they use.[4] However, experts are in general agreement about the components that are important for a good capital management system. A long-term comprehensive capital plan should be developed and updated regularly, based on thorough analysis of needs, service demands, and capacity. In addition, managers must monitor capital projects closely to minimize cost overruns and delays. Asset maintenance is another crucial component of capital management; appropriate routine and preventive maintenance can save money over the long run. Each of these three components requires the existence of good information systems to provide the necessary data relating to capital assets.

Several characteristics are considered crucial for good capital planning. Capital planning should extend over a longer horizon than operating budgets, because capital assets have long-term costs and benefits. Capital expenses are large, multiyear, and nonrecurring, which makes them "lumpy." For example, it may take several years to plan for and build an office building, but following its completion it might not require any additional major capital expenses for a number of years. Long-term comprehensive capital planning enables a government to better budget its scarce resources over time.[5]

Capital needs and service demands often require more resources than are available, so managers must compare competing capital requests and choose which projects to include in the capital plan. Coordination with a strategic plan and consideration of capital project effects on future operating and maintenance costs can enhance this process.[6] A formal ranking system also may be used to evaluate and compare projects; this approach can force the inclusion of additional information in the decision-making process and improve objectivity and justification of decisions.[7]

Citizens also play an important role in the capital planning process. Public participation in budgeting processes may help governments determine service needs, educate citizens in the complexities and costs of government services, and reduce citizens' distrust of government.[8] Making the capital improvement plan widely available and informative enhances citizen understanding and involvement. Some jurisdictions use participative approaches, such as holding decentralized public hearings throughout the community, conducting public opinion surveys, providing greater access and input to public databases, and appointing citizens to capital planning committees.[9]

Once a government has adopted a capital plan, project implementation requires careful oversight. The objective is to ensure high performance while reducing cost overruns and delays by setting goals and performance objectives and closely monitoring the project to completion.[10] Project management is facilitated by some level of centralized project tracking with regular detailed reporting.

Asset maintenance is another important component of capital management. Deferring capital maintenance can result in excessive long-term costs and require asset replacement sooner than would otherwise be necessary. For example, preventive maintenance has been found to reduce infrastructure replacement costs by 75 to 90 percent.[11] To adequately maintain their assets, jurisdictions need up-to-date inventories that record assets' age and maintenance history, and they should perform condition assessments on a regular basis, including data on the cost of maintaining assets in good condition.

Issues relating to capital reporting on financial statements have long been the subject of debate. In the past, governments have not been required to report depreciation, or even the value of their assets, which may have skewed the consideration of capital project requests.[12] Some have argued that having a capital budget will not by itself solve the infrastructure problems because the real issue is the underinvestment in maintenance, and capital budgeting methods do not show maintenance needs adequately.[13] However, the Governmental Accounting Standards Board (GASB) recently adopted new financial reporting standards (Statement 34) that require state and local governments to report the value of their infrastructure assets in annual financial statements. Depreciation expense is also now recorded for all capital assets, unless the government uses an asset management system and documents that assets are maintained at a predetermined condition level. To comply with these new requirements, governments have made significant changes in the way they track and manage their assets.[14]

Does use of these recommended capital management practices lead to better outcomes for governments that use them? Little research has been done in this area, owing to the difficulty of developing meaningful, standard capital performance measures for a large sample of governments. Adoption of individual elements by themselves may have limited effects. For example, one study of municipal capital budgeting found that the capital process tends to be more political than rational, even with a capital plan.[15] Others point out that although most state and local governments have capital plans, there are numerous instances of poor information and decision making in these jurisdictions.[16] However, the importance of capital management is only reinforced by examples of poor planning, such as the state agency that spent more than $2 million for a pedestrian walkway that was demolished shortly after being built because the buildings it connected were replaced.[17] For this reason, scholars and professional organizations continue to stress the need for long-range capital planning, project management, and asset maintenance. Rating agencies also consider management practices, such as the existence of a formal capital improvement plan, in determination of credit ratings, because in recent decades "the only significant credit difficulties that general governments have had have been due to bad management."[18]

Capital management was evaluated by the Government Performance Project against three overall criteria, representing capital planning and budgeting, project management, and asset maintenance, respectively:

- Government conducts thorough analysis of future needs.
- Government monitors and evaluates projects throughout their implementation.
- Government conducts appropriate maintenance of capital assets.

Tremendous variation was found within and across the three types of government. Overall, though, project management was found to be the strongest component. Long-term capital planning is common, but the decision-making process could be improved in many places. Asset maintenance is the weakest of the three capital management "pillars," owing largely to lack of information and inadequate funding.

Capital Management in States, Cities, and Counties

This section summarizes the capital management grades for each of the three types of government evaluated; detailed comparisons between states, cities, and counties are presented in the next section. Owing to differences in the surveys over the years of the project, the focus of analysis varies somewhat across the government types. However, comparing the grade ranges provides a rough estimation of differences in management capacity (see Table 3.1).

The 1998 grades included nine states in the A range (Kentucky, Maryland, Minnesota, Missouri, Nebraska, Utah, Virginia, Washington, and Wisconsin). Twenty-two states received grades in the B range, sixteen in

Table 3.1. Aggregate Capital Management Grades

| | States | | | | | | | |
| | 1998 | | 2000 | | Counties | | Cities | |
Grade range	N	%	N	%	N	%	N	%
A	9	18	5	10	4	10	5	14
B	22	44	28	56	17	43	22	63
C	16	32	15	30	16	40	8	23
D	3	6	2	4	3	7	0	0

the C range, and three in the D range. The distribution was somewhat similar in 2000, although only five states (Maryland, Michigan, New Jersey, Utah, and Washington) received A-range grades in this round. Twenty states improved their grades in the second round, twenty-one received lower grades, and nine states had the same grade in both rounds.

Direct comparisons between state capital management systems in the first and second rounds of the GPP project are difficult for two reasons. First, the 1998 round focused almost exclusively on public facilities. During that process, however, it became clear that transportation is a major component of capital management in the states and that management systems for transportation often are different from those for other assets. (For example, federal transportation grants mandate such elements as a minimum time period for transportation plans and specific types of public participation in the state planning process.) Therefore, transportation was included more comprehensively in the second-round evaluation, with general assets and transportation assets receiving equal weights in scoring. Second, no quantitative coding was done in the first evaluation; the Maxwell grading was based on qualitative evaluations of the survey responses and documentation. Owing to these dissimilarities, this chapter focuses primarily on the scoring in the second (2000) round of state evaluations.

Thirty-five cities were included in the GPP city sample. Phoenix received the only A grade, while four other cities received a grade of A− (Austin, Honolulu, San Jose, and Virginia Beach). Twenty-two cities received grades in the B range, and eight were in the C range.

Forty counties were evaluated in 2001. Four counties (Baltimore, Fairfax, San Diego, and Westchester) received the highest grade, A−. Seventeen others were in the B range, sixteen in the C range, and three counties received grades in the D range.

Overall, cities had higher grades than the states and counties. Seventy-seven percent of cities received grades in the A or B range, compared with 66 percent of states in the second round and 53 percent of counties. No cities received a D grade, and overall the cities had a smaller proportion of C grades than the other two government types. The sample of counties received the lowest grades: 7 percent received grades in the D range, and 47 percent were in the C and D range, compared with 23 percent of cities and 34 percent of states in 2000. The state grades in the second round ranked between the cities and counties.

Components of Capital Management Systems

As noted earlier, the focus of the Government Performance Project evaluation changed over time, as did the survey questions and the way researchers coded and weighted the responses. However, many of the major questions were similar, so some comparisons can be made that are useful in understanding similarities and differences in management capacity in these areas. This section highlights the key lessons and themes within and across the levels of governments in the three primary components of capital management: capital planning, project management, and asset maintenance. These comparisons can be used by government managers to gauge how their own practices compare with other jurisdictions. Scholars and professional organizations can use this information to understand which prescribed activities are common and where additional efforts may be needed to assist in improving capital management.

Capital Planning

Long-range capital improvement plans are common in the cities, counties, and states evaluated in the Government Performance Project. Development of a long-term plan is considered to be a crucial element of capital management, in order to adequately budget scarce resources among competing large and long-term capital needs. Table 3.2 compares the time horizons of capital improvement plans for states, cities, and counties. Cities were strongest in this area; 89 percent of the sample cities had a capital improvement plan covering five or more years, and plans of all of the cities

Table 3.2. Number of Years in Capital Improvement Plans

	States (2000)				Counties		Cities	
	General assets		Transportation					
	N	%	N	%	N	%	N	%
No CIP	5	10.4	1	2.2	4	10.8	0	00.0
1 year	3	6.2	2	4.4	1	2.7	0	00.0
2–4 years	9	16.6	15	33.3	3	8.1	4	11.4
5 or more years	32	66.8	27	60.1	29	78.4	31	88.6
N	48	100.0	45	100.0	37	100.0	35	100.0

covered at least two years. Seventy-eight percent of the sample counties had a plan for five or more years, but almost 14 percent of the counties had either no comprehensive capital improvement plan at all or only a one-year plan. States scored slightly lower; 67 percent had a five-year or longer capital plan for general assets, 17 percent had no capital improvement plan or had only a one-year plan, and the remaining states had plans that covered two to four years. For transportation needs, 60 percent of states had a plan for five or more years, 7 percent had no plan or a one-year plan, and one-third had a plan for two to four years. Overall, then, the vast majority of these governments had long-term plans, although four counties and five states lacked capital improvement plans entirely.

Information included in the capital improvement plan tends to vary widely within and across the three types of governments. As noted earlier, the availability and readability of the capital improvement plan document may enhance transparency in government and citizen understanding of governmental decision making. Table 3.3 summarizes the frequency of use of various types of information. Summary tables of the projects was the most common element of a capital improvement plan, included in 92 percent of counties, 91 percent of cities, 90 percent of state general asset plans, and 70 percent of state transportation plans. Detailed descriptions of capital projects were also widely used, but to a smaller extent in cities. Debt ratio projections, which provide information on the relative

Table 3.3. Information Included in CIP (percentage)

| | States (2000) | | | | | | | |
| | General assets | | Transportation | | Cities | | Counties | |
	%	N	%	N	%	N	%	N
Summary tables	90	45	70	35	91	35	92	35
Financing plan summary	68	34	66	33	n.a.		87	33
Debt ratio projections	24	12	8	4	14	5	34	13
Detailed project description	80	40	78	34	57	20	92	35
Project justifications	62	31	28	14	9	3	58	22
Glossary of terms	42	21	48	24	51	18	42	16
Planning process description	48	24	62	31	n.a.		71	27
Capital spending amounts	46	23	26	13	n.a.		66	25
Operating cost impacts	50	25	10	5	31	11	58	22

amount of the government's outstanding debt, were the least common item (of those included in the survey instrument); these were included in only 34 percent of counties, 24 percent of state general asset plans, 14 percent of cities, and 8 percent of state transportation plans. Overall, though, there is little consistency in the capital improvement plan document across the governments surveyed in the GPP. The extent to which citizens and other stakeholders actually read these plans is not known; nor do we know much about what types of information are most beneficial to these users. Having the data available, however, at least provides the opportunity for its use.

Many of these jurisdictions do not use recommended methods of capital project selection. Scholars and professional organizations suggest using a ranking system to compare proposed capital projects to ensure that essential information will be included in the decision process. Use of a committee also is recommended to obtain a variety of perspectives, including those of citizens. In addition, projects should be coordinated with the government's strategic plan and linked to the operating budget so that future impacts of capital decisions are taken into consideration.

The use of formal, detailed ranking criteria was minimal in all three types of governments studied: 23 percent in cities, 20 percent in counties, 10 percent for state general assets, and 32 percent for state transportation planning (table 3.4). Examples are provided later in this chapter. Many of the other jurisdictions did use some type of general criteria (for example, 71% of states). However, a number of these governments did not use any type of ranking at all, including nine states (18%) and seven counties (20%).

Committees comprising more than central office staff were used in 38 percent of states for general assets and 55 percent for transportation planning but in only 39 percent of counties. Other jurisdictions used committees made up only of central office staff, such as a finance or transportation department, but some—46 percent of the counties sampled, for example—had no committee evaluation process at all.

With the exception of state transportation planning, citizens appear to rarely be involved in the planning process (in only 23% of the sample cities, for example). Coordination with a government-wide strategic plan was fairly high for cities, at 80 percent, but it occurred in only 47 percent of counties and less than 30 percent of states. States do appear to ensure linkages with agency-wide plans, however; 64 percent claimed to do so for general assets and 68 percent for transportation assets. At all three levels, slightly more than half of the governments used informal methods of esti-

Table 3.4. Capital Project Evaluation and Management (percentage)

| | States (2000) | | | | | | | |
| | General assets | | Transportation | | Cities | | Counties | |
	%	N	%	N	%	N	%	N
Evaluation								
Formal ranking criteria	10	5	32	14	23	8	20	8
Committees	38	18	55	24	n.a.		36	14
Coordination with government-wide strategic plan	21	10	27	11	80	28	50	19
Management								
Centralized tracking	96	48	78	39	87	30	87	32
Monthly or quarterly management reports	74	37	64	34	71	25	74	26
Supportive information system	86	43	90	44	66	23	77	27

mating and reporting the impact of capital requests on operating and maintenance costs, but formal published estimations were infrequent.

Project Management

Capital project management is strong in the sample cities, counties, and states. Project monitoring is important to ensure high performance and to minimize cost overruns and delays. Most of the jurisdictions included in this project appear to have good systems in place in this area (table 3.4). The vast majority had formal tracking procedures that included some degree of central control: 87 percent of cities and counties, 96 percent of state general assets, and 78 percent of state transportation assets. A minority of these governments performed project tracking at the agency level only.

Most of these governments prepared formal project reports monthly or quarterly: 71 percent of cities, 74 percent of counties, 74 percent of states for general assets, and 64 percent of states for transportation assets. In the remaining sample governments, project reporting was generally done, but less frequently. Project reports often include information such as the originally scheduled date of completion, project delay estimates, change orders and revised cost estimates, and explanations for overruns. Responses indicate that between 82 percent and 98 percent of states and cities included these items in their project management reports.

In addition, most of these governments rated their information systems for project management as being more supportive than other capital management systems. Sixty-six percent of cities reported that their project management systems support their needs, and the systems either partially or fully met needs in 77 percent of counties, 86 percent of states for general assets, and 88 percent for state transportation assets.

Asset Maintenance

Asset maintenance is generally the weakest area of capital management. Capital assets need to be maintained in good working order to prevent excessive long-term costs and safety hazards. This requires good information systems and regular, comprehensive condition assessments to determine the status of assets, the cost of maintaining them in good condition, and the financing available to pay for the maintenance needs. Many of the governments the GPP evaluated have had difficulties with asset maintenance, although this is an area to which these jurisdictions have given increasing attention in recent years.

Information on condition assessments and maintenance cost needs among the responding jurisdictions was frequently unavailable or out of date. Table 3.5 summarizes the use of condition assessments in the sample

Table 3.5. Use of Condition Assessments in Cities

	N	%
Public buildings		
None	2	5.7
Informal	15	42.9
Formal, infrequent	10	28.6
Formal, regular	8	22.9
N	35	100.0
Streets		
None	0	0
Informal, infrequent	5	15.2
Annual visual inspection	22	66.7
Annual mechanical inspection	6	18.2
N	33	100.0

cities. Only eight (23%) of the cities reported that they conduct formal, regular building inspections. Two cities performed no condition assessments for public buildings. Most either did informal assessments or had conducted formal assessments at some point but not on a regular basis. The same is true for counties and states; some did intermittent assessments for certain types of assets, but most did not perform assessments on a regular, frequent basis. Fifty percent of counties and 28 percent of states claimed to conduct assessments at least annually.

The situation appears slightly better for streets and roads. All of these cities did some type of assessments. Two-thirds conducted visual inspections of streets on an annual basis, while six cities (18%) performed annual mechanical inspections. Forty-eight percent of states also claimed to do annual inspections or assessments of streets and roads.

Upon inspection of documents and detailed survey responses, however, it appears that these numbers were often overstated. In some cases, for example, assessments were done only when a capital project request was prepared; since the planning process occurs each year, governments may consider this to be an annual assessment, even though all assets are not assessed each year. When regular assessments were made, they sometimes consisted of cursory visual inspections. With the exception of streets, roads, and bridges, it appears to be relatively unusual for these governments to conduct regular, comprehensive condition assessments. As a result, many governments did not have estimates of what it would cost to bring their assets up to good condition. Several governments said they know this is an issue and have been working to obtain the information they need to understand and better manage asset maintenance.

These subnational governments have substantial unmet maintenance-funding needs. Many did not have precise information about the level of maintenance needs in their jurisdictions. For example, more than one-third of the states and one-half of the counties either could not or would not answer a question about their level of funding relative to maintenance needs. However, many reported that they know they have a great deal of deferred maintenance they have not been able to fund. Only 35 percent of cities and 37 percent of counties reported having funded 50 percent or more of their needs in recent years. Sixteen percent of states reported funding 50 percent or more of their general asset needs, and 18 percent reported the same for transportation assets. Only five states (10%) claimed to have funded 75 to 100 percent of annual maintenance needs for general assets in the past two years, and six to have funded this level of need for transportation assets. However, the good economic environment of the late 1990s allowed many governments to start making a dent in the backlog by using dedicated funding sources or increased general revenues for this purpose.

Information technology systems are frequently inadequate for asset maintenance support. Asset maintenance requires the ability not only to collect regular information but also to have systems in place to support ongoing data needs. This is a weakness for many of the governments in this sample. Table 3.6 summarizes the proportion of inventory and condition or maintenance systems that are considered to either partially or fully meet the needs of state and county governments. Sixty-three percent of the counties stated that their condition and maintenance systems either partially or fully meet their needs, but 31 percent had no automated system at all. Condition and maintenance systems at least partially met the needs for state general assets for 58 percent of states, but 26 percent did not have an IT system in this area. For transportation assets, 72 percent of states' systems were partially or fully supportive, but 20 percent had no IT system for maintaining these assets.

The situation is slightly better for inventory systems. Sixty-six percent of counties had systems that partially or fully met their needs, compared with 79 percent of states for general assets and 80 percent of states for transportation assets. Again, though, ten of the counties (29%) had no inventory management system, along with six states (12%). The situation is similar in cities, only 17 percent of which reported having supportive systems for maintenance and inventory tracking. Many governments noted this as a concern, especially as they attempt to implement the new accounting requirements of GASB Statement 34. A number of them noted that they

Table 3.6. States and Counties Reporting Asset Information System Partially or Fully Meets Capital Management Needs (percentage)

| | States (2000) | | | | Counties | |
| | General assets | | Transportation | | | |
	%	N	%	N	%	N
Inventory management	79	38	80	35	66	23
Condition and maintenance	58	28	72	34	63	22

were in the process of upgrading their systems or installing new systems to better meet their information needs.

Capital Management Capacity

Overall, there appear to be more similarities than differences across the three types of governments. All three tend to be strongest in capital project management and weakest in asset maintenance. Most of these governments, with some exceptions, have long-range capital plans but could improve their use of ranking criteria, evaluation committees, and citizen participation in the project selection process. Information systems are very important in capital management, especially in light of new accounting standards that require governments to maintain additional information related to their assets. In response, a number of jurisdictions are in the process of implementing new or updated information systems for capital management purposes. Efforts to improve capacity in other areas, especially in asset maintenance, also were noted.

Environmental and institutional factors might affect capital management capacity and performance. For example, initial analyses indicate that smaller states are more likely to use detailed evaluation criteria and committees but have less adequate information systems than larger states. Counties in the West were less likely to have a comprehensive capital improvement plan, and larger counties tended to score lower overall than did smaller counties. City and county structures and functions also vary significantly, in ways that can affect capital management. For example, some counties in our sample had little responsibility for roads; others were responsible for airports, hospitals, and schools. The effect of these factors on capital management capacity requires further analysis.

Capital management was evaluated as one of the five separate components of the GPP. However, a strong relationship between the management areas clearly exists. Managing for results relates to planning and measuring performance, both of which are important in capital management. Therefore, the capital management evaluation process considered the system's linkages with strategic plans and monitoring asset condition and project implementation. The other three areas relate to management of specific types of assets: employees, finances, and information. The capital management grading process did not explicitly consider human resource issues, but governments without sufficient numbers of well-trained employees would be less likely to be able to maintain strong capital systems. Similarly, without supportive automated information systems, governments will find it difficult to plan, manage, and adequately maintain their capital assets. Finally, financial management is directly connected to capital management. Operating and capital budgets must be integrated to some extent to consider the jurisdiction's total costs; and sufficient financial resources are imperative for the ability to acquire and maintain capital assets. Capital management, then, does not stand alone but is highly reliant on the other four systems studied in the GPP.

Innovations in Capital Management

Cities, counties, and states that exhibit good capital management systems can serve as models for other governments. A number of governments received high grades in the Government Performance Project. As noted earlier, Maryland, Michigan, Utah, and Washington all received grades in the A range. High-performing counties were Baltimore, Fairfax, Hennepin, San Diego, and Westchester. Among the cities, Austin, Honolulu, Phoenix, San Jose, and Virginia Beach deserve particular note for the overall quality of their capital management practices.

These and other governments in the sample have introduced innovative methods for improving capital management. This section highlights these innovations across the three types of government in each of the criteria areas.

Capital Planning

At the time of the surveys, most of the governments evaluated by the GPP had long-term capital plans; many of those that did not were in the process of developing them or creating a regular process for updating them. Linkages to strategic plans and to operating budgets also were being improved in a number of jurisdictions. One of the weakest remaining areas in capital planning is the project selection process. These governments did not commonly use criteria to evaluate and compare capital project requests. Box 3.1 includes examples of several governments that were using innovative approaches to project selection.

Minnesota had the most rigorous ranking method of the governments reviewed in the GPP. The state used a detailed scoring system with three

Box 3.1 Innovation Approaches to Capital Project Selection

- *Fairfax County* prioritizes facility requests based on asset age, condition assessment, health and safety issues, user-identified needs, and compliance with mandates. The Board of Supervisors also adopted seven categories of prioritization for storm drainage projects.

- *Franklin County* uses a matrix to rank transportation projects, based on factors such as need, growth, safety, funding availability, environmental requirements, and cooperative agreements.

- *Louisiana* uses three levels of priorities. Highest priority is given to emergencies, implementation of court orders, repairs and renovations to preserve life and property, and highway overlay, repairs, and construction. The second level is for continuation of projects that were previously funded but require additional funding for completion. The lowest priority is given to requests for new projects without previous funding.

- *Virginia* uses eight criteria to rank general asset project requests. Projects are assessed based on the degree to which they are associated with legal or judicial mandates; supplement projects for which funds have already been appropriated; are associated with the governor's funding priorities; are associated with standards or certification requirements, such as life safety code requirements or space guideline deficiencies; involve major repairs necessary for continued use of a facility; involve improvement or modification of the use of existing facilities; involve replacement or additions to existing facilities; and involve the construction or acquisition of new facilities.

- *Seattle* requires fiscal notes for capital projects in excess of $500,000. The notes must include the project's operating and maintenance costs, life span, and impact on private investment, as well as the estimated cost of denying the project.

decision-making screens. First, a technical scoring system evaluated projects against statewide scoring criteria. Then a project's statewide, regional, or local significance was determined. Finally, the project was weighed against specific funding criteria established by the governor. The governor's seven criteria are as follows:

- Protect the life and safety of residents and state employees.
- Provide responsible stewardship of existing state assets and facilities.
- Select projects that are urgent and necessary.
- Complete important projects that have received only partial funding.
- Clarify the state's funding role versus that of the private sector or other governments.

- Take advantage of unique financing opportunities.
- Promote initiatives consistent with the state's strategic plan and smart growth principles.

For transportation projects, the state was moving toward using performance measures to determine how well the system meets the needs of the public.

The use of committees to evaluate capital project requests varies substantially among these governments. Central office personnel, such as budget directors, often were included on these committees, in addition to professional staff with specific expertise (for example, engineers, architects, and planners). Private citizens and legislative members or staff were also involved in some cases. Box 3.2 notes specific examples of how governments made use of committees for project evaluation.

Project Management

Project management was the strongest area of capital management across the governments evaluated in the GPP. Most of these governments had a good process for tracking projects through implementation with regular reporting. Some of those that had weaknesses in this area were working to strengthen their processes. For example, the city of Los Angeles created a position to direct all capital projects and also had a Citizen's Oversight Committee. Philadelphia recently developed a Capital Program Office to improve project monitoring.

Several innovations in project management are allowing governments to develop even better processes for keeping down costs and complete projects in a timely manner. One of these is a design-build approach to contracting. Fulton and Maricopa counties both used this method successfully for several recent projects. Using design-build contracts, Massachusetts reduced project completion time by up to six years, and Utah expected this method to reduce construction time for a $1.6 billion highway project by five years.

Performance contracting is another method increasingly used to improve project management. For example, Fairfax County's energy performance contract used utility cost savings to finance improvements through a master lease agreement; annual cost savings were estimated at $485,000. Tennessee was also using performance contracting for energy work as part of a strategic energy plan adopted in 1999. The state of Hawaii had begun using a performance-based procurement system for roofing and painting and was expanding the system to other areas.

Box 3.2 Use of Project Evaluation Committees

• *Fairfax County* uses several formal committees. A Capital Improvement Program Committee includes the county executive; deputy executive; chief financial officer; and staff from the Departments of Management and Budget, Planning and Zoning, and Public Works. The Planning Commission conducts a workshop and public hearing on the proposed CIP and makes recommendations to the board of supervisors. The Transportation Advisory Commission is a citizen committee appointed by the board of supervisors to develop recommendations for transportation improvements.

• *Hennepin County* has a Capital Budgeting Task Force, an eleven-member citizens' advisory committee appointed by the county board that reviews requests and makes recommendations to the board.

• *Idaho's* Permanent Building Fund Advisory Council includes one member each from the state's Senate and House and three citizens, from the contracting business, banking business, and another business. The Idaho Transportation Board includes six members, one from each administrative district and a statewide chairman.

• *New Hampshire* uses several committees. The Governor's Advisory Committee on the Capital Budget includes the commissioners of administrative services and transportation, the chairperson of the Senate Capital Budget Committee, and the chairperson of the House Public Works and Highway Committee. The Governor's Advisory Commission on Intermodal Transportation includes members of the Executive Council and Department of Transportation. The Long-Range Capital Planning and Utilization Committee includes a member appointed by the governor and four members each from the Senate and House.

• *Utah's* State Building Board prioritizes project requests in the building program and includes seven private citizens, with the budget director acting as a nonvoting member. A seven-member transportation commission, which the governor appoints, prioritizes transportation requests.

• *Chicago* has a fifteen-member Capital Improvement Advisory Committee that includes citizens with expertise in areas such as planning, engineering, and finance, as well as community leaders. This committee conducts public hearings throughout the capital planning process.

Establishment of partnerships between the public and private sectors helped governments with capital management. Fairfax County entered into partnerships for a government center complex, a human services center, and affordable housing initiatives. Public-private partnerships helped Shelby County save money and generate revenue. Boston successfully used this tool to create a multiseason water facility, and Seattle estimated savings of $50 million by contracting out the construction and operation of a new water filtration system.

Several other methods were noted as well. Baltimore County was using a gain-sharing approach that was estimated to have saved $1.5 million in capital spending to date. In this plan, cost savings are shared for two years between the general fund and the team generating the savings. For example, the construction contracts administration team implemented solicitation of temporary agencies for bidding on construction inspection projects, which costs less than hiring full-time workers. San Diego County adopted a job-order contracting approach, filing individual work orders with on-call contractors, to implement its major deferred maintenance program without hiring additional staff. This saved 75 to 85 percent of the time maintenance would otherwise have taken. Fairfax County required value engineering studies for construction projects exceeding $2 million, which had saved about $7 million since 1997. In addition, Fairfax developed a manual for fire station design standardization, with savings of about 19 percent in design costs for three new fire stations.

Asset Maintenance

Asset maintenance was the weakest area overall in the capital management evaluation. Many of the governments surveyed did not conduct regular condition assessments of their assets and were not knowledgeable about their maintenance needs. Supportive automated systems were lacking in many places. However, many governments have shown some improvement in this area, especially through implementation of new or updated systems.

Funding of maintenance needs is another common problem. The economic expansion of the late 1990s allowed many cities, counties, and states to use additional revenues to catch up on their backlogs of deferred maintenance. Many of these governments still have a long way to go, however. A number of jurisdictions developed funding mechanisms to focus on maintenance needs in recent years. These include maintenance reserve funds, maintenance policies, and dedicated revenue sources. Several examples are listed in box 3.3.

Conclusion

Overall, the governments surveyed in the GPP tended to manage capital projects well. Long-term capital planning was also strong in many places,

Box 3.3 Asset Maintenance Funding Innovations

- *Clark County* implemented a voter-approved Fair Share tax program in 1990 to support roadway improvements and mass transit. Funding sources include a hotel room tax, motor vehicle privilege tax, development tax, sales tax, motor vehicle fuel tax, and jet aviation fuel tax. In addition, parks are funded partially by a residential construction tax of $1,000 or 1 percent of valuation.

- *Dallas County* has established a permanent improvement fund for maintaining county buildings from an annual property tax levy of $0.18 per $100 of assessed value, and a $10 vehicle registration fee is used to fund county road improvements.

- *Los Angeles County* began funding a deferred maintenance budget in 1994 and attempts to spend 2 to 4 percent of property value annually for this purpose.

- *Maricopa County* is developing a policy that will establish a designated reserve fund to finance long-term maintenance of jail facilities from a dedicated criminal justice sales tax.

- *San Diego County* is moving to an activity-based cost model, whereby facility maintenance will be paid for by departments located in county buildings. Over the past several years, the county has been eliminating deferred facility maintenance through a major maintenance program.

- *Santa Clara County* has adopted a policy to fund building maintenance based on replacement cost. It is currently funding this initiative at 1.7 percent of value, or $27.98 million over four years.

- In *Iowa*, a citizen advisory committee was created in 1999 to oversee the inventory and assessment of buildings. The committee also makes annual recommendations on how to use the Rebuild Iowa Infrastructure Fund, which includes a revenue stream of $100 million to $130 million from gambling receipts and interest from state reserve funds.

- *Missouri* is phasing in a facilities maintenance reserve fund, which will include 1 percent of net general revenues each year.

- *New Mexico* created a public building repair fund in 1998 that is funded from the Severance Tax Bonding Fund.

- *North Carolina* has a reserve for repairs and renovations to fund deferred maintenance; the reserve is 3 percent of the value of state buildings, allocated to specific projects.

- *South Carolina* has a capital reserve fund for general assets, equal to 2 percent of general fund revenue from the prior year; the legislature determines how this fund is used.

- *Utah* funds capital improvements at the level of 0.9 percent of the replacement cost of state facilities before it may appropriate funds for capital development projects.

- *Seattle* has created a major-maintenance reserve for its new facilities.

but the process of evaluating capital project requests could be improved. Asset maintenance was the weakest area of capital management, owing to the lack of comprehensive information related to asset condition and the costs of needed maintenance, as well as inadequate funding. There was a great deal of variation in capacity across governments, however.

Some progress in capital management area was evident in the governments assessed in the GPP. Many of these jurisdictions were in the process of implementing or updating automated information systems that will help them to better evaluate their capital needs. Some of these changes were driven by a desire to comply with GASB Statement 34, which will require enhanced accounting for capital assets. In addition, the economic boom of the late 1990s allowed many of these governments to increase maintenance funding levels, and quite a few developed designated funding sources for this purpose. The recent downturn in the economy could have an adverse effect on this trend, though. Studies have shown that capital spending can increase dramatically in periods of economic growth but is also frequently among the first areas to be reduced in recessionary periods.[19]

The evaluation methodology was somewhat different in each of the four years of the GPP because of redesigned surveys and differences in capital functions and structure in different types of governments. However, the three major criteria remained the same in each of the last three years, so the overall grading parameters were similar. Cities received the highest grades, while counties had the greatest proportion of low grades. The second state evaluation results ranked somewhere between those of the cities and counties. Further research is necessary to explore the relationship of distinguishing factors other than government type to capital management capacity. These may include, for example, size, structure, and functional responsibilities.

In 2005 *Governing* published results of a new study of performance across states.[20] Infrastructure was one of the four categories included in the study. Because of changes in the criteria and emphasis used, the new grades cannot be directly compared with the results reported in this chapter. Also, a number of changes that have occurred since the earlier study of states may have affected the 2005 grades. For example, most states have undergone significant fiscal stress in the past few years. In addition, states are further along in implementation of the GASB 34 reporting requirements. However, most of the states were found to be in the same grade range in the more recent survey as in the earlier GPP study. Asset maintenance was still the major difficulty for capital management across the states, validating the earlier results.

The Government Performance Project found strong relationships between capital management systems and the other management areas. Capital management systems overlap substantially with information technology and financial management. As noted throughout this chapter, supportive automated information systems are vital to all three components of a good capital management system: planning, project management, and asset maintenance. The financial management connection is important in two particular respects: Capital plans need to be linked to the operating budget to ensure consideration of long-term costs. In addition, an organization's financial condition, constraints, and management practices determine the availability of resources for capital projects and asset maintenance. Capital management capacity and performance are highly interdependent with these other important systems.

These findings can be helpful to managers at all levels of government. Throughout the project, numerous inquiries were received from government officials interested in knowing how closely their practices compare with others. The GPP data allow governments to evaluate themselves in this manner. Dissemination of information on innovative practices is also important in helping governments improve their management capacity.

The GPP results are also of tremendous value to scholars. This project provides the basis for discerning the relationship between management capacity and performance. Data are now available that measure capital management capacity. The next step is to explore the connections between these practices and actual performance in this area: do governments that scored well in the GPP in fact make better capital decisions, follow their long-term plans, have fewer implementation delays and cost overruns, and maintain assets better than the governments that did not score so well? The lack of available, consistent, standardized data is the major stumbling block to this effort, even within a single government. The implementation of GASB Statement 34 may enhance the ability to make better comparisons across governments regarding asset values and maintenance, but these rules still allow a certain amount of discretion. Measurement of performance in other areas, such as capital project overruns, would require in-depth case studies, extensive interviews, or surveys beyond the scope of the GPP.

The direct linkage, then, between capital management practices and outcomes remains untested. However, it is difficult to imagine that a state, county, or city could perform well in the capital management area without having the underlying "infrastructure" of supportive information systems and strong monitoring and decision-making processes. Anecdotal evidence is strong for this relationship. Governments that were rated by the GPP as high performing tend to be those that also were able to give specific examples of saving money through new innovative methods or that received additional funding for maintenance, for example, because they were able to clearly demonstrate needs in this area. These governments also appear to have leaders in capital management who are constantly striving for improvements. There is some preliminary support for this hypothesis: in-depth analysis of the counties in this sample reveal that those with the highest capital management scores were more likely to have higher bond ratings, which are based to some extent on indicators of financial performance.[21] Capital management capacity, as analyzed in the GPP, may not be sufficient, but is almost certainly necessary for high government performance.

APPENDIX

Capital Management Methodology

The capital management evaluation criteria represent the three primary components of capital management: capital planning, project management, and asset maintenance. Survey design changed somewhat over the four years of the project. The 1998 state survey consisted of eleven open-ended questions. The 1999 city survey also included eleven open-ended questions, but many of the questions had multiple parts, with more detailed questions designed to increase the specificity of the responses. The 2000 state survey attempted to improve the comparability of responses across jurisdictions by using a number of closed-ended questions; for example, one question listed possible types of information in a capital improvement plan and asked the respondent to indicate which applied to his or her state. This survey was made up of twelve questions, most of which had multiple parts. The 2001 county survey also included twelve multipart questions, many of which were closed ended.

The changes in survey design resulted from several factors. First, lessons learned from the first years of the project were used to improve the instrument in following years. The first survey, for example, asked general questions about capital project monitoring and the use of information technology in capital management; states answered these questions in a variety of different ways, making comparisons difficult. These questions were more explicit and detailed in later surveys. Second, functional differences across levels of government necessitated different emphases. For example, while highways and bridges are a major component of capital management for states, this is not always the case for counties and cities. Third, because managing transportation infrastructure is an important concern for state governments, the 2000 GPP process addressed it separately from management for general capital assets.

Survey responses were reviewed by a faculty specialist and research assistants from the Maxwell School. Key survey questions were converted into quantifiable weighted variables. Pretests were used to check for reliability across raters, and the faculty specialist reviewed the coding against the survey responses to detect errors or inconsistencies.

Governments also provided supporting documentation, such as capital improvement plans, capital asset inventories, sample project management reports, and condition assessments. These documents were used to confirm some information in the survey responses and to supplement incomplete survey responses. *Governing* reporters and the Maxwell staff also shared information; in some cases, data from the reporters' interviews were used to assist in coding. In spite of these efforts, however, the lack of data for some survey questions prevented complete coding for all governments, and not all survey responses could be verified for accuracy.

The Maxwell team based its grades on the coding scores. (See table 3.A.1 for the weighting of the criteria. Scores were not compiled for the first round of states.) The weights were determined through discussions among the faculty specialist, research assistants, and *Governing* reporters, based on the relative importance of the various components of a capital management system. Weighting differed across the years primarily because of changes in survey design. For example, data management was a separate category for coding purposes in 2001, because survey questions related to this area overlapped across the three major criteria.

Table 3.A.1. Capital Management Criteria Weighting

	Cities	States (2000)	Counties
Capital planning	59	60	50
Project management	10	15	10
Asset maintenance	31	25	20

NOTES

1. U.S. Department of Commerce, Bureau of the Census, *State and Local Government Finances: 1999–2000,* www.census.gov/govs/estimate/oosloous.html (accessed January 2003).

2. For example, Pat Choate and Susan Walters, *America in Ruins: Beyond the Public Works Pork Barrel* (Washington, DC: Council of State Planning Agencies, 1981).

3. American Society of Civil Engineers, "2001 Report Card for America's Infrastructure," www.asce.org/reportcard/index.cfm?reaction=fullfull&pages=∧ (accessed October 2001).

4. Beverly S. Bunch, "Current Practices and Issues in Capital Budgeting and Reporting," *Public Budgeting and Finance* 16, no. 2 (1996): 7–25.

5. John Mikesell, *Fiscal Administration: Analysis and Applications for the Public Sector,* 5th ed. (Fort Worth, TX: Harcourt Brace, 1999).

6. On coordination with a strategic plan, see Arie Halachmi and Alex Sekwat, "Strategic Capital Budgeting and Planning: Prospects at the County Level," *Public Budgeting and Financial Management* 8, no. 4 (1997): 578–96; and Jane Beckett-Camarata, "An Examination of the Relationship between the Municipal Strategic Plan and the Capital Budget and Its Effect on Financial Performance," *Public Budgeting, Accounting, and Financial Management* 15, no. 1 (2003): 23–40.

7. Roland Calia, "Are All Public Spending Programs Equal? Priority Setting Approaches for Governmental Budgeting," *Government Finance Review* 17, no. 4 (2001): 18–23.

8. For an overview of this literature, see Carol Ebdon, "Citizen Participation in the Budget Process: Exit, Voice, and Loyalty," in the *Encyclopedia of Public Administration and Public Policy* (New York: Marcel Dekker, 2003, 173–76).

9. Susan A. MacManus, "Democratizing the Capital Budget Planning and Project Selection Process at the Local Level: Assets and Liabilities," *Public Budgeting and Financial Management* 8, no. 3 (1996): 406–27.

10. U.S. General Accounting Office, *Executive Guide: Leading Practices in Capital Decision-Making,* GAO/AIMD-99-32 (Washington, DC, December 1998).

11. Daniel L. Dornan, "GASB 34's Impacts on Infrastructure Management, Financing, and Reporting" (Bethesda, MD: Infrastructure Management Group, June 2000).

12. Beverly S. Bunch, "Current Practices and Issues in Capital Budgeting and Planning: Prospects at the County Level," *Public Budgeting and Financial Management* 8, no. 4 (1997): 578–96; Henry Thomassen, "Capital Budgeting for a State," *Public Budgeting and Finance* 4, no. 3 (1984): 31–40.

13. Michael A. Pagano, "Notes on Capital Budgeting," *Public Budgeting and Finance* 4, no. 3 (1984): 31–40.

14. For further information on GASB Statement 34, see the symposium in *Public Budgeting and Finance* 21, no. 3 (2001): 1–87.

15. John P. Forrester, "Municipal Capital Budgeting: An Examination," *Public Budgeting and Finance* 13, no. 2 (1993): 85–103.

16. Cameron Gordon, "The Fables and Foibles of Federal Capital Budgeting," *Public Budgeting and Finance* 18, no. 3 (1998): 54–71.

17. Donald Darr, "The Benefits of Long-Range Capital Planning: The Virginia Experience," *Public Budgeting and Finance* 18, no. 3 (1998): 42–53.

18. John E. Petersen, "The Management Factor," *Governing* 14, no. 9 (June 2001): 64.

19. See, for example, Michael A. Pagano, "Municipal Capital Spending during the 'Boom,'" *Public Budgeting and Finance* 22, no 2 (2002): 1–20; John Bartle, "Coping with Cutbacks: City Response to Aid Cuts in New York State," *State and Local Government Review* 28, no. 1 (1996): 38–48; and Charles Levine, Irene Rubin, and George Wolohojian, eds., *The Politics of Retrenchment* (Newbury Park, CA: Sage, 1981).

20. Katherine Barrett and Richard Greene, "Grading the States 2005: A Management Report Card," *Governing* 18, no. 5 (2005): 24–95.

21. Carol Ebdon, "Capital Management Practices in U.S. Counties," *Public Works Management and Policy* 8, no. 3 (2004): 192–202.

CHAPTER 4

Government's Largest Investment

*Human Resource Management
in States, Counties, and Cities*

SALLY COLEMAN SELDEN AND WILLOW JACOBSON

Effective human resource management is one of the more important management components in creating and maintaining an effective and efficient government operation. Recent research in the private sector demonstrates a link between coherent and strategic HRM practices and organizational performance.[1] Most public officials agree that HRM is essential for obtaining desired results in public organizations as well. However, they might disagree about how to make that happen. Moreover, examining the connections between human resource management practices and overall measures of government performance is difficult because scholars and practitioners have been unable to derive definitive and agreed upon standards of government performance or outcomes. Despite the challenge, the need to assess and understand governments' implementation of their human resource management tools remains.

Human resource management refers to the policies, systems, and practices that influence employees' behaviors, attitudes, and performance and, thereby, the performance of the organization. The operational activities of HRM practices are extensive, including strategic and workforce planning, recruiting prospective employees, selecting employees, training and developing employees, managing employee rewards and recognition, evaluating employee performance, classifying positions, creating a positive and safe work environment (employee relations), and administering employee benefits.

While the focus in human resource management has begun to shift from tactical and day-to-day management to strategic management, many organizations continue to view HRM as administrative in nature. Organizations that take a strategic perspective tend to be forward thinking and to conceive of human capital as a valuable asset, and their HRM staff are integral members of the strategic planning community. As a result of this shift, the role of HRM departments is changing from a narrow focus policing the merit system and rules toward a broader focus that emphasizes collaboration and partnership with leaders and managers to achieve organizational goals.[2] Human resource managers are moving away from making operational decisions to acting as consultants to other departments and managers by designing and delivering policies and programs that give managers the tools and training they need to effectively perform in their positions.

The Government Performance Project (GPP) proceeded from the assumption that a human resource management system is a critical and integral component of a government's management capacity.[3] This chapter contributes to a small but growing body of work that explores ways to assess different human resource management systems.

Evaluation Criteria

The key components of good human resource management systems include workforce and strategic planning, the ability to facilitate timely and quality hiring, sophisticated professional development programs, and meaningful reward and evaluation structures and disciplinary procedures. The GPP study used five criteria, embodying these components, to characterize sound human resource management in state, county, and city governments.[4]

Criterion 1: Government conducts strategic analysis of present and future human resource needs. This criterion measures the extent to which a government addresses its personnel capacity over time, particularly the sophistication with which the government conducts strategic analysis of present and future human resource needs and availability. It includes the extent and nature of planning tools such as strategic planning, performance measurement, and information technology.

Criterion 2: Government obtains a skilled workforce. This criterion addresses the extent to which the government is able to obtain the employees it needs. To acquire a skilled workforce, a government must be able to conduct effective recruiting efforts and to hire employees in a timely manner.

Criterion 3: Government maintains an appropriately skilled workforce. This criterion concerns the government's ability to maintain an appropriately skilled workforce by providing training to develop employee skills, retaining experienced employees, disciplining poor performers, and terminating employees who cannot or will not meet performance standards.

Criterion 4: Government motivates the workforce to perform effectively in support of the government's goals. This criterion focuses on whether a government is able to encourage employees to perform effectively in support of its goals. Effective motivation typically rests on the use of appropriate cash and noncash rewards and incentives, an effective performance appraisal system, and sound mechanisms that facilitate employee feedback.

Criterion 5: Government structures the workforce. This criterion captures the degree to which the government's human resource structure supports its ability to achieve its workforce goals. This includes having a coherent and appropriately sized classification system reinforced by personnel policies that are flexible in terms of promotion and compensation.

Government Grades

Governments were graded on a scale from A to F. Governments receiving an A grade demonstrated excellence in their human resource management capacity across all five criteria. The grade of B indicates that the government's human resource management system, while not excellent, was distinguished in several ways. It demonstrated mastery in some but not all of the criteria, and it focused on building capacity by changing existing systems, rules, laws, and practices. The grade of C references a broad range of moderate, but satisfactory, human resource management capacity. It signifies that the government had implemented the basics of the criteria and that its capacity, though not impressive, was adequate to maintain daily operations. The grade of D indicates that the government met an acceptable level of capacity on a few of the criteria but had noticeable deficiencies in other areas. The grade of F indicates that the government was below the minimum standard in all five criteria. As shown in table 4.1, only two governments, Rhode Island in the first survey of states, and New Orleans in the second, received failing grades. Similarly, only two governments, South Carolina in 2000 and Phoenix in 1999, demonstrated the highest level of capacity in human resources. Most of the governments studied demonstrated varying levels of capacity across the criteria, with some operating at the highest levels of capacity in their ability to motivate employees, such as Washington State, and others demonstrating great capability in their capacity to hire employees, such as Fairfax County.

Table 4.1. Human Resource Management Grades

State	Grade 1999	Grade 2001	City	Grade	County	Grade
Alabama	C−	D+	Anchorage, AK	C	Alameda, CA	D+
Alaska	C−	C	Atlanta, GA	B−	Allegheny, PA	D−
Arizona	C+	C	Austin, TX	A−	Anne Arundel, MD	C
Arkansas	C+	C	Baltimore, MD	C+	Baltimore, MD	B−
California	C−	C	Boston, MA	C−	Broward, FL	B+
Colorado	B	B−	Buffalo, NY	D	Clark, NV	C−
Connecticut	C−	C	Chicago, IL	C−	Contra Costa, CA	B−
Delaware	B	B	Cleveland, OH	C−	Cook, IL	D
Florida	C+	B−	Columbus, OH	C−	Cuyahoga, OH	C−
Georgia	B−	B−	Dallas, TX	C	Dallas, TX	B+
Hawaii	C−	C	Denver, CO	B−	Erie, NY	C−
Idaho	C	B	Detroit, MI	B−	Fairfax, VA	A−
Illinois	B	B	Honolulu, HI	C	Franklin, OH	B−
Indiana	C+	B	Houston, TX	C	Fulton, GA	C
Iowa	B+	B+	Indianapolis, IN	A−	Hamilton, OH	B
Kansas	B+	B+	Jacksonville, FL	C+	Harris, TX	C+
Kentucky	B	B+	Kansas City, MO	B−	Hennepin, MN	B−
Louisiana	C+	B	Long Beach, CA	C	Hillsborough, FL	D
Maine	C+	B−	Los Angeles, CA	C−	King, WA	D+
Maryland	B	B	Memphis, TN	D	Los Angeles, CA	B−
Massachusetts	C+	B−	Milwaukee, WI	C+	Maricopa, AZ	B+
Michigan	B+	B+	Minneapolis, MN	B	Mecklenburg, NC	B
Minnesota	C+	C+	Nashville, TN	B	Miami-Dade, FL	B−
Mississippi	C+	B-	New Orleans, LA	F	Milwaukee, WI	C+
Missouri	B	B+	New York City, NY	B−	Monroe, NY	C−
Montana	B−	C+	Philadelphia, PA	B−	Montgomery, MD	B+
Nebraska	B−	C	Phoenix, AZ	A	Nassau, NY	D
Nevada	D	D+	Richmond, VA	C	Oakland, MI	B
New Hampshire	B	C+	San Antonio, TX	B+	Orange, CA	B−
New Jersey	C−	C−	San Diego, CA	C	Palm Beach, FL	C
New Mexico	B−	B−	San Francisco, CA	C	Prince George's, MD	B−
New York	C	C+	San Jose, CA	C	Riverside, CA	B
North Carolina	B−	B+	Seattle, WA	B	Sacramento, CA	C
North Dakota	B+	B	Virginia Beach, VA	B	San Bernardino, CA	C−
Ohio	B	B	Washington, DC	B−	San Diego, CA	B−

(continued)

Table 4.1. Human Resource Management Grades (*continued*)

State	1999	2001	City	Grade	County	Grade
Oklahoma	C−	C−			Santa Clara, CA	C+
Oregon	C+	C			Shelby, TN	B
Pennsylvania	B	B+			Suffolk, NY	C−
Rhode Island	F	C−			Wayne, MI	B−
South Carolina	A−	A			Westchester, NY	D+
South Dakota	C+	B−				
Tennessee	C+	B−				
Texas	B	B				
Utah	B+	B−				
Vermont	B−	C				
Virginia	B	B+				
Washington	B+	A−				
West Virginia	C+	C+				
Wisconsin	B+	A−				
Wyoming	B−	C+				

Trends in Public Human Resource Management Practices by Criteria

Conducting Strategic Analysis of Human Resource Needs

A decade ago, scholars and practitioners suggested that human resource management should be a strategic partner to management because it would help organizations achieve their strategic and organizational goals.[5] Where strategic planning is conducted, officials articulate a clear mission and goals for the HRM department and link the mission and goals to the organization's strategic plan. The diffusion of strategic human resource management has been slower in the public sector than in the private sector. The GPP research shows, however, that strategic human resource management practices in government are on the rise as selected public organizations shift their focus from short-term to long-term workforce needs that are integrated with the strategic planning process.[6] We found that strategic HRM planning is more often conducted in state than in county governments: about 78 percent of state HRM departments and 60 percent of county HRM departments conduct strategic planning.[7]

Strategic human resource management in the public sector includes other factors, such as tools necessary to plan, decisions about how to implement and distribute HRM functions and responsibilities, and actions taken to monitor progress toward a government's goals and objectives. An important and central tool is workforce planning, which is defined as a strategy and set of procedures by which the state's future personnel needs are assessed. Workforce planning enables agencies to ascertain their need for and availability of human resources to meet their objectives.

Our research shows that formal workforce planning is increasing in states. In the two-year period between the state surveys, the most dramatic change in state human resource management practices was in the area of workforce planning. Since 1998, numerous states, such as Connecticut and Oklahoma, have adopted workforce planning. In 1998 most states did no workforce planning, and only five had implemented a comprehensive, formal plan. In 2000 this number rose dramatically: 46 percent of states developed and used formal workforce plans either approved by the legislature or governor or developed and used by its central human resource office. Washington State, for example, created an Office of Workforce Planning to oversee and implement its process. A key component of Washington's balanced scorecard performance management system was internal capacity, which ensures that appropriate staffing and competencies exist to achieve the goals of the organization.

Many cities and counties have not invested in formal workforce planning. Only about 20 percent of the cities surveyed in 1999 and 19 percent of the counties in 2001 noted that they conduct formal, government-wide workforce planning. Of those cities that did not conduct formal workforce planning in 1999, 72.2 percent did not identify workforce planning as a need. This percentage is double that found among counties who had not adopted formal workforce planning in 2001 (35%). We found no associations between the perception of need for workforce planning and the size of government.

A few cities conducted targeted workforce planning as needed. When Virginia Beach decided to hire employees for information technology positions, it developed a hiring plan, constructed a retention plan, and formulated a training plan. A few places felt that workforce planning is captured in the budgeting process when they plan for the next fiscal year's workforce needs. Several local governments noted that their workforce planning process takes the form of a biennial or annual examination schedule.

An important component of workforce planning is access to and use of comprehensive information and data about employees. We found that many governments, particularly in cities, were struggling to keep technology up to date. We found that only 35 percent of cities operated an integrated HRM information system. Most cities operated multiple HRM systems. Baltimore maintained different systems that track training, benefits, job applications, job classification, safety and injuries, and unemployment insurance claims. At the time of the 1999 survey the city was planning to adopt Oracle's HRIS. Several cities, such as Jacksonville, Los Angeles, and San Antonio, maintained their payroll systems separately. Denver noted that having multiple IT systems has led to data anomalies and delayed generation of reports. A few cities, such as Dallas and Nashville, continued to operate antiquated mainframe systems.

The statistics in counties and states are a little better. Fifty percent of counties and 68 percent of states reported that they operate an integrated HRM information system. Of the states operating integrated systems, 29 percent developed their systems internally. Like the states, many counties have integrated systems that were developed internally. Fairfax, for example, is in the process of updating its custom-developed HRM information technology system. Across governments, the vendor most often used for HRM information technology systems was PeopleSoft. Other included American Management System, GEAC, HRIS, Integral Systems, Lawson, and SAP. As indicated above, some county and state governments operate multiple systems. Illinois, for example, operates multiple systems that are integrated at key points by means of batch-processing technologies. The state has considered online integration, but because of "the uniqueness of the State of Illinois business rules, costs to customize a vendor supplied-solution could not be justified."

Looking across the levels of governments, we found considerable variation in how well governments conduct strategic analyses of present and future human resource needs. Some governments engage in the process fully, others lack adequate tools, and still others have not prioritized planning as part of their role. Overall, states appear to be setting the benchmarks on this criterion.

Obtaining a Skilled Workforce

Because human capital represents the largest asset of public organizations, the selection process continues to be a critical human resource function, supplying persons with specific talents, knowledge, skills, and abilities needed to perform public services. The selection process starts with recruitment and is officially over when a new employee successfully completes his or her probationary period.

Governments at all levels encounter multiple challenges when recruiting and hiring employees. The most common barriers include the following:

- tight labor market
- uncompetitive salaries
- budget constraints
- procedures constraints (testing, certification, and advertising regulations)
- residency requirements
- slow hiring processes
- collective bargaining agreements

Franklin County's statement reflects the sentiments of many of the surveyed counties:

> A highly competitive labor market and low unemployment rates in this area dramatically affect the recruitment of new employees, especially social workers. . . . Candidates with in-demand skills, such as IT professionals, usually have many high-paying private sector jobs from which to choose. This makes it harder for Franklin County to become the Employer of Choice, as wages in the public sector are generally lower than in the private sector.

In Montgomery County, the problems are more procedural: "Current personnel regulations require all positions to be advertised for a minimum of two weeks, require an examination for all positions, and prohibit direct hiring." In Santa Clara County, "merit system rules require applicants to fail to show for an interview, waive an interview or participate in 3 interviews within a 6-month period (with the same department) in order for the department to access other names beyond the first seven for a vacancy." Alaska's obstacles are multiple, including "inadequate applicant pools, state resident hiring preferences, artificial delays in the process by approval chain, [and] lack of training and experience in selection techniques for hiring managers."

Our research shows that technology has enhanced recruiting processes in the states and counties more than in city governments. All states (in 2000) and counties posted job openings online, and 90 percent of states and 86 percent of counties provided applications online. Only 65 percent of cities posted job openings online, and just 45 percent of cities made applications available online. Florida's Web-based application system allows applicants to file and store their state employment applications and then apply for as many vacancies as they choose. Indiana's Web site and job bank provide Spanish translation. The Tennessee Employment Application Monitoring System allows applicants to conduct job searches, submit applications, and take employment examinations online. Job applicants receive their examination scores the same day. According to its survey response, South Carolina's Web site generated more than a million hits each month.

Compared with states and counties, cities have not invested as heavily in recruiting new employees. For every recruitment technique listed in table 4.2, a lower proportion of cities than counties and states use the technique. For example, none of the cities allowed for direct hires, and just over one-third advertised in trade publications; on the other hand, one-third of counties and two-thirds of states authorized direct hires, and more than 88 percent of counties and states advertised in trade publications. San Jose's response noted that "recruiting is insufficient . . . and is not centrally monitored for quality." Houston indicated that it did not have the resources to

Table 4.2. Use of Recruiting Techniques (percentage)

	Cities (N = 33)	States (2000) (N = 50)	Counties (N = 36)
Twenty-four-hour telephone job line	29	64	81
Online job posting	65	100	100
Job bulletin	26	84	94
Commercial Internet site	42	54	64
External job fair	63	98	94
Virtual job fair	n.a.	24	14
Open house	3	36	39
College site visit	36	96	75
Letter campaign	4	48	56
Trade publication ad	36	88	97
Professional recruitment firm	10	54	61
Satellite office	10	56	28
Walk-in job counseling	7	72	50
Application available online	45	90	86
Direct hire	0	63	36
Paying travel expense for interview	0	60	50

recruit for all city departments. New York City revealed that most of its efforts to recruit were internal; open positions are posted first within the department in which the vacancy is located and then made available to other city employees. Positions are opened externally only if there is an inadequate pool of internal applicants. Los Angeles did not assign "dedicated" staff to general recruitment activities; instead, it used student interns as recruiters.

Our research shows that many states implemented changes in the procedural requirements of laws that govern hiring between the 1998 and 2000 surveys. Several states, such as Iowa, passed legislation to eliminate the so-called Rule of X (requiring that a prescribed number of candidates be considered for a position or to expand the number of names or scores on certified lists). States also implemented other procedural changes to improve the hiring process. To keep the register of eligible candidates current, Idaho shortened the length of time its list is valid. Indiana made agencies responsible for the hiring of entire occupational categories, enabling them to receive and evaluate applications directly. Both Iowa and Indiana eliminated testing. Wisconsin repealed its residency requirement and restrictions on out-of-state recruiting and eliminated the restrictions on the number of qualified candidates that could be interviewed.

Civil service rules in many cities limit hiring flexibility and slow hiring processes. In some cities, such as Milwaukee, state laws govern aspects of the hiring process. A few cities participate directly in the state civil service. In Buffalo, the state provides and evaluates 95 percent of the tests administered to city applicants. Many cities, including Buffalo, Chicago, Houston, Honolulu, and Los Angeles, require hiring from a certified list with a specified number of applicant names and scores. In Philadelphia, the applicant pool is limited to the top two candidates; a voter referendum is necessary to change this requirement. Detroit has to justify a decision not to hire the top-scoring candidate. The systems in some cities, Boston, for example, require completion of numerous procedural steps before vacancies may be posted or an offer of employment extended. A number of other cities, Cleveland and Denver among them, have residency requirements that limit the pool of potential employees. Detroit noted that verifying residency often create delays in the city's hiring process.

More than 85 percent of the governments surveyed used testing to screen job applicants. However, testing is not always perceived as a barrier in the hiring process. As shown in table 4.3, only 2.8 percent of counties and none of the states responded that the testing process always delayed the

Table 4.3. Prevalence of Delays in Government Hiring Process Owing to Testing (percentage)

	States (2000)	Counties
Always	0	3
Often	6	14
Sometimes	40	61
Rarely	44	19
Never	10	3
N	48	36

Table 4.4. Time Required to Fill Positions (percentage)

Average number of days	Cities	States (2000)	Counties
1–30	16	19	3
31–60	40	58	61
61–120	36	21	36
121	8	2	0
N	32	47	36

hiring process. Sixty-one percent of counties and 40 percent of states perceived that it sometimes does.

The length of time it takes to fill positions is a process measure of effectiveness. We found that states, on average, hired slightly more quickly than cities and counties (see table 4.4). Cities took the longest time to fill open positions. That cities used fewer recruitment tools and were impeded by different civil service rules may have been a factor.

Another proxy of the effectiveness of the hiring system is the percentage of new hires terminated during their probationary period. States fired about 5.3 percent of new hires in 2000, compared with 4.6 percent of new hires in cities and 3.7 percent in counties. This finding suggests that while states may fill positions more quickly, they may not necessarily be getting the fit that counties are able to achieve by taking more time.

Because of the difficulties associated with filling some positions and the need for seasonal employees in government, many governments employ temporary staff. In 2000 approximately 5.8 percent of all state employees were temporary, and in 2001 approximately 8.3 percent of county employees were classified as temporary. In 2000 Georgia employed the largest share of temporary employees (20% of its workforce), followed by Mississippi and North Dakota. South Carolina developed the TempO initiative to help state agencies meet short-term staffing needs. According to the state respondent, TempO reduces the time and costs associated with filling temporary jobs. Moreover, as a recruitment tool it allows agencies to review candidates' work while considering them for permanent positions. Since the program was introduced in early 2000, 13 percent of TempO's workers received permanent positions with the state. Similarly, Nebraska, in partnership with the Omaha Workforce Development Office, operates the Specialized Office Services program, which serves as a clearinghouse for all temporary jobs in the state.

Looking across the governments, we found differences in how effectively the governments recruited and selected their workforces. These differences may be because of variations in the use of recruiting techniques across governments, states and counties being much more aggressive in their efforts to compete for human capital than city governments. Such investments appear to have paid off, because states and counties were able to hire more quickly than city governments. Speed is only one dimension of effectiveness, however; it needs to be balanced with quality. Counties terminated a smaller proportion of new hires during the probationary period, giving the leadership in recruiting and selection processes to county governments. This is a tough comparison, however, because of the sheer differences in size and complexity in county and state governments.

Maintaining a Skilled Workforce

A government's training infrastructure is an important tool for ensuring that its workforce fits with its ever changing needs. Challenging opportunities for professional development can also serve to attract new talent and to retain current workers. Governments invest in training and development to ensure that workers have the necessary skills and opportunities to perform in their current and future positions. Training builds individual skills and competencies and thereby organizational capacity. The GPP argued that capacity is linked to overall organizational performance.[8]

To provide appropriate training, governments need to understand what training has been offered and what employees have participated. How governments track employee participation varies; employees' training can be tracked centrally or at the departmental level. The central personnel department keeps records on individual employee training in 76.0 percent of cities, 88.6 percent of states (2000 data), and 76.0 percent of counties. Individual departments maintain records in 66.6 percent of the cities, 91.4 percent of the states, and 98.0 percent of the counties surveyed. For cities, records kept by the central office were more often computerized (82.6%) than those kept at the department level (50.0%). Among counties and states, the records kept at the departmental levels (87.8 and 87.5%, respectively) were more frequently computerized than those kept at the central level (71.4 and 78.1%, respectively). Computerized records are more easily accessible to managers and policy makers for planning and analysis. In the cities surveyed, the central HRM department plays a more prominent role than individual departments in tracking and automating individual training records. However, states were more likely to maintain records at a central personnel office than either cities or states. This may reflect, in part, the quality of states' information technology systems as well as their increased attention to workforce planning.

Despite the advances in tracking individual participation in training programs, many states still lack systematic, centralized information on training and development. In 2000, twenty-two states were unable to estimate their total or per employee training expenditures. More than 80 percent of counties were able to provide information on total training expenditures, and 75 percent had information on per employee expenditure.

Table 4.5 presents information about the proportion of governments providing different types of training. The data indicate that states consistently provide the most training. The data for states and counties represents training that is offered centrally, by departments, and by contractors; the city data represent training offered centrally. While the comparison is not perfect, we believe it captures a great deal of the training that is occurring, because more than 90 percent of the cities indicated that the central HRM department was responsible for providing citywide training. However, to make the data more comparable, table 4.5 also presents data about types of training offered by the central personnel office at state and county levels.

As can be seen in table 4.5, cities consistently offer less training than counties or states. Centrally, states and counties were more likely to provide employees with performance management, leadership, supervisory, and management training. Less than a majority of cities, counties, and states provided technical, first aid, or basic skills training centrally.

The data suggest that all governments are committed to leadership development. We found that 60.6 percent of cities, 91.7 percent of counties,

Table 4.5. Training Offered (percentage)

	Central training			All training[a]	
	Cities	States (2000)	Counties	States (2000)	Counties
Technical (apprenticeship)	30.3	22.0	22.2	98.0	88.9
First aid	33.3	33.3	42.0	96.0	86.1
Performance management	36.4	91.8	77.8	98.0	91.7
Basic skills	48.5	32.0	27.8	72.0	61.1
New employee orientation	48.5	40.0	94.4	100	100
Leadership	60.6	84.0	77.8	98.0	91.7
Supervisory skills	60.6	90.0	91.7	100	97.2
Computer	66.7	57.1	75.0	98.0	100
Management	75.8	90.0	83.3	100	97.2
Other	75.8	40.8	27.8	44.0	27.8
N	33	50	36	50	39

Source: R. D. Behn, "The Big Questions of Public Management," *Public Administration Review* 55 (1995): 313–24.
Note: Data are for thirty-three cities, thirty-six counties, and fifty states.
[a]Training offered either centrally, through departments, through outside contractor, or a combination of the three.

and 98.0 percent of states provided leadership training opportunities to employees. Missouri, for example, initiated a series of one-day programs for managers and supervisors. The program brings in well known authorities in the areas of management and leadership, such as Bruce Patton on negotiations and Chip Bell on mentoring. Pennsylvania offers a series of seminars to executives on the best contemporary management thinking. Working with Iowa State University, Iowa developed a leadership academy that offers an Executive Development Program and a Certified Managers Program. Mecklenburg County instituted the Leadership Education and Development Academy to identify and develop up-and-coming talent within the county. Orange County offers Enlightened Leadership training to county supervisors and managers.

In addition to offering a variety of classes, it is important to have a good sense of what training is needed. We found that counties and states typically assess training needs when the training responsibility is centralized. Training needs assessments are more frequently conducted by counties than by states.[9] However, the data are not encouraging. We found that most governments do not complete training needs assessments before developing and implementing their training programs. The data are summarized as follows:

- 23.5 percent of counties conducted training needs assessments for the entire county government annually, compared with 18.4 percent of states that conducted training needs assessments for the entire state government annually
- 25.8 percent of counties conduct training needs assessments for county departments annually, compared with 16.7 percent of states that conduct training needs assessments for state agencies annually
- 9.4 percent of counties conduct training needs assessments for specific job classifications annually, whereas no states conduct needs assessments for specific job classifications annually

However, governments mentioned an array of other techniques they used to ascertain their training needs. For example, Baltimore County uses departmental needs assessment surveys collected by central HRM, focus group results, recommendations from departmental training liaisons, and training course evaluations. Wayne County determines its training needs using data on Training Counsel probationary failures, succession planning, and recruitment needs.

If employees are to understand the training opportunities available to them, governments must disseminate training information. Our research shows that only 50 percent of cities distributed a training catalog, and only 23.1 percent had a training catalog available on the Internet in 1999. These numbers are higher for counties, with 68.6 percent distributing catalogs, 62.9 percent having online catalogs, and another 22.9 percent developing online catalogs. States are the most likely to provide employees access to such data, with 96 percent of states distributing catalogs to all employees, 80 percent posting training catalogues online, and 18 percent developing online capacity at the time of the survey.

Our results demonstrate that states are providing employees with more opportunities and greater access to training than cities and counties. States provide the greatest array of training courses, followed closely by counties. Leadership and management courses are more likely to be provided at all levels of government than more general courses. However, states continue to lack important information about training spending patterns, in part because much of the spending is decentralized and not necessarily captured in the budgeting process.

In addition to developing skills and competencies, to maintain an effective workforce governments need to be able to remove employees who are not performing well or are engaging in behaviors that violate government rules. Appropriate discipline is a necessary component of an effective management infrastructure.[10]

A progressive discipline system is the dominant model used at all levels of government; that is, a system that involves a gradual increase in the severity of punishments for every rule violation. Martin Levy notes that a good discipline policy includes progressive discipline, in combination with unbiased implementation and standardized documentation.[11] The data indicate that 78.8 percent of the cities, 75 percent of counties, and 80.9 percent of the states have progressive discipline systems in place.

As shown in table 4.6, our data suggest that states were better able to address behavioral problems than performance problems. Counties noted that that they can address both behavioral and performance problems at approximately the same speed. However, more than 40 percent indicated that the discipline system did not allow the county to discipline or remove employees quickly for either performance or behavioral problems. States were more positive about their ability to discipline behavioral problems, with 77.1 percent of the states agreeing or strongly agreeing that the discipline system in place allowed managers to discipline behavior problems quickly. States were less optimistic, however, about their efforts to remove poor performers.[12]

Table 4.6. State and County Positions on Discipline (percentage)

	Strongly disagree	Disagree	Neutral	Agree	Strongly agree	(N)
Discipline system allows managers to discipline performance problems quickly						
States (2000)	0	26	28	36	11	47
Counties	8	39	11	39	3	36
Discipline system allows managers to discipline behavior problems quickly						
States (2000)	0	2	21	50	27	48
Counties	6	31	19	36	8	36

Although states indicated that they still face obstacles, including the lack of consistency and uniformity in disciplinary actions across state agencies and departments, they reported being more likely to undertake progressive discipline than cities or counties, though cities were not far behind. Compared with states, counties have slightly more trouble using their systems effectively.

States may be in a better position than cities or counties to maintain an appropriately skilled workforce because of their greater training opportunities and more effective disciplinary processes. Counties do not lag far behind. State governments disseminate materials to employees more systematically than other levels of government. However, many cities and counties have good systems in place for tracking training information other than course participation—an area in which states can clearly benefit. States and cities are more likely than counties to undertake progressive discipline, though a majority at all levels employed this practice.

Motivating Workforce Performance

To maximize human capital, a government must be able to motivate its employees to perform at high levels and in ways that contribute to its goals.[13] This can be accomplished using a variety of tools and techniques. Two important mechanisms in this regard are awards, both monetary and nonmonetary, and formal feedback. Examples of the former are listed in table 4.7.

Our research shows that states and counties used a greater diversity of monetary rewards than cities (see table 4.8 and figure 4.1). A shift in the types of remuneration used by the states occurred between the 1998 and

Table 4.7. Employee Rewards Used in Government

Nonmonetary rewards	Monetary rewards
Job flexibility related to performance	Individual performance bonus
Time flexibility related to performance	Group performance bonus
Performance recognition program	Gain sharing
Public service recognition week	Merit pay
Employee of the month	Skill-based pay
Commendation award	Competency pay
Governor's award	Pay-for-performance

Table 4.8. Use of Monetary Employee Rewards in Government (percentage)

	Cities	States (2000)	Counties
Pay-for-performance	26	74	75
Individual performance bonus	26	64	58
Group performance bonus	3	38	42
Skill pay	3	54	53
Competency pay	n.a.	42	28
Gain sharing	6	18	19
Annual step increase	n.a.	78	89
Cost-of-living payment	10	66	64
N	31	50	36

2000 surveys. There was a dramatic increase in the use of individual and group performance bonuses by states: in 2000 about 64 percent of states used individual performance bonuses and 38 percent used group bonuses, compared with 14.3 and 2.0 percent, respectively, in 1998. Counties were more likely than states to employ group bonuses (41.7%). Cities were the least inclined to employ this tool, with only 3 percent offering bonuses for group performance. Maricopa County's Share the Savings incentive plan allowed departments to define their criteria for developing a departmental incentive strategy. Many departments in the county adopted a group performance incentive to reward achievement of specific departmental

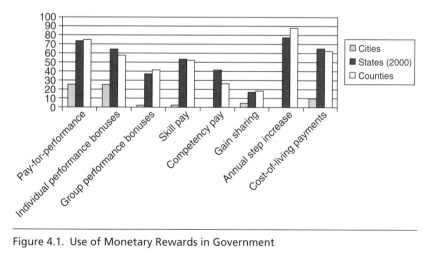

Figure 4.1. Use of Monetary Rewards in Government

goals that require teamwork. Mecklenburg County implemented the Quality Achievement Award Program, which recognizes individual employee accomplishments with monetary awards up to $500. Managers working in Kentucky state government have the authority to award a lump-sum bonus to an employee who has participated in a significant project outside the scope of his or her normal work.

Our research shows that cities primarily use traditional compensation techniques, while states and counties were more likely to employ a variety of techniques. Only about a quarter of the cities surveyed used pay-for-performance techniques or individual performance bonuses citywide. A number of cities mentioned that they used merit pay to recognize a limited group, typically their managerial workforce. Other cities noted that their compensation strategies were constrained by labor contracts. Eighty-five percent of Milwaukee's employees, for example, are represented by one of nineteen bargaining units. Boston, also highly unionized, noted that "there are no reward systems or practices in place." States and counties both used a variety of techniques and did so at similar levels, although many unionized counties and states also noted bargaining difficulties in the development of their reward and recognition systems.

States employed both skill pay and competency pay in 2000. Indiana allows agencies to customize their compensation strategies by selecting the appropriate methods from among competency-based pay, skill-based pay, gain sharing, and pay-for-performance. An analysis of Indiana's Department of Financial Institution's workforce revealed that most of its financial examiners were leaving between the four- and seven-year service marks—a point at which examiners had attained a highly technical skill set thanks to expensive training paid for by the state. The agency's investment was not paying off. As a result, the department structured a variable competency pay program to target employees at the four- to seven-year mark. Only a few counties were experimenting with competency pay, but more than 50 percent used skill pay in 2001. Although states and counties used a diversity of techniques, the most common way to reward employees in both was an annual step increase.

In addition to cash and pay rewards, governments offer a variety of nonmonetary rewards (see table 4.9). Cities used the fewest nonmonetary tools to motivate employees. Performance recognition programs were one of the most common nonmonetary rewards used by all levels of government. The least used tool was job flexibility. We found governments at all levels trying new efforts to enhance their nonmonetary rewards programs. Mari-

Table 4.9. Use of Nonmonetary Employee Rewards in City Government (percentage)

	Never	Rarely	Sometimes	Often or very often[a]	N[b]
Job flexibility					
Cities	14	18	50	18	28
States (2000)	23	17	42	19	48
Counties	39	14	36	11	36
Performance recognition program					
Cities	46	15	12	27	26
States (2000)	0	8	40	52	48
Counties	11	6	33	50	36
Public service recognition week					
Cities	100	0	0	0	19
States (2000)	19	11	21	49	47
Counties	56	3	19	22	36
Employee of the month					
Cities	95	0	5	0	19
States (2000)	2	4	46	48	48
Counties	14	3	53	31	36
Commendation award					
Cities	77	9	5	9	22
States (2000)	2	9	32	57	47
Counties	14	6	53	28	36
Other					
Cities	64	8	20	8	25
States (2000)	0	9	32	59	22
Counties	3	63	6	38	32

[a]For states and counties, the categories "often" and "very often" were combined so that the scales were consistent across the three years.
[b]If a city, state, or county did not respond to a question, the response was treated as missing for that question.

copa County implemented its Share the Savings program, which allows a department to recognize employees who have consistently met or exceeded their performance goals. The county also recognizes individual employees with nonmonetary awards, such as the Sparkplug Award for boosting morale and the Hang In There Award for perseverance.

Montgomery County initiated Montgomery's Best Honor Awards Program, featuring seven competitive awards presented annually by the county executive and chief administrative officer. Michigan's Quality Recognition System provides recognition and incentives to state agencies, employees, and retirees for process improvements that improve the quality of state services. South Carolina utilizes several types of nonmonetary rewards, including job and time flexibility, performance recognition week, public service recognition week, employee of the month recognition, and commendation awards. The state also provides agencies with flexibility to establish reward and recognition programs; some agencies are being particularly creative in this effort (for example, the Department of Vocational Rehabilitation). Washington uses a diversity of monetary and nonmonetary rewards, such as pay-for-performance, individual performance bonuses, skill and competency pay, performance recognition week, commendation awards, and the governor's award.

Of the three groups surveyed, states consistently implement a greater number of monetary and nonmonetary rewards. Counties used these techniques less often than states, with some minor exceptions, but the level of use was not significantly different. Cities, on the other hand, use fewer tools; only a handful of them use rewards at all.

Performance appraisals are also an important tool in motivating performance. Formal performance evaluations give feedback and directions to employees and provide managers with information that can help them in making decisions.[14] Both state and county governments use multiple instruments to assess employee performance (see table 4.10; on the other hand, 62.1 percent of cities used a single performance appraisal system for all employees.) Iowa, Virginia, Washington, Wisconsin, and Maricopa County all use seven different types of performance appraisal instruments (listed in table 4.10).

Maricopa County is creating a new performance management appraisal system consisting of an alignment worksheet, which stresses the importance of achieving departmental goals; performance factors, which encompass elements of essential work behaviors directly related to the job; and an employee development plan, which outlines training, education, and individual skills development. Westchester County introduced an integrated performance management and evaluation application, allowing employees, supervisors, and managers to use a unified system to create and track goals, log events to document individual performance, and create performance

Table 4.10. Use of Performance Appraisal Instruments (percentage)

	States (2000)	Counties
360-degree appraisal	42	25
Appraisal linking individual and organizational performance goals	96	83
Peer evaluation	48	19
Customer evaluation	52	25
Supervisor's evaluations of team	44	14
Subordinates' evaluation of supervisor	42	19
Subordinates' evaluation of manager	40	14
N	50	36

Note: Comparable data were not collected in the 1999 city survey.

Table 4.11. Frequency of Formal Evaluation of Civil Service Employees (percentage)

	States (2000)	Counties	Cities
Annually	86	81	75
Semiannually	12	8	3
No formal evaluation required	0	6	13
Other	2	6	10
N	50	36	32

evaluations. Most of the state and county governments surveyed use performance appraisal instruments linking individual goals with organizational goals. Approximately half of the states use customer and peer evaluations as part of their performance appraisal systems.

As shown in table 4.11, all states require a formal evaluation for civil service employees, and 88.9 percent of counties require a formal evaluation annually or semiannually. Approximately 12.5 percent of cities and 5.6 percent of counties require no annual formal evaluation of employees.

Feedback from employees is equally important. Employee feedback can yield suggestions or data that can be used to improve the system by empowering employees, improving morale, and increasing understanding of the system from the front lines. Twice as many states (74%) and cities (71.9%) have formal government-wide suggestion programs as counties (36.1%). A significantly larger percentage of cities (53.3%) than states (34.0%) or counties (25.7%) conduct formal government-wide employee surveys. Governments are becoming more innovative in collecting employee feedback. The Kentucky Employee Suggestion System (ESS) is fully automated. Each agency has an ESS coordinator who is networked to the system. Coordinators receive, evaluate, and respond to employee suggestions online. The system ensures timely evaluation and action on suggestions by the ESS Council. In 1999, fifty-eight awards were presented to employees, which represented a first-year savings of more than $2.2 million. Dallas County surveys new employees to assess their first three months of employment in order to audit its orientation program. North Carolina conducts an annual formal statewide employee survey that covers a broad set of topics, including pay, benefits, family-friendly services, and satisfaction with central human resource services.

Monetary and nonmonetary rewards encourage employees to participate in suggestions programs. Half of the counties, 80 percent of the states, and 69 percent of the cities provided monetary rewards for suggestions. The amount of the monetary reward varies with a high for states of $50,000 (New York) and a state average of $5,587 individual rewards within a year. Recognition for employees' suggestions is provided by 80.0 percent of the states, 61.8 percent of the counties, and 56.7 percent of the cities. Clark County uses a formal countywide employee suggestion program, in which about 10 percent of county departments participate and employee recognition and monetary awards of up to $25,000 are available. Santa Clara uses a formal countywide employee suggestion program, which offers a monetary award equivalent to 10 percent of the first year's savings, to a maximum award of $10,000.

Looking across governments, we found that states consistently demonstrated a greater sophistication in their ability to motivate a workforce to perform effectively. In particular, states have more sophisticated performance appraisal systems in place and use a great variety of instruments. All states require formal employee evaluations. Counties also employ a number of instruments, though at a significantly lower level, and not all require formal employee evaluations. More than 10 percent of cities do not require a formal evaluation of employees. Additionally, states use a great number and diversity of reward instruments, both monetary and nonmonetary. Cities lag behind states and counties in terms of the diversity of rewards and performance appraisal systems, but more consistently require mechanisms designed to elicit employee feedback.

Structuring the Workforce

Many public human resource management systems were created under a strong belief that rigidly, centrally controlled systems are the best way to exclude undue partisan influence and pressure on public employment systems. Some thought of the HRM system as a way of making government more businesslike. Many of the components of the personnel systems that emerged during the mid-1900s contributed to increasingly centralized, standardized, and rule-based civil service systems that provided great job protection to employees. Graded authority structures and public compensation systems, for example, were structured on principles of centralization and hierarchy. In their favor, centralized, hierarchical structures promoted standardization, stability, and predictability. They did not, however, allow for the discretion and flexibility that many public organizations and their leaders now find critical to long-term effectiveness. Compared with states, city and county governments more often operate traditional, centralized human resource management systems; Cleveland and Wayne County are two examples.

One indicator of centralized hierarchy is central control of recruiting, testing, and hiring. In some cities and counties, the state plays a significant role in the design and implementation of its HRM system. The city of Buffalo's HRM system, for example, is governed in part by state civil service rules. This greatly limits the city's flexibility in hiring and classification, because New York State civil service law governs the processes. We examined three components of the selection process; our results are shown in table 4.12. The study found that primary responsibility varies, depending on the stage of the selection process, and that centralized systems of recruiting and hiring still exist. However, the study found no evidence to suggest that the personnel authority of the overall process is moving toward total decentralization. Broadly speaking, the data indicate three trends:

- While responsibility for recruiting is the most shared component of the selection process, in cities and counties recruiting responsibility is almost as likely to be centralized within HRM departments.
- Testing is centralized in most of the cities, counties, and states surveyed. However, about a third of these governments share testing authority.
- Employee selection is typically decentralized to hiring departments in cities, counties, and states.

Table 4.12. Managerial Responsibility for Components of Selection Process

	Centralized			Shared			Decentralized		
	Cities	States[a]	Counties	Cities	States[a]	Counties	Cities	States[a]	Counties
Recruiting	39	6	42	46	64	47	15	24	8
Testing	67	50	61	30	34	28	3	16	8
Hiring decision	9	4	8	16	4	14	75	88	69
N	33	50	36	33	50	36	33	50	36

Note: Some of the percentages are less than 100 percent because of missing data.
[a]From 2000 survey.

Looking at the trends over time in states, we found that changes in authority shifted toward shared authority. The proportion of states that reported centralized recruiting fell from 18 percent in 1998 to 6 percent in 2000. Sixteen percent of states shared authority for recruiting in 1998; two years later, that figure had risen to 64 percent. In the 1998 survey, 53 percent of states responded that a central authority conducted testing; in 2000 the figure fell slightly, to 50 percent.

A government's classification system is important because it reflects not only the complexity of the hiring system but also the flexibility of the compensation system. On average, states have fewer titles per employee than cities and counties. Moreover, 48 percent of states used broad banding of related jobs, compared with 22 and 28 percent of cities and counties, respectively. Although some states, counties, and cities have reformed their inflexible, graded, step-based models, many governments' classification systems remain complex and rigid. New York State, for example, with approximately 158,000 employees, has 4,000 classification titles (down from an earlier high of about 7,000). Pennsylvania, a strong advocate of the centralized model, has 89,000 employees and 2,838 classification titles. Hillsborough County has 4,300 titles, almost one title per employee. Some governments, such as those in Baltimore and Seattle, have not updated their centralized classification systems in years. Despite some decentralization, Minneapolis retains 480 classification titles for its 4,903 permanent and 2,552 temporary employees (down from 640 titles in 1996). By contrast, South Carolina works with 452 classification titles for its nearly 72,000 employees; and Cuyahoga County maintains 30 titles in its system, an average of 1 title for every 366 employees.

Traditional classification systems are also linked to narrow and rigid compensation guidelines and procedures. For example, the practice of small, annual, and within-grade step increases for employees is a common indicator of a traditional system and the dominant approach used by counties. The interlocking complexity and rigidity of these components of the personnel system are often exacerbated in traditional systems, such as Buffalo's, by labor-management agreements, which create additional constraints on hiring, promotion, discipline, and compensation.

State governments are moving toward shared responsibility for their HRM functions between central HRM offices and agencies. Both cities and counties, on the other hand, lean toward centralization of HRM functions. There are no examples of totally decentralized HRM systems in the cities and counties surveyed and only one such system among the states (Texas). Our data indicate that HRM systems in cities are more centralized than those in counties, but county systems are more centralized than most state HRM systems. As governments move away from traditional, centralized civil service systems, there are increasing variations in governmental human resource management systems. Many differ in how they structure responsibility, provide for flexibility, and ensure that they have a professional and responsive cadre of employees. Such sharing allows continued consideration of broad governmental concerns, such as equity, but combines them with the customization necessary for better agency and departmental performance. The differences across public HRM systems are likely to continue to increase as governments respond to changing global, political, and economic environments.

Governments That Lead the Way

This section examines governments with high-capacity human resource management systems at the city, county, and state level. Systems are considered to have high capacity if they received a grade of B+ or higher; these are listed in table 4.13. Our examination of these high-performing governments across government level yielded five important lessons:

- High-capacity governments are technologically sophisticated.
- High-capacity governments have the information they need for decision making and planning.
- High-capacity governments use a diversity of selection and reward HRM tools.

Table 4.13. High-Performing Governments

States (2000)	Counties	Cities
Iowa (B+)	Broward, FL (B+)	Austin, TX (A−)
Kansas (B+)	Dallas, TX (B+)	Indianapolis, IN (A−)
Kentucky (B+)	Fairfax, VA (A−)	Phoenix, AZ (A)
Michigan (B+)	Maricopa, AZ (B+)	San Antonio, TX (B+)
Missouri (B+)	Montgomery, MD (B+)	
North Carolina (B+)		
Pennsylvania (B+)		
South Carolina (A)		
Virginia (B+)		
Washington (A−)		
Wisconsin (A−)		

- High-capacity governments engage in planning.
- High-capacity governments are able to hire and fire quickly.

Along with a brief discussion of each lesson, examples and innovations are noted; other examples of the practices and lessons highlighted in this section are also noted throughout the chapter.

Technological Sophistication

The governments with higher capacity increasingly use technology to provide better services to their employees and customers. The high-capacity governments had integrated HRM information technology systems in place and demonstrated increased use of the Internet for a variety of activities, including recruiting, application posting, application submission, and advertising and registration for training courses. Additionally, the high-capacity governments were automating a variety of functions, including testing and suggestion programs.

Eighty-five percent of the high-capacity governments have integrated HRM information technology systems. In this context, *integrated* means a single system that performs multiple human resource management functions using common software and common data.

The governments indicated that they have expanded their use of technology for recruiting as well as the entire selection and hiring process, making the process more accessible and expeditious. All high-capacity governments make applications available online and either currently have or are in the process of developing the capacity to submit them online. Missouri implemented the Management and Applicant Information Resource System, which provides online, real-time access to applicant information for agencies throughout the state. Any authorized agency can access the applicant information. A tremendous advantage of using this system is that special skills and competencies can be identified to help agencies fill specific positions, and to choose applicants with specialized skills and abilities within broad classifications.

High-capacity governments also realize the importance of developing a technologically sophisticated workforce. These governments noted a host of training courses associated with technology, such as computer training.

In summary, automation was an area of keen interest for these governments as they undertook integrating many of their human resource functions. The application process, employee surveys and suggestion programs, and even training courses have been automated by many of these governments.

Access to Information

High-capacity governments collect and keep a diverse set of data used in decision making and planning. All of the governments' central human resource departments collect data about their performance or the outcomes of their efforts. These governments are developing sophistication in deciding which measures to collect data for and how to use of these measures. Many of the high-capacity governments have begun to link output measures to outcome measures and are able to organize the data in a manner that allows them to be easily integrated into the planning process. The data from output measures collected by Broward County, for example, are well organized and broken into frames of quarters, allowing comparison between the programmed and the actual data. The categories include human resource programs, employee assistance programs, and employee benefit services. Following the output measures, the county provides a description of strategic outcomes. The information collected is compiled in a Quarterly Performance Measurement Form. Broward County uses an automated database to track employee participation in training and development courses.

The high-capacity governments not only collect organizational performance measures but also collect information on individual employees, in reference to both performance and training. Most of the high-capacity governments noted that they maintain databases to track employee training and development data to use in planning and decision making. High-capacity governments recognized the importance of information gathered through employee feedback. Most of these governments—all but one state (the overall state average was 74%), all cities, and almost 50 percent of the counties (compared with the overall county average was 36.1%)—indicated that they used employee suggestion programs. Those that had a suggestion program offered rewards for suggestions.

Engagement in Planning

Planning related to human resource management was undertaken by all of the high-capacity governments in the form of workforce planning, strategic planning, or a combination of both. San Antonio was the only high-capacity city that does not conduct workforce planning. Eight of the eleven high-capacity states have a formal workforce planning process in place, while the remaining three undertake workforce planning informally. Three of the five county governments with high capacity have informal plans, one has a formal plan, and one requires workforce plans from its departments. The topics covered in workforce plans are diverse. North Carolina's workforce plan covers nineteen different areas, while Fairfax County's covers five. On average, for the high-capacity governments, fifteen areas of planning are covered.

For example, in November 1999, a Workforce Planning Advisory Committee in Iowa began operations with priorities in recruitment, compensations and succession planning. Later, in July 2000, workforce planning was legislatively added to the functions of the human resource department. The position of workforce planning coordinator was created to oversee this function. Phoenix's personnel and operating departments meet each spring to develop annual forecasting plans. The departments identify upcoming retirements and vacancies, newly budgeted supplemental positions, and reorganizational needs. The personnel department provides a forecast plan in the form of a list of job classifications based on the expiration date of the existing list. Together, the departments develop a recruitment plan for the upcoming fiscal year. The city of Phoenix received an award from the Public Technology Institute in 1989 for this program.

With the exception of Broward County, all the high-capacity governments have a strategic plan for their human resource departments. Although Broward County's human resource department does not have a strategic plan, it requires all departments to conduct workforce planning.

Diversity of Selection and Reward Tools

High-capacity governments consistently employed a wider array of tools and techniques across different HRM functions, such as recruiting, rewarding, and compensation, than did the sample in general. High-capacity counties, on average, used 18.6 techniques, compared with the overall county average of 16.1. The average figure for high-capacity states was 19.8, compared with the average for all states of 17.1. Examples of recruiting techniques include external job fairs, online resume banks, internal job fairs, commercial Internet sites, virtual job fairs, twenty-four-hour telephone job lines, local newspaper ads, open houses, national job fairs, college site visits, online job postings, on-site interviews, job bulletins, letter campaigns, ads in trade publications, direct hires, partnerships with professional associations, walk-in job counseling, travel expenses for interviews, radio advertisements, satellite offices, postings in community centers, listings with professional recruitment firms, television advertising, use of full-time recruiters, and reimbursement of relocation expenses. In addition to these and other traditional recruiting efforts, many governments were trying new and innovative recruiting practices.

High-capacity governments were also more likely to employ a variety of testing techniques, recognizing the need to appropriately match the test with the needs of the position. Formal tests are administered primarily for clerical, fire, and police positions. Applications for other positions are reviewed and evaluated in a manner appropriate to the position under consideration. Phoenix, whose stance is a common view for the governments, noted that it "uses a full range of testing types, including written examinations, training and experience evaluations, equipment demonstration tests, in-basket exercises, assessment centers, and oral boards (for Public Safety positions). Testing and selection methods are not standardized; they are chosen based upon the job analysis."

All the high-capacity governments use a complementary mix of monetary and nonmonetary rewards, some as many as fifteen different types. Iowa uses a performance recognition program, holds a public service recognition week, recognizes an employee of the month, and awards commendations and a special governor's award for exemplary employees. The state's monetary rewards include gain sharing, competency pay, cost-of-living payments, individual performance bonuses, and pay-for-performance.

The high-capacity governments also employ a variety of compensation practices. Many of them were pushing to align pay with market rates and to provide managers with more options and discretion. Although broad banding has received considerable attention and was used in some form by half the high-capacity governments, these governments also looked to other appropriate compensation systems and used a variety of them, often employing different systems for different groups of employees. For example, Broward County has recently implemented a new performance, goal-driven compensation system that includes bonus eligibility for executives, professionals, and managers. In 2000 Fairfax County launched a new pay-for-performance compensation system for all employees (other than public safety workers), a move that dramatically changed the existing compensation and evaluation process.

Fast Hiring and Firing

High-capacity governments consistently took less time to perform many fundamental human resource functions. On average, they were able to fill a vacant position in fewer days and terminate for performance and behavioral problems in less time than other governments. Both areas were a concern for many governments at the time of the surveys.

In response to the tight labor markets of the late 1990s, governments refined and developed their selection systems. They tried to adjust salaries to be more commensurate with market wages, provided more flexibility in starting salaries, and allowed for signing bonuses.

In addition to the increased use of the Internet, Phoenix is using theme-oriented recruiting. This tool explores the attitudes of current successful employees to enable governments to recruit similarly motivated employees. In partnership with the police department, Phoenix has conducted an open house for potential police communication operators to tour the city's communication bureaus. This allows potential operators to experience the work environment in advance, giving them a better understanding of the job. Since Phoenix was experiencing immediate demand, this recruitment process was expedient. During the open house, applications were distributed, and applicants registered for test dates. Approximately 450 people were processed. The open house was followed by a series of One-Stop Shop testing and interview dates. For the convenience of the applicant, the One-Stop Shop combined written and typing tests, interviews, and simulator testing. Following completion of the tests and interviews, applicants were placed on a list and received tentative job offers, contingent upon background checks. All the strategies that have been employed aim at creating a streamlined and convenient application process.

Using technology, training, new techniques, structure, and other tools, high-capacity governments tend to have shorter durations to hire (on average, thirty to sixty days). Among the high-capacity counties, 80 percent took less than sixty days to hire, compared with the county average of 63.8 percent. The difference for the high-capacity states is even more dramatic. All the high-capacity state governments were able to fill a vacant position in less than sixty days, whereas 77.1 percent of all the states needed between 61 and 270 days to fill a vacant position.

A traditional complaint is that managers in government are highly restricted in their ability to fire inadequate employees and that, for those that are authorized, the termination process takes an inordinate amount of time. High-capacity governments are able to terminate employees in much less time than the average—most in less than ten days for either performance or behavioral problems. Specifically, all the high-capacity states were able to terminate employees in less than thirty days for performance problems, 81 percent doing so within the first ten days; and 100 percent were able to terminate an employee for behavioral problems in less than ten days.

Excellence in Public Human Resource Management Systems at All Levels of Government

While all governments face challenges, most of those surveyed performed well in one or more areas of human resource management. Similarly, many governments, including those that did not make it into the high-performing category, are undertaking a number of innovative practices. Numerous governments demonstrated their ability to overcome environmental constraints and perform effectively. For example, Pennsylvania manages its state human resources well, though it operates under a traditional, centralized civil service structure.

As governments move away from traditional, centralized civil service systems, we find increasing variations in government human resource management systems. Many systems differ in how they structure responsibility, provide for flexibility, and ensure a cadre of professional and responsive employees. These differences are likely to increase as governments respond to changing global, political, and economic environments. Furthermore, because the HRM systems within and across governments are complicated and varied, questions arise about the portability of HRM reforms and practices and the inherent challenge of studying systems externally. Reforms in human resource management are more easily implemented in governments in which the political or administrative leadership champions change. Reforms are not as likely to succeed, even in the name of good governance, in places without such guidance.

High-performing governments are more likely to assume a strategic human resource management role. They articulate a clear mission and goals that are linked to the government's strategic plan; they plan for their immediate and long-term workforce needs in light of those priorities and goals; and they collect the necessary data to assess achievement of their intended goals. While the GPP study shows that HRM-related planning has not yet become universal, there is considerable momentum in that direction at the state level of government.

APPENDIX

Multicomponent Scaling Used to Analyze Criterion-Based Evaluation Approach

The Government Performance Project partnered journalists from *Governing* magazine with academic faculty experts in HRM. The journalists relied on their academic partners to analyze the survey data and supporting documentation. The journalists conducted follow-up interviews, during which they contacted state, county, and city HRM officials and solicited additional information. In the end, *Governing* published an evaluation summary and rating using letter grades for each government's HRM system. This appendix focuses only on the data and the methods used by the academic partner and identifies trends and lessons by criterion based on those analyses.

The study followed two basic approaches in analyzing, comparing, and ranking public human resource management systems, the appropriate methodology being determined by the nature of the data collected. When primarily qualitative data was collected to assess the criteria, we employed fuzzy logic. When the data collected was primarily quantitative, we created a series of quantitative multicomponent additive scales. Fuzzy logic was used to evaluate state HRM systems in 1998, and a multicomponent scaling technique was used to analyze city systems in 1999, state systems in 2000, and county systems in 2001.[15] Thirty-two cities returned completed surveys, for a response rate of approximately 91.5 percent in 1999.[16] All states returned completed surveys in 2000. Thirty-six counties, or 90 percent, submitted complete survey responses and were included in the analysis in 2001.[17]

Multicomponent Scaling Technique

After analyzing the 1998 data for states, we changed the survey design considerably, to incorporate primarily quantitative responses. As a result, a different analytical strategy was employed in the subsequent evaluations of city, county, and state human resource management systems.

Most of the data collected during these three years were quantitative. To analyze and quantify the qualitative data, researchers

- designed a coding scheme for systematic conversion of the qualitative survey responses into quantified variables
- pretested the coding scheme, using the survey responses and supporting documentation from five states
- revised the coding scheme, reflecting feedback from the pretest
- coded the survey responses, using two raters for each question
- computed interrater reliability, first, computing the pairwise percentage agreement, then computing the correlation between the two coders' ratings[18]
- developed and employed a process for resolving coding discrepancies between raters[19]

In this study, the human resource management variables were grouped by criteria, explicitly assigned weights, and summed to create an index per criterion and an overall HRM capacity index.[20] The next step was to choose a coherent structure that assigned appropriate weights to evaluation indicators. To construct the indexes, the research team first linked the quantified human resource variables to each criterion and assigned weights to each variable. The weighted variables were summed, and the scales standardized. Researchers then computed a measure of human resource management capacity for each government by summing the five standardized scales. Finally, they applied two other weighting schemes to determine the sensitivity or robustness of the HRM capacity measure. The final grades were calculated within a possible range of 0 to 100. Innovations and barriers were identified by analyzing the open-ended questions using QSR NUD*IST—a qualitative data analysis tool.

NOTES

1. Rosemary Batt, "Managing Customer Services: Human Resource Practices, Quit Rates, and Sales Growth," *Academy of Management Journal* 45, no. 3 (2002): 587–97.

2. Sally Coleman Selden, Patricia Ingraham, and Willow Jacobson, "Human Resource Practices: Findings from a National Survey," *Public Administration Review* 61, no. 5 (2001): 598–607; U.S. General Accounting Office, *A Model of Strategic Human Capital,* GAO-02-3735P (Washington, DC, March 15, 2002).

3. Patricia Ingraham and Sally Coleman Selden, "Human Resource Management and Capacity in the States," in *Public Personnel Management: Current Con-*

cerns, Future Challenges, ed. Carolyn Ban and Norma M. Riccucci, 3d ed. (New York: Longman, 2002), pp. 210–24.

4. In 1998 states were evaluated on six criteria. Criteria 1 and 6 were later combined and are now captured in criteria 5.

5. James W. Down, Walter Mardis, Thomas R. Connolly, and Sarah Johnson, "A Strategic Model Emerges," *HR Focus* 74, no. 2 (1997): 22–24.

6. Gary E. Roberts, "Issues, Challenges, and Changes in Recruitment and Selection," in *Public Personnel Administration: Problems and Prospects,* ed. Steven W. Hays and Richard Kearney, 4th ed. (Upper Saddle River, NJ: Prentice-Hall, 2003), pp. 89–104.

7. The GPP survey did not ask this question of cities.

8. Willow Jacobson, Ellen Rubin, and Sally Selden, "Examining Training in Large Municipalities: Linking Individual and Organizational Training Needs," *Public Personnel Management* 31, no. 4 (2002): 485–506.

9. Comparable data were not collected in the 1999 city survey.

10. Leon C. Megginson, *Personnel Management: A Human Resources Approach* (Homewood, IL: Richard D. Irwin, 1985).

11. Martin Levy, "Discipline for Professional Employees," *Personnel Journal* 69, no. 12 (1990): 27–28.

12. Comparable data were not collected in the 1999 city survey.

13. R. D. Behn, "The Big Questions of Public Management," *Public Administration Review* 55, no. 4 (1995): 313–24.

14. Wayne F. Cascio, *Managing Human Resources: Productivity, Quality of Work Life, Profits,* 4th ed., McGraw-Hill Series in Management (New York: McGraw-Hill, 1995).

15. For a thorough discussion of the fuzzy logic approach, see Sally Coleman Selden, Salwa Ammar, Willow Jacobson, and Ron Wright, "A New Approach to Assessing Performance of State Human Resource Management Systems: A Multi-Level Fuzzy Rule-Based System," *Review of Public Personnel Administration* 20, no. 3 (2000): 58.

16. Anchorage did not return a survey. Atlanta, Long Beach, and San Diego provided abbreviated responses.

17. Alameda, Nassau, San Bernardino, and Suffolk Counties did not return completed surveys.

18. On computation of pairwise percentage agreement, see Rikard Larsson, "Case Survey Methodology: Quantitative Analysis of Patterns across Case Studies," *Academy of Management Journal* 36, no. 6 (1993): 1515–47.

19. A Syracuse University graduate student and the designer of the coding scheme reexamined the observations, discussed the responses, conducted follow-up interviews with state officials where necessary, and reached a joint consensus on how to code them. Larsson, "Case Survey Methodology," 1532.

20. Robert F. DeVellis, *Scale Development: Theory and Applications* (Newbury Park, CA: Sage, 1991).

CHAPTER 5

The Performance Challenge
Information Technology Management in States, Counties, and Cities

B. J. REED, LYN HOLLEY, AND DONNA DUFNER

Information technology has become central to government operations. Governments are largely service oriented, and service activities depend increasingly on the quality, accuracy, and timeliness of information. Information technology systems not only support substantive activities of government such as public safety, public transportation, and public works, they also are essential to financial, human resource, and capital management endeavors. The Government Performance Project model of government performance and management capacity included IT as one of the pillars of management capacity, equal in importance to finance, human resource, and capital management.

Technology permeates all aspects of government performance, from World Wide Web applications that provide services for citizens to legacy systems that process payroll. This dependence on technology was underscored by the threat of information systems failure owing to the phenomenon known as Y2K.[1] The looming crisis riveted the attention of elected officials everywhere on the need to prepare legacy systems for the turn of the century, prompting state and local governments to accelerate information technology decisions and adjust budget priorities. It awakened governing bodies to the centrality of IT in government performance and management capacity.

The story of IT management in U.S. government began as a story of operating practitioners adapting successful private sector technologies for use in their respective public sector functions.[2] Public sector IT managers relied on private sector models, and private sector research and best practices were also adopted by the public sector.[3] Researchers and educators interested in public sector IT management came late to the information management party.[4] In 1986 a special issue of *Public Administration Review* focused attention on the need for research on public sector IT, a need confirmed by subsequent studies.[5] Until the GPP study, comprehensive data about IT in U.S. governments simply did not exist.

This chapter discusses findings from analysis by a multidisciplinary team of the GPP data specifically related to IT management. The first section places the analysis in the context of the project. The next presents a framework for considering variations in IT infrastructure in state, county, and city government. The third section explores characteristics of IT management capacity in states, counties, and cities and how they measure up in relation to the GPP criteria along with crosscutting discussions of e-government and geographic information systems (GIS). The chapter ends with conclusions and a suggestion for future research. The chapter appendix contains a glossary of the technical terminology used in this chapter and describes in detail the criteria used in IT assessment.

To explore IT management capacity in the states, counties, and cities selected for study, GPP surveys tapped the seven key criteria shown in table 5.1. The data underpinning assessments of government IT capacity consisted of survey responses and information from multiple other sources, including publicly available information and the interview data gathered by journalists from *Governing* magazine. The rating and ranking phase of assessment was guided by the weights shown in table 5.1. The analyses discussed in this chapter are based on these assessments ad the new data.

Table 5.1. Criteria for Grading Government IT Management Capacity

Criterion	Weight (%)
Government-wide and agency-level IT systems provide information that adequately supports managers' needs and strategic goals	25
Government's IT systems form a coherent architecture	25
Government conducts meaningful, multi-year IT planning	15
IT training is adequate	15
Government can evaluate and validate the extent to which IT system benefits justify investment	10
Government can procure the IT systems needed in a timely manner	5
IT systems support the government's ability to communicate with and provide services to its citizens	5

A Framework for Considering Variations in IT Infrastructure

The degree of IT integration determines the degree to which state, county, and city systems can share data and information.[6] It dictates the quality of management information, the coherence of IT architecture, the adequacy of IT planning, the efficacy of IT training, the content and scope of IT cost-benefit analyses, the nature of IT procurement, and the government's ability to serve its citizens.[7] In other words, the level of systems integration underlies capacity for IT performance for all seven GPP criteria. The following discussion of variations in IT infrastructure and management capacity is organized around the overarching theme of systems integration. Integrated IT systems are the outcome of IT inclusion in the process of strategic planning.[8]

The seminal IT planning literature consistently maintains that strategic information systems planning (SISP) is crucial to achieving a strategic competitive advantage or profitability for a business enterprise.[9] Strategic competitive advantage requires maintaining market share, ensuring customer satisfaction, managing continuous improvement of process and product quality, and maintaining legal compliance and ethical stature.[10] In the case of U.S. state, county, and local governments, organization goals are expressed as laws or ordinances, and success is measured in terms of efficient, effective, and ethical program delivery. To integrate IT with organization goals, IT must be incorporated in the process of establishing the strategic organization goals.[11]

Information Technology at the State Level

Some of the conditions currently considered necessary for integration of information systems and technology may not exist in many state governments. Integration of IT systems requires engagement of IT at the strategic level of management and as part of the process of establishing organization objectives.[12] Formalization of structures, techniques, written procedures, and policies also is required.[13] Loosely coupled structures of governance often prohibit the degree of formalization necessary for IT integration in state government.[14]

The barriers to IT integration at the state level are many. Technological barriers range from obsolete or disparate hardware and software to inadequate transmission speeds. These barriers are costly to overcome and are made more formidable by the often distressed condition of state budgets.

Data ownership and turf issues also constrain integration, especially since within states, the state agencies, counties, and cities have many different interests, along with some autonomy. County and city governments have a much heavier service delivery requirement than state governments. They also may receive some funding directly from the federal government. The time constraints inherent in government election and budget cycles are yet another barrier to the long-term planning horizon characterizing IT system integration at strategic organization levels.[15]

Strategic Information Systems Planning

A long-term focus, comprehensiveness, formalization (established procedures), approach (innovation versus integration), flow (top-down locus of authority), executive participation, and consistency (frequency of the planning activities) are regarded as essential features of strategic information systems and technology planning.[16] Planning is an activity used to identify strategic applications and align IT with organizational goals and objectives.[17]

In state government, the objectives that guide planning and systems integration are set by politically elected or appointed officials who typically focus on achieving visible results in two years or less.[18] Short planning horizons are implicit in the election and budget cycles that frame the work of elected and appointed officials in U.S. state governments.[19]

Stephen Bajjaly's nationwide study found the only long-term objectives communicated to state IT resource managers focused on budgetary and operational efficiency, tactical objectives that serve strategic organization objectives.[20] The level of IT integration attainable is limited by the level at which the strategic objectives are established.

In addition to elected executive and legislative officials, state governments' strategic IT decisions involve a host of other stakeholders, including citizens, government employees, technology vendors, other external constituencies, and interest groups.[21] In public organizations, large numbers of internal and external stakeholders are engaged in the decision process to ensure that no individual or group presents obstacles to implementation.[22] Inclusion of stakeholders who have conflicting interests, however, may weaken the coherence of objectives set and plans made and may ultimately reduce the level of IT integration.

The pattern of stakeholder level of involvement in key IT management functions is the signature of IT integration. The two key strategic-level IT functions are making state IT policy and strategic information systems planning. The governor and the state legislature are at the top or strategic level of the administrative hierarchy in state government and, for strategic IT planning, should be very involved in functions such as making policy and developing IT strategic plans. Table 5.2 shows the mean level of involvement for each set of stakeholders in each key state IT management function.

The mean levels of involvement, however, for the governors' office in making IT policy and strategic information systems planning are 3.48 and 3.44, and for state legislatures, 2.29 and 1.54, respectively. These low levels of involvement by strategic-level actors suggest that IT integration is not occurring at the strategic level in state government.

On the other hand, high mean levels of involvement in SISP characterize officials subordinate to the governor—the chief information officer, the central IT office, and individual state agencies have means of 4.96, 4.44, and 4.38, respectively. These high mean levels of involvement indicate that strategic functions such as planning and setting policy are conducted below the strategic level, which in state organizations is composed of elected executive and legislative officials. A small group of actors—CIOs, central IT offices, and individual agencies—conduct state IT planning, most likely without benefit of the executive involvement specified by SISP models in the private sector.[23] The standard deviations of involvement for CIOs and state agencies in SISP are low, at 0.21 and 0.87 respectively, suggesting the same pattern of involvement is consistent across states.

Two characteristics of government may contribute to the lack of top-down strategic planning. First, loosely integrated state structures may prohibit the degree of formalization necessary for SISP initiated at the uppermost levels of state administration. Second, formalization of structures, techniques, written procedures, and policies necessary for SISP may be missing.[24] State agencies, counties, and cities often receive funding in the form of grants directly from the federal government. This may also serve as a constraint for setting integrated statewide objectives from the top down.

Integration within Functional Areas

Integration of IT systems within and across functional areas at the statewide level is disappointing, ranging from a low of 37 percent to a high of 79 percent (see table 5.3). Most functional areas are reported to lack IT integration with other functional areas. These findings are hardly surpris-

Table 5.2. Stakeholder Involvement in Key State IT Management Functions

	Making IT policy		SISP		Designing and developing IT systems		Approving IT procurement		Implementing IT systems		Overseeing implementation	
	Mean	SD	Mean	SD	Mean	SD	Mean	SD	Mean	SD	Mean	SD
State legislature	2.29	1.43	1.54	0.87	1.21	0.68	2.2	1.47	1.17	0.48	1.96	1.30
Legislative committee	2.23	1.21	1.60	0.80	1.19	0.53	2.19	1.41	1.32	0.72	2.17	1.21
Governor's office	3.48	1.39	3.44	1.41	1.64	0.86	2.52	1.41	1.67	0.95	2.73	1.38
Executive committee	3.30	1.47	3.38	1.52	1.85	1.12	2.38	1.58	1.80	1.11	2.60	1.55
CIO	4.93	0.25	4.96	0.21	3.67	1.29	4.44	0.92	3.47	1.42	4.31	0.90
Central IT office	4.33	1.01	4.44	1.03	4.27	1.07	4.28	1.19	4.10	1.22	4.00	1.22
IT steering committee	3.93	1.25	3.73	1.34	2.40	1.32	2.40	1.42	2.06	1.36	2.80	1.47
Individual agencies	3.56	1.22	4.38	0.87	4.67	0.63	3.85	1.34	4.71	0.61	4.52	0.85
IT end users	2.17	1.17	2.60	1.19	3.42	1.23	2.06	1.48	3.19	1.30	2.54	1.41
External consultants	1.51	0.77	1.75	0.77	3.43	0.87	1.11	0.31	3.43	0.85	2.66	1.04
External vendors	1.25	0.48	1.35	0.56	3.04	1.25	1.04	0.20	3.38	1.12	2.46	1.18
Citizens	1.73	1.19	1.31	0.79	1.38	0.67	1.40	0.61	1.15	0.30	1.10	0.92

Source: Donna Dufner, Lyn Holley, and B. J. Reed, "Can Private Sector Strategic Information Systems Planning Techniques Work for the Public Sector?" *Communications of the Association of Information Systems* 8, no. 28 (2002): 413–31.

Note: Rated on a scale of 1 to 5, where 1 = not involved and 5 = very involved.

Table 5.3. Statewide Functional System Integration

	Integration[a]		No integration	
	N	%	N	%
Budgeting	25	52	23	48
Specialized financial reports	28	58	20	42
Financial accounting	29	60	19	40
Cost accounting	19	40	29	60
Fraud control	15	31	33	69
Payroll	30	63	18	37
Hiring	18	38	30	62
Managing human resources	19	40	29	60
Managing training	8	17	40	83
Procurement	21	44	27	56
Tracking capital projects	11	23	37	77
Tracking asset conditions	10	21	38	79
Inventory management	14	29	34	71
Contract monitoring	10	21	38	79
Using performance data[b]	11	23	37	77

[a]System is fully operational and integrated with other systems.
[b]Tracking performance to provide information needed to manage for results (MFR). In other words, using IT to capture performance data.

ing, since IT planning occurs at levels below the state legislature and the governor's office, that is, below the level of strategic decision making. Strategic information systems planning is requisite to IT integration.

Functional areas with direct relationships to the tracking of pecuniary expenditures have the highest presence of integrated IT systems. Fifty-two percent of systems supporting budgeting, 58 percent of the systems supporting specialized financial reports, and 60 percent of the financial accounting systems at the statewide level are reported to be integrated. The highest level of integration reported is for systems supporting payroll, at 63 percent.

Some functional areas with evident strategic implications, such as using performance data, tracking asset conditions, and managing training, are reported to have relatively low levels of integration at the statewide level, at 23, 21, and 17 percent, respectively. Again, functional system integration at the state level remains disappointingly low.

Procurement

More than half (56%) of the systems that support procurement at the state level are not integrated, nor are these systems likely to become integrated. The low level of elected executive involvement relative to involvement at subordinate levels is also indicative of lack of state-level strategic planning for IT procurement. Subordinate levels are more involved. Mean levels of involvement for individual state agencies (3.85), central IT offices (4.28), and CIOs (4.44) are higher than those for state legislatures (2.2) and governors' offices (2.52), further indicating the absence of a strategic plan for IT procurement or of support of procurement through the use of integrated IT.

The proportion of states carrying out cost-benefit analyses for IT before procurement and upon implementation is high, at 92 and 80 percent, respectively.[25] Sixty percent of respondents reported having a statewide centralized IT procurement system.[26] Absent a statewide strategic frame of reference, however, centralized procurement and cost-benefit analysis may focus on tactical concerns, such as legal requirements for competitive bidding or cost containment.

Three types of bidding processes were evaluated at the state level: formal competitive bidding, negotiated competitive bidding, and negotiated noncompetitive bidding. Approximately 71 percent of the states reported that formal competitive bidding takes longer than six months. The negotiated competitive bidding processes and the negotiated noncompetitive bidding processes are reported to be faster. Only 46 and 40 percent of the respondents reported that negotiated competitive bidding and negotiated noncompetitive bidding, respectively, took more than six months. In most states (83%), developing a written request for IT procurement took less than six months.[27]

Information Technology at the County Level

As with state government, the degree of IT integration in county government determines whether systems can share data and information with one another. The extent of systems integration underlies the capacity for IT performance.[28] Conditions currently considered necessary for integration of information systems and technology may be even less likely to occur in counties than in state governments. Integration of IT systems requires engagement of IT at the strategic level of management.[29] The scope of strategic county objectives that the top-level elected county officials can set is constrained. County governments are constitutionally extensions of and subordinate to their state governments. Strategic objectives adopted by top elected county officials, therefore, must not conflict with state requirements. State governments also impose many objectives on their counties and limit the mechanisms by which their counties collect revenue.[30]

Many of the barriers to integrating IT at the county level parallel those at the state level. Time constraints inherent in county election and budget cycles truncate the long-term planning horizon needed for IT system integration at strategic organization levels.[31] Technological barriers range from obsolete or disparate hardware and software to inadequate transmission speeds and are costly to overcome. Data ownership and turf issues also constrain integration. Departments within county governments have different interests, different histories of IT development, and different IT capabilities. The following paragraphs examine data from the Government Performance Project for indications of the condition and integration of IT in county governments.

Strategic Information Systems Planning

As previously mentioned, achieving organizational objectives requires that information technology be included in the process of strategic planning.[32] High levels of involvement by actors at the executive level, such as the county board, council, or commission, and chief elected officials are necessary for strategic information systems planning to take place. An empirical study of private sector firms conducted in 1998 by A. H. Segars, Varun Grover, and J. T. C. Teng found successful strategic planning to be associated with a high degree of economic rationality, continuous planning processes, direction by top executives, and engagement of functional and operational department heads.[33]

County governance makes these conditions virtually impossible to achieve. Governing bodies typically consist of a plural chief executive officer—an elected commission, board, or council—that defines county objectives. State government further hampers strategic decision making at the county level by controlling the mechanisms of revenue collection and imposing many objectives or "mandates" on counties.[34]

As with state government, the high mean levels of involvement for CIOs and central county IT offices coupled with the low mean levels of involvement for most of the other actors confirm that information technology is lower in the hierarchies of county-level public organizations than one would expect for strategic, integrated IT management (table 5.4). Top county exec-

Table 5.4. Stakeholder Involvement in Key County IT Management Functions

	Making IT policy		SISP		Designing and developing IT systems		Approving IT procurement		Implementing IT systems		Overseeing implementation	
	Mean	SD	Mean	SD	Mean	SD	Mean	SD	Mean	SD	Mean	SD
County board, council, or commission	2.54	1.43	2.05	1.22	1.32	0.71	3.27	1.48	1.22	0.53	1.68	0.97
Legislative committee	1.93	1.14	1.66	0.94	1.35	0.81	2.03	1.52	1.17	0.54	1.34	0.81
Chief elected official	2.80	1.40	2.43	1.25	1.40	1.00	3.33	1.60	1.63	1.13	2.03	1.40
Chief administrative officer	3.21	1.23	2.78	1.11	1.62	0.79	3.19	1.35	1.51	0.83	2.22	1.08
Executive committee	3.11	1.34	2.96	1.29	1.96	1.17	2.46	1.32	1.57	0.88	2.39	1.47
CIO	4.63	1.07	4.88	0.42	3.81	1.20	4.56	0.95	3.69	1.20	4.41	1.01
Central county IT office	3.95	1.45	4.24	1.26	4.50	1.33	3.92	1.30	4.53	1.03	4.45	1.06
IT steering committee	3.55	1.31	3.52	1.31	2.94	1.34	3.03	1.49	2.71	1.40	3.26	1.41
Individual departments	2.84	1.29	3.40	1.29	3.66	1.32	3.07	1.30	3.84	1.29	3.71	1.27
IT end users	1.79	1.04	1.95	1.06	2.53	1.22	1.63	1.03	3.08	1.34	2.29	1.38
External consultants	1.74	1.03	2.29	1.09	3.03	0.97	1.29	0.69	3.11	1.09	2.21	1.02
External vendors	1.21	0.62	1.50	0.83	2.71	1.27	1.29	0.77	3.00	1.21	1.92	1.08
Citizens	1.29	0.52	1.45	0.72	1.32	0.81	1.16	0.55	1.08	0.36	1.08	0.27

Source: Donna Dufner, Lynn Holley, and B. J. Reed, "Strategic Information Systems Planning and U.S. County Government," Communications of the Association for Information Science 11, no. 13 (2003): 219–24.
Note: Rated on a scale of 1 to 5, where 1 = not involved and 5 = very involved.

utives do not perform IT planning; it is the CIO and the central county IT office that perform both strategic and tactical IT management functions. Individual agencies also are engaged in both strategic and tactical IT management functions, with mean levels of involvement of 3.40 to 3.84 in four of the key management functions: SISP, designing and developing IT systems, implementing IT systems, and overseeing implementation.

In county government as in state government, strategic objectives are selected through a process of political discourse and compromise among a wide variety of external and internal interest groups, typically with diverse needs and goals.[35] The objectives of county government are expressed either as county ordinances or as mandates from state or federal government that county government must implement. Information technology issues often are not considered in the process of establishing county objectives. In government, these processes for setting and implementing strategic objectives are loosely coupled.[36] The separation between setting and carrying out objectives in the public sector, although imperfect, is supported by extensive research and scholarship.[37]

The structure of intergovernmental relations further impedes consideration of operational issues at the time objectives are established. For example, an objective that no citizen should be on the welfare rolls for longer than two years, or that public transportation should be accessible to handicapped citizens, might be expressed as a nationwide or statewide mandate.[38] At the time such objectives are set by elected officials at the national or state level, the feasibility and operational aspects of implementing them at the county level may not be fully considered. In the private sector, however, the processes of setting strategic objectives and then making relevant budget allocations are more likely to be integrated.

The separation of setting objectives and planning implementation, to the extent it exists, precludes strategic information technology planning. In county governments, the county CIO or equivalent IT expert may not be consulted to provide the information necessary for creating an integrated and feasible SISP linked to the achievement of strategic objectives expressed as county ordinances or mandates. County officials almost certainly will not be consulted when mandates affecting counties are set by higher levels of government.[39]

At the county level, patterns of stakeholder involvement in key IT management functions are similar to those at the state level. Levels of involvement in key strategic functions such as making IT policy and SISP are low for the strategic-level elected officials on county boards, councils, or commissions, with means of 2.54 and 2.05, and for chief elected officials, with means of 2.80 and 2.43, respectively (see table 5.4). These patterns of involvement suggest little IT integration at the county level.

Countywide planning efforts, by definition, are not strategic.[40] The structure and function of county government tend to distance functional and operational department heads from strategic county-level decisions. In both state and county governments, the strategic IT roles of elected executives and unelected mid-level administrators are reversed: mid-level administrators reported more involvement in key IT strategic management functions such as making IT policy and SISP. Involvement of IT actors in state and county governments show similar patterns, differing primarily in the level of intensity of involvement across actors.

Integration within Functional Areas

The pattern of integration across functions in counties mirrors that in the states. The highest levels of integration are in areas of pecuniary responsibility. As in state government, county financial systems such as budgeting, specialized financial reports, financial accounting, payroll, and procurement have the highest degree of integration with other systems, with 67, 68, 76, 55, and 68 percent of counties, respectively, having fully integrated IT systems (table 5.5). The level of systems integration within functions, however, is higher in counties than at the state level.

Procurement

When asked about the degree of centralization of IT procurement, 95 percent of respondents reported some county-level involvement in procurement. About 58 percent (22 respondents) reported the county and the departments jointly handle the procurement of information technology. About 37 percent (14 respondents) reported that IT procurement is handled mainly at the county level.

Generating a request for proposal for both countywide (68%, or 26 respondents) and departmental (84%, or 32 respondents) systems typically takes less than six months. Only 2 percent (5) of countywide and 3 percent (1) of departmental requests took longer than one year. Generating a request for proposal requires time to plan procurement (determine what to procure and when), to plan solicitation (document product requirements and identify potential sources), and for solicitation itself (obtaining quotes,

Table 5.5. Countywide Functional System Integration

Functional area	Integration[a]		No integration	
	N	%	*N*	%
Budgeting	25	67	12	32
Specialized financial reports	26	68	12	32
Financial accounting	29	76	9	24
Cost accounting	16	42	22	58
Fraud control	13	36	23	64
Payroll	21	55	17	45
Hiring	10	26	28	74
Managing human resources	17	45	21	55
Managing training	4	11	33	89
Procurement	26	68	12	32
Tracking capital projects	16	42	22	58
Tracking asset conditions	8	22	29	78
Inventory management	10	26	28	74
Contract monitoring	12	32	26	68
Using performance data[b]	5	14	32	87

[a]System is fully operational and integrated with other systems.
[b]Tracking performance to provide information needed to manage for results (MFR). In other words, using IT to capture performance data.

bids, offers, or proposals). This procurement scenario and timing is similar in large private sector organizations.[41]

When asked about the nature, type, and duration of the procurement process, most respondents reported using a variety of procurement processes, including formal competitive bidding, negotiated competitive bidding, and negotiated noncompetitive bidding. As shown in table 5.6, durations ranged from less than six months to more than one year.

Information Technology at the City Level

Cities are municipal corporations created by and for local communities. Counties are political subdivisions of the state, created to administer state functions. That being said, cities and counties experience a continual ebb and flow of shared responsibilities for significant services such as law enforcement, emergency response, and public welfare.

Table 5.6. County Procurement Process and Duration
to Project Implementation (percentage)

	Less than six months	Six months to one year	More than one year	Response N
Formal competitive bidding	51	41	5	36
Negotiated competitive bidding	52	24	10	25
Negotiated noncompetitive bidding	73	4	8	22

Given the symbiotic relationship between cities and counties and their parallel positions in relation to federal and state mandates and revenue constraints, it is not surprising that conditions challenging citywide IT integration mirror those at the county level. Conditions challenging citywide IT integration include planning horizons curbed by short election and budget cycles, separation of strategic policy setting from planning implementation, data ownership and turf issues, obsolete or disparate hardware and software and slow transmission speeds, and inadequate funding.

The thirty-five cities surveyed in 1999 are large cities, selected, as were the counties, based on the total revenue. The IT survey instrument administered to the cities was an early version and did not include items that would have permitted evaluation of IT integration between counties and cities. Specifically comparable items were added later to the county and state questionnaires. Nonetheless, the GPP study has created an essential stepping-stone to investigation of that increasingly important permeable interface between cities and counties.

Strategic Information Systems Planning

As in state and county governments or in any organization, achieving organizational objectives in city government requires that information technology be included in the process of strategic planning.[42] Since the survey instrument administered to the cities did not address the question of strategic information systems planning directly, the data were examined in relation to the SISP model discussed earlier. The most relevant item on the city questionnaire was, "Do you have both strategic-level and tactical-level (annual operating or business) plans? If so, please describe the relationship between these plans."

Among the thirty-three cities that returned surveys, nine—27 percent— gave a positive response. However, given the wording of the question, it is quite possible that some of these cities did not have strategic plans in place. This would be the case if respondents referred to plans that are tactical rather than strategic or to plans that have been in place without revision, whereas strategic planning requires structured processes that are repeated on a periodic basis.[43] That no planning horizon was given also makes it difficult to ascertain whether the "plan" in question was a strategic plan.

The established SISP model calls for consideration of IT during the process of setting strategic organization objectives as well as the involvement of elected city officials in strategic-level IT functions such as making IT policy and SISP. Table 5.7 shows actor involvement with the city plan.

For the thirty-three cities responding, the best-case scenario would be that 67 percent (twenty-two) of the mayors and 49 percent (sixteen) of the legislatures are involved with city IT planning. However, in addition to the possibility that the plans referred to may be tactical rather than strategic, there is no indication that IT is a part of the city plan. Furthermore, the data gathered for the county and state GPP surveys show a lack of involvement of elected officials in strategic IT planning activities. The city pattern approximates the county pattern.

Integration within Functional Areas

The data available from the city surveys address the extent of IT integration in two functional areas—human resource management and financial management. Human resource systems are integrated in about 46 percent (fifteen) of the cities, and financial management systems are integrated in approximately 27 percent (nine cities). As with state and county systems,

Table 5.7. Stakeholder Involvement with City Plan

	n of cities	% of cities (*N* = 33)
Mayor	22	67
Legislative branch	16	49
Citizens	13	39
City agencies	16	49
External stakeholders (nonprofit organizations, consultants, and others)	5	15

the level of IT integration within city functional areas indicated by these data is low.

Geographic Information Systems and E-Government

The adoption of costly IT systems such as geographic information systems and electronic government bears witness to the acknowledged importance of IT to government at the state, county, and city levels.[44] The GPP survey data provide a baseline for studying these technologies.

Geographic information systems are designed to provide access to place-based information. They provide significant managerial information to aid in decision making at a tactical level and can inform policy development. They can be used to create knowledge in real time to assist in the deployment of resources such as police officers and to direct maintenance of existing implemented physical plant such as sewers and water pipes. Through GIS a wide variety of place-based information can be made available. Applications can have capabilities that range from tracking the location of utilities to mapping the incidence of violent crimes in particular neighborhoods. Despite repeated rounds of budget cutting, GPP data indicate widespread adoption of these systems. Forty-five states, twenty-two counties, and fifteen cities surveyed had such systems in place (see table 5.8).

E-government initiatives provide electronic access to government information and services and are likely to figure prominently in future governance.[45] Adoption of e-government characterizes the states with high IT capacity. Those that received a grade of A or A——Utah, Kansas, Michigan,

Table 5.8. Presence of Geographic Information Systems

	N	%
Has geographic information system		
States	45	90
Counties	22	59
Cities	15	45
Has only partial or no geographic information system	5	10
Counties	15	41
Cities	18	54

Source: B. J. Reed, "Information Technology Management," 2002, e-mail attachment, 2002, College of Community Affairs and Public Service University of Nebraska at Omaha and the Government Performance Project Information Technology Committee.

Missouri, and Washington—provide access to information through the use of intranet, extranets, and data warehousing.

Interactive access is provided to managers in Utah for tracking budget, revenue, expense, and payroll data. Utah also has a human resources data warehouse that provides access to employee information. The state offers more than a hundred interactive Web-based services for its residents, employees, and managers through its home page.[46] The Information Network of Kansas provides user-friendly access to electronic government, streamlines internal functions, and enables businesses to interact with government through the Web.[47] A wide variety of information and services relating to human resources, legal and legislative matters, licensing, medical insurance, property, and tax payment is available through the network.

Michigan provides a wide variety of information and interactive services to its citizens, who can file unemployment claims, apply for licenses, search criminal histories, track offenders, renew license plates, and obtain certificates of birth, marriage, and death online. Approximately a hundred information and service links are provided at the state's Web site.[48]

In Missouri, the Internet and data warehousing provide citizens and government managers and employees with access to information and services. A small subset of the interactive service offerings available through the Web portal includes child support payment information, a calendar of events, a senior prescription program, the *Guide to Missouri State Government,* information and resources for state employees facing layoffs, the *Fiscal Year 2004 Executive Budget,* information and resources for long-term care of elderly and disabled persons, road conditions, state holidays, and school and government office closings.[49] Citizens also can renew driver's licenses, register new businesses, file taxes, obtain copies of birth or death certificates, apply for hunting and fishing permits, file unemployment insurance claims, apply for veterans' benefits, and register to vote at the state's Web site.

The Washington State home page is also a Web portal through which a citizen can order copies of birth certificates, renew a building trades license, obtain a business license, pay child support, find a contractor, renew a corporation license, replace a driver's license, order a fish or game license, find a job, hire someone, find missing money or property, buy a daily Sno-Park permit, buy a state parks parking permit, file and pay state taxes, file for unemployment insurance, renew a vehicle or boat license, and report a vehicle sale.[50]

These high-capacity states gain productivity and provide citizens with time-saving opportunities and increased access to information while reducing travel and frustration through Web-based information and services that can be accessed from the comfort and privacy of home. States with high IT capacity are distinguished from other states in providing a much broader scope of such services. The Web sites of states with lower capacity provide fewer services. For example, Colorado's site primarily provides access to information, and the Massachusetts Web site offers information but only eight services.[51]

The five high-capacity counties, those that received grades of A or A−, are Baltimore, Fairfax, Maricopa, Oakland, and Orange. These counties provide citizens with user-friendly access to customizable information and offer a few interactive services. The Fairfax County database-searching capability is a feature that eliminates travel time for citizens and increases productivity by providing a consistent interface over a variety of databases for county legacy systems. Oakland County provides a substantial list of interactive services through a Web portal in addition to static information. Orange County's Web site provides approximately twenty interactive services, mostly form-based transactions, ranging from pet adoption to voter registration.[52]

The primary difference between the high-capacity states and the high-capacity counties is that the counties offer fewer interactive services. Most county-level Web pages provide information in a one-directional or broadcast mode that is comparable to a book or television. The interactive services provided by high-capacity governments use the Web interface to allow completion of transactions such as tax payment or license renewal. Web pages in high-capacity states are being used as portals through which interactive services are provided. Web portals also provide access to a variety of legacy systems through data warehouses.

Providing services plus information through a Web-based interface requires an IT architecture that is significantly more complex and expensive than that used to provide information through Web pages using a Web server. The Web server is the front end for applications programs that process input from the citizen. Data warehouses with Web-based access are a step beyond static Web pages and are typically used to store groups of related data. Generally, the user can perform operations on the data, such as sorting or grouping of related items. The data warehouses must be fed data from legacy systems on a periodic basis.

The Web portals used to access legacy systems and data warehouses are expensive and require skilled personnel for successful development. Many state and local governments simply do not have the funding or the resources to develop and support the more complex IT applications. Only two cities in the research sample—Minneapolis and Phoenix—have high IT capacity, and they are approaching the Web portal level of service. Phoenix now provides minimal services, focused mainly on revenue collection. A Web portal is envisioned for Minneapolis, along with data warehouses supported by intranets to provide Web-based services for both citizens and employees.[53]

Key Findings: How States, Counties, and Cities Measure Up

Adequate Information

In respect to effective use of IT to support management, findings show that the information provided by IT systems at the state and county levels provides support primarily for tactical functions. At these levels, strategic IT planning does not generally involve elected officials. Strategic goals are simply not set at top levels of government.[54] Only one state legislature and sixteen governors' offices (of the forty-eight states studied, in both cases) reported high levels of involvement in strategic IT planning, the level of planning that would be required for integration efforts and data sharing to work on a broad scale. Only two county boards, councils, or commissions and two county chief elected officials (of the thirty-seven counties responding) reported being very involved in strategic planning. Results from the cities are ambiguous.

Whether information systems adequately support the achievement of strategic goals in general is suggested by the types of functional systems listed in tables 5.3 and 5.5. These systems predominantly support tactical functions, tracking the movement of money, and are not designed for management information systems reporting.

Only eleven states (of forty-eight) and five counties (of thirty-seven) are using data to evaluate performance, a process necessary to determine whether strategic goals are being achieved. The numbers of states and counties that do not use performance data indicate the extent to which IT supports the achievement of tactical rather that strategic goals.

In many states, mechanisms to integrate IT systems that support key management functions are not in place (see table 5.3). The picture is not much better at the county level, where absence of system integration is typical (see table 5.4). One major barrier to systems integration at the state and county levels is the prevalence of production or legacy systems, which are islands of information often lacking a management information system component. Reports generated by these systems must be combed for information and then cut and pasted together, like pieces of a puzzle, to create a complete picture—for each episode of decision making.

Despite the absence of strategic IT planning at the top levels of government and the lack of integrated information, the GPP data provide some indication of "middle-up" IT planning at the level of individual agencies or crosscutting projects. That middle-level planning seems to be coordinated or at least to involve the chief information officer. Thirty-two of the thirty-seven counties responding reported that their CIO is very involved in making policy regarding the design and use of IT systems, developing IT plans, designing and developing IT systems and projects, approving the procurement of IT systems and hardware, implementing IT systems and hardware, and overseeing the implementation of IT systems and projects. The high mean levels of involvement reported indicate that county CIOs are involved in most important strategic and tactical phases of IT and related activities (see table 5.9). A similar picture can be seen at the state level.

Stakeholder involvement in the IT strategic and tactical key management functions departs from the model defining SISP planning in both state and county government (see tables 5.2 and 5.4). Most elected officials making strategic decisions are not involved in IT policy or planning. The mean levels of involvement for tactical-level actors and functions are consistent with the model.[55] The model also predicts the low levels of involvement among citizens, vendors, and consultants.

Table 5.9. Mean CIO Involvement in Strategic and Tactical IT Activities

	States (N = 45)	Counties (N = 32)
Making policy about design and use of IT systems	4.93	4.62
Developing IT strategic plans	4.96	4.87
Designing and developing IT systems and projects	3.66	3.81
Approving procurement of IT systems and hardware	4.44	4.56
Implementing IT systems and projects	3.46	3.69
Overseeing implementation of IT systems and projects	4.31	4.40

Note: Means are measured on a scale of 1 to 5, where 1 = not involved and 5 = very involved.

Coherent Architecture

When asked about specific functional areas such as finance, human resources, and procurement, a substantial majority of respondents at the state level reported these systems lack integration. The picture is much the same at the county level (see tables 5.3 and 5.5).

As with state and county IT systems, the data indicate a low level of IT integration within city functional areas. Unintegrated information systems—systems that do not share information with other systems—are the norm for both state and local government. Based on these findings, IT architectures of state and local governments can be defined as not coherent in today's world.

Information sharing at state and local levels is being encouraged and supported through grants from the federal government. Information sharing by criminal justice systems is a federal priority for state and local governments to enable more effective tracking of offenders.[56] Information sharing improves productivity by eliminating the amount of time required to find information stored in disparate systems and provides more intelligence, since the user is able to see the big picture. Finally, because this technology provides more reach and scope, increased cohesion among groups is achieved.[57]

The private sector learned early that islands of information can lead to disaster. In the 1980s, most major banking institutions were not aware of their global loan exposure because of the stand-alone systems in various functional areas of the bank, such as private banking, international banking, and commercial loans. Today, these systems are integrated, and the total loan exposure for the bank, an individual, or a country is known and tracked closely. The push for enterprise-wide systems or solutions and the emphasis on knowledge management are other examples of the attempt to integrate and share information.[58] Unfortunately, the public sector lags behind in this respect.

Multiyear Planning

The GPP queried the existence of multiyear planning with the question, "Does your state [or county] have a statewide [or countywide] information technology strategic plan?" Although responses to the question did not vary, grades on IT capacity did. State and county IT grades ranged from high to low, A+ through D.[59] The criteria used by the GPP to rate IT performance address aspects of IT considered critical to public organizations' capacity for performance.[60]

Information technology planning is one of the criteria for assigning grades. Although all respondents reported that a statewide IT strategic plan was either in place or in progress (see table 5.10), the lack of strategic planning raises questions about what strategic planning means to these respondents.

Forty-eight of the fifty states returned completed surveys. All nine states receiving an IT grade of B+ or higher reported having a statewide IT strategic plan in place. Four of the seven states with IT grades of C or lower also reported having a statewide IT strategic plan in place, and the remaining three reported that their plan was in progress. The remaining states, those receiving grades of B through C+, indicated having a statewide IT plan either in place (twenty-five states) or in progress (seven states).

The assigned grades are only slightly related to having a statewide IT strategic plan in place. Although the numbers are small and many factors

Table 5.10. Government-wide IT Strategic Plans, State and County, by IT Capacity

	In place	In progress	Nonexistent	N
High capacity				
States	9	0	0	9
Counties	7	1	0	8
Middle capacity				
States	25	7	0	32
Counties	14	2	3	19
Low capacity				
States	4	3	0	7
Counties	4	4	3	11
Total				
States	38	10	0	48
Counties	25	7	6	38

Source: Donna Dufner, Lyn Holley, and B. J. Reed, "Can Private Sector Strategic Information Systems Planning Techniques Work for the Public Sector?" Communications of the Association of Information Systems 8, no. 28 (2002): 413–31.
Note: High-capacity states are those that were assigned an IT grade of B+ or higher; middle-capacity states, B through C; and low-capacity states, C– or lower.

contribute to the overall state IT grade, the data hint at a slight relationship between having a statewide IT strategic plan in place and higher grades for overall performance. All states with high IT grades reported having a plan in place, but only 78 percent of states with middle IT grades and 57 percent of states with low IT grades did so. The relationship between having a plan in place and assesssment of overall IT management capacity may be worthy of further investigation.

The realization of "strategic" information and technology planning in states is further called into question by the state responses to another GPP survey question, "Is there an information technology component to your state's overall strategic plan?" There was some discrepancy in the findings, owing to a gap between reports of having statewide SISP and reports of having an IT component in the statewide strategic plan. Although thirty-five states reported having statewide SISP, only twenty-nine reported that their overall strategic plan included an IT component. Ten states reported an IT component was "in progress." According to the business model, IT is an integrated part of strategic information systems planning, these responses indicate that strategic IT planning does not occur at the state level.[61]

Adequate Training

Information technology training does not appear to be a high priority in state and local government. Training in counties (thirty-seven reporting) is generally offered on a weekly and monthly basis. Measured on a scale of 1 to 5, the mean frequency of training is 2.54. The mean level of training for end users, on a scale of 1 to 3, is 2.21, indicating that training is a combination of mandatory and voluntary.[62] The proportion of users trained is reported to be between 26 and 50 percent. The adequacy of training cannot be determined, however, without linking training with specific IT systems.

Twenty states reported that more than 60 percent of end users participate in training each year. Only two of thirty-seven responding counties reported that more than three-quarters of their end users participate in training each year. Only eleven counties have minimum training requirements for end users. The low priority given to training by state and local government is surprising considering the acknowledged importance of IT. The findings from GPP interviews indicate that end users of IT frequently are not up to the task.[63] Training is often one of the first expenses to be sacrificed as budgets shrink.[64]

Cost-Benefit Evaluation

The data indicate that almost all state and county governments surveyed evaluate the extent to which IT system benefits justify investments (see tables 5.11 and 5.12). The validity of the evaluation may be limited by the lack of relevant strategic objectives, which would frame the value of the benefits to be achieved. The real total costs, which include overhead and ancillary services, may not be fully understood.

Conclusions and Future Directions

Potential IT benefits for government provision of services are equal to or greater than any of the benefits achieved in the private sector. The private sector SISP model is a proven path leading to the benefits of strategic IT applications. Barriers and challenges posed by government structures are so formidable as to suggest that attainment in government of strategic IT

Table 5.11. State and County IT Cost-Benefit Evaluation

	States		Counties	
	N	%	N	%
Evaluates before procurement	46	92	31	84
Evaluates upon implementation	40	80	23	62
Does not evaluate, or only partially evaluates, before procurement	4	8	6	16
Does not evaluate, or only partially evaluates, upon implementation	10	20	14	38

Source: B. J. Reed, "Information Technology Management," 2002, e-mail attachment, 2002, College of Community Affairs and Public Service University of Nebraska at Omaha and the Government Performance Project Information Technology Committee.

Table 5.12. City IT Cost-Benefit Evaluation

	N	%
Has cost-benefit system	14	45
Does not have cost-benefit system	17	55

Source: B. J. Reed, "Information Technology Management," 2002, e-mail attachment, 2002, College of Community Affairs and Public Service University of Nebraska at Omaha and the Government Performance Project Information Technology Committee.

applications using a business model may be impossible. Data from the GPP, however, reveal that state, county, and city governments with high performance potential have devised means of overcoming the barriers to implementing strategic IT. State and some county governments with high performance potential have established structures of IT governance separated from the short-term tides of politics and budget cycles. Another successful strategy identified by the GPP data is that of creating project or agency pockets of integrated IT applications—in other words, "middle-up" information systems planning. Findings based on the GPP data provide hope that further study will show the way for governments to realize the gains in efficiency, quality, and scope of government services that are possible through strategic IT.

APPENDIX

Glossary and IT Assessment Criteria

Glossary

broadcast. Mode in which messages and information are transmitted in one direction only to the user or client.

extranet. A private electronic network that is similar to an intranet but also allows private communication with certain registered others.

functional system. An information system designed to support a specific functional area of the organization, such as finance, human resources, or marketing.

interactive services. Services enabled by a two-way electronic communication system that allows a number of computers to communicate with one another. The user sends a command to a software application on a distant computer, which then responds to the user request. Web-based services are interactive. Web-based information (screens with hypertext links) is unidirectional, much the same as a book.

Internet. A worldwide, publicly accessible system of interconnected electronic networks. The Advanced Research Projects Agency (ARPANET) was a collection of computer networks designed in 1969 to enable the military to transmit data. Today the Internet consists of ARPANET, CSNET (Computer Science Network), and NSFNET (National Science Foundation Network). The Internet initially offered four data-sharing or information services, all of which required some knowledge of computing and programming. The World Wide Web, the newest information-sharing service on the Internet, requires no programming skills for customers or users to access information on the Web or to use Web portals for services. The Internet is used for external communication.

intranet. A private computer network that limits access to a specific group. An intranet is used to provide internal organizational communication.

island of information. A stand-alone or unintegrated computer system that is unable to share data or information electronically with other information systems.

information technology (IT). A combination of telecommunication and computing software and hardware.

legacy system. An information system built to support a specific functional area. Legacy systems are often aging and costly to maintain.

PeopleSoft. A commercial, proprietary, off-the-shelf, enterprise-wide software system .

production system. A generally large-scale information system used for processing large volumes of data generated by a functional area, such as social security payments.

software package. A computer program that can be purchased and installed on a PC, mainframe, laptop, or minicomputer.

systems integration. The ability of information systems to communicate and share data with one another. For example, a payroll system might share data electronically with a human resources system. Integration data is transmitted electronically from one computer to another.

Web page. A hypertext document that contains information and links to services and information.

Web portal. A Web page through which access is provided to data warehouses and legacy systems

Web server. A computer used to host Web sites.

World Wide Web, the Web, WWW, or W3. An Internet service that allows simple access to electronic resources. The newest information-sharing service on the Internet, the Web requires no programming skills for customers or users to access information on the Web. Hypermedia documents stored on the Internet can be accessed through a universal resource locator (URL) or Web address such as www.maxwell.syr.edu/gpp/.

Y2K. The turn of the century to the year 2000. The term was generally used in reference to the expected impact on legacy IT.

IT Assessment Criteria for States and Counties

1. Government-wide and agency-level information technology systems provide information that adequately supports managers' needs and strategic goals.
2. Government's information technology systems form a coherent architecture; strategies are in place to support present and future coherence in architecture.
3. Government conducts meaningful, multiyear information technology planning.
   - The information technology planning process is centralized.
   - Government managers have appropriate input into the planning process.
   - Formal government-wide and agency information technology plans exist.

4. Information technology training is adequate.
   - Information technology end users are adequately trained to use available systems.
   - Information technology specialists are adequately trained to operate available systems.
5. Government can evaluate and validate the extent to which information technology system benefits justify investment.
6. Government can procure the information technology systems it needs in a timely manner.
7. Information technology systems support the government's ability to communicate with and provide services to its citizens.

IT Assessment Criteria for Cities

1. Government-wide and agency-level information technology systems provide information to support managers' needs and strategic goals, with a particular emphasis on financial management, human resource management, capital management, and managing for results
2. A coherent architecture for information technology systems
3. Meaningful multiyear information technology planning, including centralized technology planning, appropriate input from managers into the process, and the existence of formal government-wide and agency IT plans
4. Information technology training adequate for end users and information technology specialists
5. Capacity to evaluate the extent to which benefits of an information technology system justify investment
6. Procurement of needed information technology systems in a timely manner, both for commodity-type items and those that are more complex
7. Information technology systems that support the government's ability to communicate with and provide services to its citizens.

Components of IT Assessment Criteria for States and Counties

The Government Performance Project assessment of information technology focused on seven key criteria: architecture, management support, planning, citizen involvement and engagement, cost-benefit analysis, procurement, and training. The specific elements that helped frame the components of each criterion are noted below.

Architecture

- appropriate mix of centralized and decentralized hardware and software systems for consistency of capacity across the state government in support of key functions such as human resource management and financial management

- quality and level of integration across various management systems that include timely access to information
- standardization of hardware and software systems across state government agencies and divisions necessary to support management processes
- consistent enforcement of architecture policies and systems to ensure standardization and integration

Management Support

- mechanisms by which integrated and timely IT systems support key management functions
- quality of integrated tools such as geographic information systems in improving support for state agency activities
- level of centralized executive leadership in the form of a chief information officer or equivalent
- level of clarity and understanding of appropriate centralized and decentralized functions of IT
- appropriate mix of executive, legislative, internal, and external stakeholders in the design, improvement, and implementation of state IT systems
- quality and design of management systems that track implementation and resolve problems associated with implementation of IT systems
- integration of telecommunications with other IT and state management systems

Planning

- completeness and comprehensiveness of the state's strategic plan
- frequency with which that plan is reviewed and revised
- extent to which IT components are included in that statewide strategic plan
- level of IT planning that occurs statewide and within individual agencies
- mechanisms in place to ensure adequate review and assessment of IT planning efforts

Citizen Involvement and Engagement

- overall capacity of information technology to support state government's ability to communicate with and provide services to its citizens
- quality of the transmission and receipt of information to citizens about policies and services
- quality of the transmission and receipt of information to local, state, and federal agencies
- quality of the transmission and receipt of information to school districts and nongovernmental agencies
- quality of geographic information system and its ability to support state agencies and their efforts to serve citizens

Cost-Benefit Analysis

- capacity of state government to evaluate and validate the extent to which IT system benefits justify their costs
- level of evaluation of both monetary and nonmonetary costs and benefits before purchase and at full implementation
- frequency of evaluation of costs and benefits
- processes developed and used to link cost-benefit analysis to decision making on IT systems

Procurement

- capacity of state government to procure the IT systems needed in a timely manner
- level of centralization of procurement processes for both large- and small-scale IT systems
- participation by end users in the procurement process
- timing of procurement process, including development of requests for proposal and length to award
- use of master contracts and length of time from development to award

Training

- quality and level of IT training for both end users and IT specialists
- requirements for IT training of end users and IT specialists
- frequency of IT training for end users and IT specialists
- level of standards for IT training

NOTES

1. "Y2K" was the popular term used for the year 2000 legacy system conversion problem and refers to information systems' inability to process data after midnight on December 31, 1999, owing to dating programming that was not able to process years beginning with the numeral 2.

2. Donna Dufner, Lyn Holley, and B. J. Reed, "Can Private Sector Strategic Information Systems Planning Techniques Work for the Public Sector?" *Communications of the Association of Information Systems* 8, no. 28 (2002): 413–31; Lyn Holley, Donna Dufner, and B. J. Reed, "Got SISP? Strategic Information Systems Planning in U.S. State Governments," *Public Productivity and Management Review* 25, no. 4 (2002): 398–412; Bruce A. Rocheleau and Laingfu Wu, "Public Sector vs. Private Information Systems: Do They Differ in Important Ways? A Review and Empirical Test," *American Review of Public Administration* 32, no. 4 (2002): 379–97; Barry Bozeman and Stuart Bretschneider, "Public Management Information

Systems: Theory and Prescription," *Public Administration Review* 46, no. 6 (1986): 475–87.

3. Bruce A. Rocheleau, "Prescriptions for Public-Sector Information Management: A Review, Analysis, and Critique," *American Review of Public Administration* 30, no. 4 (2000): 414–35; J. M. Bryson, *Strategic Planning for Public and Nonprofit Organizations: A Guide to Strengthening and Sustaining Organizational Achievement*, rev. ed. (San Francisco: Jossey-Bass, 1995); S. L. Caudle, W. L. Gorr, and K. E. Newcomer, "Key Information Systems Management Issues for the Public Sector," *MIS Quarterly* 15, no. 2 (1991): 171–88; Bozeman and Bretschneider, "Public Management Information Systems."

4. Bozeman and Bretschneider, "Public Management Information Systems."

5. Ibid.; Stuart Bretschneider, "Management Information Systems in Public and Private Organizations: An Empirical Test," *Public Administration Review* 50, no. 5 (1990): 536–45.

6. In this chapter, *IT infrastructure* is used to refer inclusively to all IT facilities and resources needed to provide services that are pervasively available for use. The source for this definition is S. D. Burd, *Systems Architecture: Hardware and Software in Business Information Systems*, 2d ed. (Cambridge, MA: COURSE Technology, 1998).

7. Maurice Estabrooks, *Electronic Technology, Corporate Strategy, and World Transformation* (Westport, CT: Quorum, 1995).

8. Bernard Boar, *The Art of Strategic Planning for Information Technology*, 2d ed. (New York: Wiley and Sons, 2001); S. T. Bajjaly, "Managing Emerging Information Systems in the Public Sector," *Public Productivity and Management Review* 23, no. 1 (1999): 40–47; N. F. Doherty, C. G. Marples, and A. Suhaimi, "The Relative Success of Alternative Approaches to Strategic Information Systems Planning: An Empirical Analysis," *Journal of Strategic Information Systems* 8, no. 30 (1999): 263–83; A. H. Segars, Varun Grover, and J. T. C. Teng, "Strategic Information Systems Planning: Planning System Dimensions, Internal Coalignment, and Implications for Planning Effectiveness," *Decision Sciences* 29, no. 2 (1998): 303–45; J. M. Bryson and F. K. Alston, *Creating and Implementing Your Strategic Plan: A Workbook for Public and Nonprofit Organizations* (San Francisco: Jossey-Bass, 1996); Bryson, *Strategic Planning*.

9. M. P. Drennan, *The Information Economy and American Cities* (Baltimore, MD: Johns Hopkins University Press, 2002); Boar, *Art of Strategic Planning*; Rocheleau, "Prescriptions"; Bajjaly, "Managing Emerging Information Systems"; Doherty, Marples, and Susaimi, "Alternative Approaches"; A. L. Lederer and V. Sethi, "The Implementation of Strategic Information Systems Planning," *MIS Quarterly* 12, no. 3 (1988): 445–61; A. L. Lederer and V. Sethi, "Key Prescriptions for Strategic Information Systems Planning," *Journal of Management Information Systems* 13, no. 1 (1996): 35–62; Segars, Grover, and Teng, "Strategic Information Systems Planning"; Bryson and Alston, *Creating and Implementing Strategic Plan*; Bryson, *Strategic Planning*; F. Neiderman, J. C. Brancheau, and J. C. Weatherbe,

"Information Systems Management Issues for the 1990s," *MIS Quarterly* 15, no. 4 (1991): 475–500.

10. Estabrooks, *Electronic Technology*; Robert Bryce and Molly Ivins, *Pipe Dreams: Greed, Ego, and the Death of Enron* (New York: Public Affairs, 2002).

11. U.S. General Accounting Office (GAO) and David McClure (project manager), "Maximizing the Success of Chief Information Officer: Learning from Leading Organizations," CIO Executive Guide, GAO-01-376G (Washington, DC, 2001); A. P. Balutis and P. J. Kiviat, "Best IT Practices in the Federal Government," CIO Council, 1997, www.cio.gov/docs/iac.htm).

12. S. L. Caudle, "Strategic Information Resources Management: Fundamental Practices," *Government Information Quarterly* 13, no. 1 (1996): 83–97; GAO and McClure, "Maximizing Success"; Balutis and Kiviat, "Best IT Practices."

13. Lederer and Sethi, "Key Prescriptions"; Rajiv Sabherwal and W. R. King, "An Empirical Taxonomy of the Decision-Making Processes Concerning Strategic Applications of Information Systems," *Journal of Management Information Systems* 11, no. 4 (1995): 177–214.

14. Dufner, Holley, and Reed, "Can Private Sector Techniques Work?"; Holley, Dufner, and Reed, "Got SISP?"; Segars, Grover, and Teng, "Strategic Information Systems Planning"; J. M. Ward and P. M. Griffiths, *Strategic Planning for Information Systems*, 2d ed. (Chichester, U.K.: Wiley and Sons, 1996).

15. Segars, Grover, and Teng, "Strategic Information Systems Planning."

16. Lederer and Sethi, "Key Prescriptions Planning."

17. National Commission on the State and Local Public Service, *Revitalizing State and Local Public Service: Strengthening Performance, Accountability, and Citizen Confidence*, ed. F. J. Thompson (San Francisco, CA: Jossey-Bass, 1993).

18. Ibid.

19. Caudle, Gorr, and Newcomer, "Key Issues for the Public Sector."

20. Bajjaly, "Managing Emerging Information Systems."

21. S. S. Dawes, T. A. Pardo, D. R. Connelley, and C. R. McInerney, "Partners in State-Local Information Systems: Lessons from the Field" (Albany, NY: Center for Technology in Government, 1997), www.ctg.albany.edu.

22. Bryson and Alston, *Creating and Implementing Strategic Plan*; Bryson, *Strategic Planning*; K. E. Newcomer and S. L. Caudle, "Evaluating Public Sector Information Systems: More Than Meets the Eye," *Public Administration Review* 51, no. 5 (1991): 377–84.

23. Segars, Grover, and Teng, "Strategic Information Systems Planning."

24. Lederer and Sethi, "Implementation"; Sabherwal and King, "Empirical Taxonomy."

25. B. J. Reed, "Information Technology Management," e-mail attachment, 2002, College of Community Affairs and Public Service University of Nebraska at Omaha and the Government Performance Project Information Technology Committee.

26. Ibid.

27. Ibid.

28. Estabrooks, *Electronic Technology.*

29. Balutis and Kiviat, "Best IT Practices"; GAO and Mcclure, "Maximizing the Success."

30. F. J. Coppa, *County Government: A Guide to Efficient and Accountable Government* (Westport, CT: Praeger, 2000).

31. Segars, Grover, and Teng, "Strategic Information Systems Planning."

32. Boar, *Art of Strategic Planning*; Bajjaly, "Managing Emerging Information Systems"; Doherty, Marples, and Suhaimi, "Alternative Approaches"; Segars, Grover, and Teng, "Strategic Information Systems Planning"; Bryson and Alston, *Creating and Implementing Strategic Plan*; Bryson, *Strategic Planning.*

33. Segars, Grover, and Teng, "Strategic Information Systems Planning."

34. Coppa, *County Government.*

35. Ibid.; Dufner, Holley, and Reed, "Can Private Sector Techniques Work?"; M. E. Guy, "Public Management," in *Defining Public Administration*, ed. J. M. Shafritz (Boulder, CO: Westview, 2000), pp. 166–68; H. G. Rainey and Barry Bozeman, *Journal of Public Administration and Research Theory* 10, no. 2 (2000): 447–69; Rocheleau, "Prescriptions"; G. T. Allison, "Public and Private Management: Are They Fundamentally Alike in All Unimportant Respects?" in *Public Management and Private Perspectives*, ed. James L. Perry and Kenneth L. Kraemer (Palo Alto, CA: Mayfield, 1983), pp. 72–92.

36. Holley, Dufner, and Reed, "Got SISP?"; Rocheleau, "Prescriptions."

37. Nicholas Henry, *Public Administration and Public Affairs*, 8th ed. (New Jersey: Prentice-Hall, 2001); B. D. Wood and R. W. Waterman, *Bureaucratic Dynamics: The Role of Bureaucracy in a Democracy* (Boulder, CO: Westview, 1994); J. W. Fesler and D. F. Kettl, *The Politics of the Administrative Process* (Chatham, NJ: Chatham House, 1991); Glenn Abney and T. P. Lauth, *The Politics of State and City Administration* (Albany: State University of New York Press, 1986).

38. Coppa, *County Government*; Beverly Ciglar, "Emerging Trends in State-Local Relations," in *Governing Partners: State-Local Relations in the United States,* ed. Russell Hanson (Boulder, CO: Westview, 1998), pp. 53–74; P. T. Fletcher, S. I. Bretschneider, and D. A. Marchand, *Managing Information Technology: Transforming County Governments in the 1990s* (Syracuse, NY: School of Information Studies, Syracuse University, 1992); Caudle, Gorr, and Newcomer, "Key Issues for the Public Sector."

39. Coppa, *County Government.*

40. Segars, Grover, and Teng, "Strategic Information Systems Planning."

41. Project Management Institute Standards Committee, *A Guide to the Project Management Body of Knowledge: PMBOK Guide* (Newton Square, PA: Project Management Institute, 2000).

42. Boar, *Art of Strategic Planning*; Bajjaly, "Managing Emerging Information Systems"; Doherty, Marples, and Suhaimi, "Alternative Approaches"; Segars, Grover, and Teng, "Strategic Information Systems Planning"; Bryson and Alston, *Creating and Implementing Strategic Plan*; Bryson, *Strategic Planning.*

43. Segars, Grover, and Teng, "Strategic Information Systems Planning."

44. M. J. Moon, "The Evolution of E-Government among Municipalities: Rhetoric or Reality?" *Public Administration Review* 62, no. 4 (2002): 424–33; A. T.-K. Ho, "Reinventing Local Governments and the E-Government Initiative," *Public Administration Review* 62, no. 4 (2002): 434–43.

45. Moon, "Evolution of E-Government"; Ho, "Reinventing Local Governments."

46. Utah State Web pages, 2003, www.utah.gov/government/onlineservices.html.

47. "The Information Network of Kansas (INK) was created by an act of the Kansas State Legislature in 1990 for the purpose of providing equal electronic access to state, county, local and other public information to the people of Kansas. INK provides Kansans equal access to governmental data via the Internet. INK is . . . a model for public/private cooperation. It is a government service administered for the good of the public, while benefiting from the entrepreneurial spirit and efficiencies found in private business." See www.accesskansas.org/board/index.html for detailed information on INK.

48. Michigan State Web pages, 2003, www.michigan.gov/.

49. Missouri State Web pages, 2003, www.state.mo.us/.

50. Washington State Web pages, 2003, http://access.wa.gov/.

51. Massachusetts State Web pages, 2003, www.mass.gov/portal/index.jsp; Katherine Barrett and Richard Greene, *Powering Up: How Public Managers Can Take Control of Information Technology* (Washington, DC: CQ Press, 2000).

52. Fairfax County Web pages, 2003, www.co.fairfax.va.us/eservices/default.htm; Oakland County Web pages, 2003, www.co.oakland.mi.us/online_services/; Orange County Web pages, 2003, www.oc.ca.gov/.

53. City of Phoenix Web pages, 2003, www.ci.phoenix.az.us/; City of Minneapolis Web pages, 2003, www.ci.minneapolis.mn.us/.

54. Segars, Grover, and Teng, "Strategic Information Systems Planning."

55. Ibid.

56. T. Martin, D. Dufner, and R. K. Piper, "Juvenile Accountability Incentive Block Grant: Two Year Evaluation Report," submitted to the City of Omaha, Douglas County, and the Juvenile Accountability Coalition, June 22, 2002; J. Else, T. Martin, R. K. Piper, and D. Dufner, "Juvenile Accountability Incentive Block Grant: Year Two Evaluation Report," submitted to the City of Omaha, Douglas County, and the Juvenile Accountability Coalition, March, 2002; J. Else, T. Martin, R. K. Piper, C. Gibson, and D. Dufner, "Juvenile Accountability Incentive Block Grant: Year One Evaluation Report," submitted to the City of Omaha, Douglas County, and the Juvenile Accountability Coalition, June 22, 2001; T. Lipper and M. Hosenball, "Learning How to Share," *Newsweek,* December 9, 2002; Roslin Hauck and Suzanne Weisband, "When a Better Interface and Easy Navigation Aren't Enough: Examining the Information Architecture in a Law Enforcement Agency," *Journal of the American Society for Information Science and Technology* 53, no. 10 (2002): 846–54.

57. Hsinchun Chen, Jenny Schroeder, Roslin Hauck, Linda Ridgeway, and Homa Atabakhsh, "COPLINK Connect: Information and Knowledge Management for Law Enforcement," *Decision Support Systems* 34, no. 3 (2003): 271–85;

"reach and scope" refers to the ability of IT to extend the reach of human capability and broaden the scope or the amount and nature of work performed.

58. Tony Kontzer, "Share the Knowledge," *InformationWeek*, November 18, 2002.

59. "Government Performance Project State Survey" (A. K. Campbell Public Affairs Institute, Maxwell School of Citizenship and Public Affairs, Syracuse University, 2001), www.maxwell.syr.edu/gpp/grade/state_2001/stategrades2001.asp; "Government Performance Project County Survey" (A. K. Campbell Public Affairs Institute, Maxwell School of Citizenship and Public Affairs, Syracuse University, 2001), www.maxwell.syr.edu/gpp/grade/county_2002/grades.asp; "Government Performance Project City Survey" (A. K. Campbell Public Affairs Institute, Maxwell School of Citizenship and Public Affairs, Syracuse University, 2000), www.maxwell.syr.edu/gpp/statistics/2000%20City%20MRF%2011.06.02.htm.asp #Mix%20of%20Planning/.

60. Ibid.

61. Segars, Grover, and Teng, "Strategic Information Systems Planning."

62. For the frequency scale (thirty-seven counties reporting), 1 = daily, 2 = weekly, 3 = monthly, 4 = annually, and 5 = on demand. For level of training (thirty-five counties reporting), 1 = usually mandatory, 2 = sometimes mandatory, and 3 = usually voluntary.

63. Barrett and Greene, *Powering Up.*

64. B. J. Reed, "Information Technology Management," in *Paths to Performance in State and Local Government: A Final Assessment from the Maxwell School of Citizenship and Public Affairs,* ed. Patricia Ingraham (Syracuse, NY: Maxwell School of Citizenship and Public Affairs, 2003), pp. 133–50.

CHAPTER 6

The Reality of Results
Managing for Results in State and Local Government

DONALD P. MOYNIHAN

This chapter marshals evidence from the Government Performance Project to examine the progress and challenges in implementing managing-for-results systems in state and local governments. These findings confirm the current popularity of results-based reform, despite the apparent failure of similar reforms in the past. The GPP found that governments at all levels are devoting significant energy to creating and distributing performance information. However, practical problems in the creation of these performance information systems are common. Frequently, governments engage in multiple types of planning that are not well coordinated, and translating high-level goals into quantitative measures also proves problematic. Over the past decade, state and local governments have made considerable progress with managing for results, but if MFR is to realize its potential, public leaders need to ensure that they learn the right lessons from other public innovators. Too often, they have been satisfied with creating and improving a performance information system. A more telling performance measure for MFR is whether performance information is actually used in making decisions. Despite progress in creating performance information, governments struggle to incorporate these data into regular decision-making processes.

A Decade of Results-Based Reform

The idea of managing for results has dominated the public management reform agenda for more than ten years. The prevalent reform idea, whether cast in terms of New Public Management or Reinventing Government, justifies changing management in the public sector to improve performance. Performance itself has been defined in increasingly narrow terms as measurable outputs and outcomes, with much less attention to competing definitions of performance than in the past.[1]

Although there is no definitive list of the elements of MFR, there appears to be a consensus about its core procedural aspects: the creation and distribution of performance information through strategic planning and performance measurement routines. Increasingly, the verification of performance information, through performance-auditing routines, also is regarded as a core element. Some management theorists argue that focusing on only these procedural aspects of MFR is limiting. They point out that the ultimate achievement of MFR goals depends on a willingness to accompany performance information with complementary organizational reform, including customer service, increased management authority, performance-based incentives, organizational learning, and process reengineering.[2]

Ultimately, the most telling standard for MFR is not whether performance information exists but whether it is used in various decision-making venues in government, from day-to-day management of programs to high-level resource allocation decisions. It is by incorporating performance data into decisions that governments move from simply measuring results to managing them. Ascertaining whether and to what degree performance data was actually used in decision processes was the most methodologically challenging part of the GPP analysis of managing for results. One method was simply to ask government officials, which was done both in surveys and interviews (see the chapter appendix). Respondents were asked to describe how the government uses performance information and how it ensures that the information is used. They were also asked to rank the degree to which MFR is applied in different types of decision making. Every state offered examples of times when performance information influenced a decision; cumulatively, these examples provided a typology of potential uses of performance information (see box 6.1). However, all states struggled to demonstrate that their examples were typical as part of a systematic application of performance information.[3]

Previous efforts to incorporate performance information into public sector decision making have shown little success. That such reforms continually reemerge is indicative of the persistent urge to search for governmental efficiency.[4] If MFR is the latest chapter in the search, the wide scope of its intended impact distinguishes it from previous efforts, which largely focused on budget decisions but neglected day-to-day management decisions.[5] It is partly because of the breadth of this scope that there is less agree-

Box 6.1 Potential Uses of Performance Information

• *Resource allocation:* Performance information can inform budget debates and questions that legislators ask agencies. However, it appears that the idea of rewarding high performers with more money is not widely accepted. A more frequent practice is to use performance information to demonstrate program distress and the need for more funds.

• *Performance contracting:* Governments at all levels employ private sector contractors to deliver public services. Evidence suggests that contractors perform well if incentives are linked to performance measures. However, problems arise when contracts poorly specify goals, incentives, and rewards.

• *Performance improvement efforts:* Performance information provides transparency of productivity, making shirking more difficult and facilitating a top-down pressure to perform. Decision makers have greater knowledge about the performance of programs and processes. Such learning informs decisions about process improvement.

• *Improved accountability:* When the uses and results of public money are transparent to the public, external accountability is facilitated. The potential for internal accountability also is improved because elected officials have information on the bureaucrats' activities. However, even if the information is widely accessible and relevant, for accountability to be exerted the target audience for this information must actually use it.

• *Improved capacity:* Performance information can inform how present management structures and rules enable or constrain performance and how changes would improve performance.

ment on what precisely MFR means. Past efforts, such as zero-based budgeting and the Planning Programming and Budgeting System, were associated with clear and understandable procedures (even if those procedures proved largely impossible to implement, as Aaron Wildavsky argues).[6]

Regardless of theoretical ambiguity, MFR has proved popular. The GPP and other surveys of government have confirmed the widespread adoption of MFR reform across different levels of government.[7] The best illustration of this popularity comes from the state level. Virtually every state government has demanded, either through legislative or administrative requirement, that government plan and report performance on a regular basis. Survey evidence confirms that, as a result, strategic planning and the creation of performance information rank as the most intensively adopted of public sector reforms in the past decade.[8]

Managing for Results as Part of the GPP

At what point does a reform become so widespread that it is no longer a reform but simply the standard way of doing things? The designers of the GPP faced this dilemma when dealing with managing for results. In public management literature, results-based reform was often characterized as a single-event treatment, something *done to* government that would result in greater efficiency and effectiveness. This approach overlooked that MFR seeks to change governmental routines and relationships in permanent ways. Once adopted, it is a part of a government's institutional procedures. Managing for results is intended to interact with and redirect other managerial systems to facilitate performance improvement. Understanding public sector efforts to achieve results, therefore, requires that MFR be treated as a permanent management system in the context of other management systems.

The black box model assumes a neutral role for management and administration and little distortion between resource allocation and program products.[9] The GPP's conceptual underpinning assumed that MFR changes traditional approaches to management (see figure A.1 in appendix A to this volume). Examining the traditional input-output model clarified the need for an MFR system in government. Traditionally, there has been a great deal of information on inputs, but the outputs of governmental efforts are rarely clearly specified in either an ex ante or an ex post fashion. As a result, the purposes of government frequently are not clearly communicated to public employees or to citizens and elected officials, to whom the employees are accountable. Without knowing what the government is intending to achieve in the future or what it actually achieved in the past, it is difficult to understand how management contributes to the production process—that is, how management matters. In management systems that are not focused on goal achievement, managers frequently find themselves working around organizational rules and structure to get things done.

In designing management systems, policy makers traditionally focused on controlling the distribution of inputs rather than the achievement of outputs. The focus on inputs not only limits direction but also results in management systems that are designed to limit the use of inputs and, therefore, the discretion of managers to reorganize for better performance. The argument for MFR is that the availability of performance information allows the creation of management systems that control for results rather than inputs. As a result, managers may be given enhanced managerial discretion to achieve goals.

Another problem with the traditional black box model is that it masks the stove-piping and lack of coordination among the multiple management systems that direct public employees. Notwithstanding the centralized nature of such systems, they are, effectively, stove-piped. The study and practice of public management has fragmented theories and analyses of different management systems so that personnel specialists know little about how budgeting works and budgeting experts do not see personnel as part of their responsibility. As a result, the incentives created by one management system could be confounded by another management system.[10] To the extent that different management systems can be coordinated, such cross-system inconsistency can be reduced.

Adding an overarching MFR system to the traditional black box model, therefore, serves a number of purposes. It provides information about the government's intended goals and a means by which performance can be judged. It also offers the potential to coordinate existing management systems in a way that facilitates the achievement of those goals.

Cross-government Lessons

An Executive Passion

Christopher Foreman's observation that "efficiency is rarely a legislative passion" holds true for results-based reform.[11] While legislatures have shown a willingness to adopt MFR legislation—at last count, thirty-two states had implemented it—the impetus for MFR tends to come from executive branch actors.[12] A similar pattern of executive dominance in the MFR process occurs across all levels of government. Of the cities surveyed by the GPP, 68.7 percent report that the mayor's office has a significant influence, followed by 48.6 percent for individual agencies and 45.7 percent for the legislative council. Detailed data from states and counties further reflect this dominance (see table 6.1). The governor's office has the highest level of involvement (on a scale of 1 to 5) in the strategic planning process (4.66), followed by the budget office (4.39), individual agencies (4.02), and other central state offices (3.84). Other governmental actors are markedly less involved in the process. In fact, the legislature's involvement (2.76) is rivaled by the involvement of interest groups (2.56) and citizen advisory groups (2.85).

Table 6.1. Cross-state Average Stakeholder Involvement in Setting Goals

Stakeholder	States (2000)	Counties
Legislature	2.76	3.17
Legislative committee	2.67	1.08
Chief executive officer[a]	4.66	2.95
Budget office	4.39	4.03
Central office	3.84	3.39
Individual agency	4.02	3.89
Local government	2.09	1.31
Interest group	2.56	1.64
Citizen advisory group	2.85	2.36
Individual citizen	2.09	1.58
Independent auditor	1.13	1.22
Consultant	1.48	2.36
Contractor	0.91	1.14

Note: Ratings are on a scale of 0 to 5, where 0 means no involvement and 5 means very active involvement.
[a]For the states, the governor; for counties, the chief elected official or chief administrative officer.

Structural arrangements for county governments differ more than for their state equivalents, creating greater variation in the relative powers and roles of different actors. Despite this variation, the findings for counties are largely similar to the state-level findings. In counties, legislative councils tend to have greater involvement (3.17), and chief executive officers have less direct involvement (2.95). However, the pattern of executive branch dominance is maintained through the high involvement of the budget office (4.03), other state central offices (3.39), and individual agencies (3.89). Given the capacity limits of local governments, it is not surprising that counties tend to rely more on consultants to define their MFR systems (2.36), but interest group involvement (1.64) is less intense than at the state level (2.56).

The Rise of Performance Information Systems

The GPP found that all levels of government have spent considerable energy developing performance information systems intended to create and distribute performance information. These systems typically require agencies to undertake strategic planning and report performance measures on a regular basis and according to specific guidelines.

A performance information system ensures that data is available to decision makers. The logic of these systems is illustrated in figure 6.1. The systems themselves do little to improve the capacity or incentives for decision makers to use this information, however, and that the systems exist tells us little about how decisions are actually made. Providing performance information is a necessary but not sufficient condition to ensure its actual use.

Why did performance information systems (PIS) become so popular? Elected officials across the ideological divide embraced the idea of making government more results oriented, and a PIS provides a convenient way to implement this goal. While elected officials claimed a mandate for making government more results oriented, in practice such a mandate tended to be quite vague. Therefore, elected officials ultimately turned to central agency officials, most frequently from the finance department, to determine how to enact reform. The relationship between the finance department and line agencies is based on formal rules that determine the type and rate of information to be reported for the budget, spending reports, and so on. In this context, it is not surprising that mandates for results-based government usually are translated into requirements for more information.

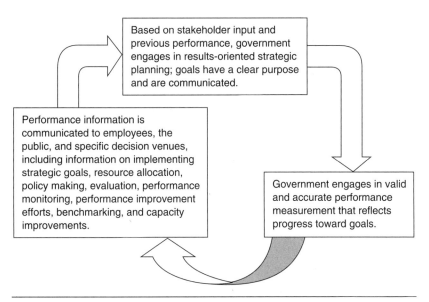

Figure 6.1. Integrating Planning, Measurement, and Decision Venues

Intergovernmental devolution of authority and demands for accountability also promote MFR. Performance standards that provide the basis of accountability between different levels of government increasingly cement intergovernmental relations.[13] County governments, as creatures of state governments, are especially prone to such mandates.

Changing professional standards reinforced the tendency to focus on the creation and distribution of performance information. During the 1990s, various public sector professional governmental organizations, including the National Academy of Public Administration, the Governmental Accounting Standards Board, and the International City/County Managers Association, advocated the creation and reporting of performance information as desirable standards for governments to pursue, standards that are increasingly necessary to receive various types of formal accreditation. Whether to maintain the appearance of professional legitimacy or simply as a good-faith effort to adopt new public management ideas, members of these organizations sought to implement performance information systems.

Types of Performance Information Systems

Among governments, a PIS typically includes similar types of information: a government-wide vision statement, a statement of core values, agency mission statements, descriptive goals, quantified performance measures, and targets.[14] The systems are designed to link strategic planning with performance measurement in order to quantify and track the government's aspirational goals. A PIS distributes this information, usually through formal documentation. This can include either specially created MFR documents or existing documents, such as the budget. Increasingly, governments are relying on Web-based technology to both collect and distribute vast amounts of information, which allows recipients to determine the type of information they wish to view (for an example, see box 6.2).

Types of Planning and Performance Reporting

While governments tend to include similar types of performance information in their performance information systems, they rely on one or a mixture of three possible ways to generate and distribute that information: performance information can be produced for government-wide, agency, or budget documentation. Each type of MFR document tends to focus on certain types of information more than others.

Box 6.2 Electronic Performance Information Systems: Virginia Results

- Virginia Results is a state government Web site, operated by Virginia's Department of Planning and Budget, that acts as a centralized resource for a variety of results-oriented information generated from state agencies. Through forms on the site, agencies can directly submit strategic planning and performance measurement information to central state performance management databases. Once submitted, this information is available to anyone who views the site.

- If decision makers or citizens also want to obtain additional planning, measurement, or evaluation information, Virginia Results provides contact information to expedite such a request.

- Also available online are a series of quality-of-life indicators. These indicators are high-level outcomes regarding issues such as the environment, economy, families, safety, education, and health.

- Part of the rationale for Virginia Results was to allow users to view the information they are interested in. Virginia noticed that different types of information are relevant to different audiences. For example, statewide strategic goals may be appropriate for the public and for legislators, while detailed agency goals may be more useful for agency budget staff. The state also designed the Web site to improve continuity between administrations, since governors in Virginia are limited to a single term and cannot succeed themselves.

- Virginia Results can be found at *http://dpb.virginia.gov/VAResults/Index.cfm*

Government-wide planning tends to be most common at the city level: twenty-three of the thirty-five cities surveyed developed citywide plans. Evidence of countywide planning was present in twenty-two of the thirty-six counties that responded to the survey. Because they have more limited functions, city and county leaders find it easier than state officials to assemble a comprehensive government-wide plan that meaningfully relates to service delivery. At the state level, government-wide plans tend to focus on setting a broad vision for the government rather than dealing with the specifics of implementation. Such statewide planning appears to be on the upswing. The 1998 GPP survey found that seventeen states had strategic plans, and this number increased to twenty-seven in 2000.

Since undertaking strategic choice at the state level has little demonstrated effect upon operational behavior and technical efficiency, the reasons for this increase in statewide MFR are worth examining. One possible reason is the rise in performance budgeting requirements. Greater accountability and transparency may be another, with statewide systems promising to offer a standardized and central format by which any interested party may access information on the goals and performance of public organizations.

Interviews with administrators in some states suggest two other possibilities: statewide systems reflect a need, first, to clarify political accountability and, second, to generate a positive image of government management. Managing-for-results systems explicitly advocate a model of accountability based on results, suggesting a move away from accountability based on political loyalty and ideology. To the degree that goals and measures created by MFR will be taken seriously, elected officials will be intensely interested in shaping those goals. Creating a clear set of objectives allows a governor to more easily clarify and communicate priorities, to emphasize some goals and results and to deemphasize others, thereby exerting policy control on cabinet and agency officials through lower-level strategic goals and performance measures. In this way, MFR tools can be used not only for performance-based accountability but also to exert political accountability. Managing-for-results systems also have great symbolic value; they enable elected officials to point to evidence that they are reforming government. Since few can object to the concept of making government more results oriented, this symbolism is significant.

City leaders rely less on agency planning because of their ability to develop comprehensive government-wide plans. However, agency planning is the most frequent mode of developing performance information at the state level. Agency plans cover much more specific information than the statewide plan allows, owing to the latter's space limitations, including performance measures and targets and identification of the actors responsible for achievement of goals. Thirty-three of thirty-six counties reported having agency-level strategic plans in place, and nineteen of these counties claimed that more than 50 percent of their agencies had such plans. In a content analysis of documents for specific county functions, the GPP found that twenty-three counties created performance information in the area of transportation, twenty in the area of corrections, and twenty in the health and human services function.

At the city level, budgets are the most popular means of collecting and distributing performance information—thirty of the thirty-five cities rely on them. Thirty-two of the thirty-six counties studied incorporate outcome measures and communicate performance information in their budget documents. This practice is gaining prominence at the state level as well. Thirty-one states incorporated strategic goals into their budget in 1998; thirty-seven states followed this strategy in 2000.

Across the different levels of government, budgets tend to reveal common formats for presenting information. This is to be expected, given common professional associations and norms. The budget also is built around individual agencies' requests. Therefore, budgets often feature agency goals and measures, but little effort is made to foster a coordinated government-wide vision or establish a common set of core values.

Coordination of Multiple Planning and Measurement Efforts

The GPP found that governments tend to use multiple forms of planning simultaneously (see table 6.2). The most common pattern is to use government-wide, agency, and budget planning at the same time. The next most popular is a combination of budget and agency planning. The most recent surveys across the three levels of government found less than 10 percent of all respondents reported using just one of these planning modes.

Using different modes of planning simultaneously results in a potential lack of coordination. What if the goals presented in the government-wide, budget, and agency plans contradict one another or simply emphasize different priorities? The GPP found that goals and measures highlighted in one

Table 6.2. Different Approaches to MFR

| | States | | | | Cities (*N* = 35) | | Counties (*N* = 36) | |
| | 1998 | | 2000 | | | | | |
Type of Planning	*N*	%	*N*	%	*N*	%	*N*	%
Government-wide, agency, and budget	7	14	20	40	9	26	16	44
Government-wide and budget	4	8	1	2	5	14	3	8
Government-wide and agency	3	6	5	10	8	23	2	6
Government-wide only	3	6	1	2	1	3	1	3
Budget and agency	14	28	17	34	10	29	11	31
Budget only	6	12	2	4	2	6	2	6
Agency only	10	20	2	4	0	0	0	0
No plan	3	6	2	4	0	0	1	3

Note: Because of rounding, totals may not add to 100 percent.

plan were frequently different from performance information in other plans.[15] This is because performance information is often produced by distinct groups of actors with different agendas, each of whom pays little attention to the other groups' efforts. While the idea of conflicting goals in public administration is not new—it is arguably an inherent characteristic of its environment—a primary purpose of results-based reform is to produce a "clarity of task and purpose" to guide resource allocation and implementation decisions.[16] Instead, MFR has often proved to be another avenue for formalizing the agendas and voices of different governmental actors.

Vertical Integration

Effective management is furthered by vertical integration—maintaining consistency between high-level goals and lower-level goals and measures. A top-down perspective on implementation decries the inability of senior managers to hold lower-level officials accountable for their actions. Performance-based accountability that relies on an explicit and logical hierarchical linkage between different levels of goals appears to offer a solution to this problem. However, breaking down broad aspirations into specific goals and measures proves difficult for many governments. The problem arises because organizations can create multiple levels of goals and measures, and there is a strong possibility that higher and lower levels will not be consistent with one another. The likelihood of inconsistency becomes more pronounced when managers seek to translate goals into measures.

Translating goals into measurements can distort the original intent of the goal, as illustrated in a case study by Carolyn Heinrich.[17] In the study, quantitative goals were tied to performance incentives that effectively motivated contractors, but those measures did not reflect the program's ultimate goal, creating a de facto implementation failure. This poses a basic problem for MFR efforts that seek to inform decision making and improve performance, since goal clarity is undermined. Assuring the consistency of goals and measures is an issue frequently overlooked in MFR literature, but analysis of the Government Performance Project data suggests it is an endemic problem. Content analysis of MFR documentation assessed the degree of consistency between goals and performance measures. Detailed analyses of state and county documents suggest that for almost all types of strategic planning and performance measurement, governments are more likely to struggle to link goals and measures than to make such linkages successfully (see table 6.3).

Table 6.3. Respondents' Assessment of Linkage between Strategic Goals and Measures

	Government-wide	Budget	Education	Corrections	Transportation
All measures are entirely consistent with and clearly contribute to specific goals					
States (2000)	10	6	6	7	7
Counties	0	1	2	0	1
Most measures are consistent with and clearly contribute to specific goals					
States (2000)	4	10	11	14	14
Counties	6	6	7	5	5
All measures are associated with specific goals but do not strongly contribute to them					
States (2000)	3	4	4	2	5
Counties	4	12	7	2	3
Measures are not clearly associated with specific goals					
States (2000)	0	8	1	0	2
Counties	1	2	3	2	1
Measures bear little recognizable consistency with goals					
States (2000)	10	9	10	9	11
Counties	11	11	4	11	11

Creating Vertical Integration

Most serious efforts to create vertical integration feature a central body that oversees the consistency of agency efforts with government-wide goals. Frequently, these are preexisting bodies, typically a government-wide office of management and budget. Sometimes, however, a special task force is convened (usually by executive order rather than statutory creation). For example, Los Angeles County established an Interagency Operations Group (IOG) to help departments integrate their individual strategic plans with the county's plan. The IOG also coordinates, collaborates, and integrates services for children and families and measures overall progress.

The state governments that received the highest GPP grades tend to be concerned with vertical integration. For example, Oregon published a *Benchmark Blue Book* that stipulates the connections between high-level state goals and lower-level programs. Indeed, a concern with vertical integration is one of a number of "integrative facilitators" high-performing states pursue that enable MFR to work as designed.[18] Integrative facilitators are practical actions designed to ensure that performance information flows to the right person in the right position at the right time and that this information is actually used. States with high MFR grades were more likely than lower-performing states to undertake actions and routines that fostered integration. Even the high-performing states candidly admit they do not fully understand whether such actions actually have the desired effect, but integrative facilitators represent what states perceive as the best way to ensure that performance information adds value to the governance process. Box 6.3 provides a short explanation of each of the integrative facilitators.

In previous work, Patricia Ingraham and I provide specific examples of how the high performers seek to use integrative facilitators.[19] One example of the balance between top-down and bottom-up results is Missouri's strategic planning process under the former governor Mel Carnahan. Political and administrative actors had clearly specified responsibilities in the process. An executive team that included the governor was tasked with defining priority results, providing directions to the subcabinet, communicating results to citizens and stakeholders, and overseeing and approving subcabinet recommendations. Department directors and deputy directors who made up the subcabinet team focused on key substantive areas, measuring and reporting performance results and overseeing research teams. Research teams consisted of planners, policy analysts, researchers, and program managers, and one or more teams were assigned to each subcabinet team. The process established how goals were set, how the detailed objectives and measures were identified and tracked, and who was responsible for answering substantive policy questions.

Utah and Virginia provide examples of the role central agencies play in processing information. Utah illustrates how central agencies facilitate the flow of information downward to ensure that agencies understand the statewide vision. The Governor's Office of Planning and Budget communicates statewide goals to the agency level, and agency goals and measures are reviewed by the agency for consistency with the statewide plan. The Virginia Results Web site offers an example of how a central agency facilitates a lateral flow of information—between agencies or within agencies—through an electronic system that collects, stores, and disseminates detailed information, offering advantages in terms of timeliness, information storage capability, and reduced transaction costs (see box 6.3). Virginia Results allows immediate access to regularly updated agency information that is disaggregated at increasingly detailed levels of agency activity.

Box 6.3 Integrative Facilitators: Characteristics Separating High-Performing and Low-Performing States

- *Comprehensiveness:* All levels of government are involved in producing relevant performance information. A comprehensive approach implies a common results framework and common language among decision makers. A comprehensive system requires a high level of coordination between different levels of government to ensure vertical integration of goals.

- *Vertical integration:* The concept of vertical integration emphasizes consistency between different levels of performance goals.

- *Balance between top-down and bottom-up approaches:* Building an MFR system that includes congruent statewide and agency-level goals requires central coordination (which offers policy coordination and political accountability) along with high levels of discretion at the agency level (which allows for the development of detailed MFR information, tapping into substantive agency expertise). Central coordination is generated through strong central administrative agencies and committed political leadership, while agency discretion provides agencies with the primary planning authority for their substantive areas.

- *Strong guidance for agency efforts:* Specific requirements can standardize the type of information agencies generate while allowing them to decide the content. A standard format makes information more understandable, transparent, and comparable to users. Another method for ensuring a standard agency approach and enhancing the quality of information is to offer informative guidelines for agency MFR efforts, including standard definitions and a how-to guide for each aspect of the state's strategic planning and performance measurement approach.

- *Information processed through a central agency:* Central agencies play an important role in communicating information downward (to ensure that agencies understand the statewide vision and that use of the information is consistent with political intention), communicating information upward (processing and selecting information for the attention of senior officials), and ensuring the lateral flow of information (creating lateral modes of distribution, such as electronic databases, and increasing discretion where information is produced).

- *Political oversight and commitment:* When elected officials are interested in using MFR to pursue better governance and are willing to take on quasi-administrative oversight roles, the system tends to work. In high-performing states where functional MFR systems were not in place when they were elected, governors made it a political priority. In states where a strong MFR system is already in place, the governor's role is to build a new vision into and improve upon the existing framework.

Transferring Ideas across Government

As more and more governments engage in a new activity, it is reasonable
to assume that learning occurs and that the governments benefit from sharing information. At the same time, there also is a risk that standardizing
an innovation will restrict learning and lead to adoption of the innovation for reasons of professional legitimacy rather than for performance
benefits.[20] As discussed previously, MFR is rapidly becoming a professional
norm in the public sector. The GPP analysis of managing for results has
found evidence of both learning for the sake of performance improvement
and learning for the sake of legitimacy; this section offers some insights
on the former.

Different governments, even different levels of governments, frequently
find ways to share information about their MFR efforts. The Clinton
administration's National Performance Review clearly influenced state and
local adoption of MFR reforms, but it was based on success stories that
emerged primarily from state and local government.[21] Similarly, the Government Performance and Results Act of 1993 is a federal reform that has
influenced the nature of performance information systems at the state and
local level but was itself based on the MFR efforts of the city of Sunnyvale,
California. The General Accounting Office surveyed leading state expo-
nents of MFR to search for lessons applicable to the implementation of
the Government Performance and Results Act at the federal level.[22]

Professional organizations and conferences provide other ways to disseminate information and standards about MFR or to develop cooperative
efforts to use and compare performance information. The International
City/County Managers Association undertakes an annual comparative
review of specific performance standards in a number of volunteer cities
and counties. Cross-government comparisons also can occur more informally, beyond the aegis of professional organizations: a government official
phones a colleague in another region or department, for example, and
begins a dialogue about implementation or standards. Such networking can
be more organized. For instance, Fairfax County instituted a Regional Performance Measurement Consortium that brings together neighboring local
governments to exchange lessons learned and innovative practices in MFR.

Perhaps the most widespread method of popularizing MFR has been the
dissemination of case studies of MFR success stories in public management
literature. These stories have appeared in popular management texts, most
notably *Reinventing Government*, by David Osborne and Ted Gaebler, and

in professional journals.[23] Such success stories persuasively portray public officials using MFR techniques to dramatically improve government efficiency and effectiveness. The focus on success stories left much of MFR literature in the field of best-practice research.[24] A key limitation of this type of research is that it generalizes management techniques as having universal application but often can overlook contextual factors that were central to the original success. Therefore, governments seeking to adapt a success story to their own contexts usually operate with extremely limited information and can easily miss the key lesson of the best practice and how it may be adapted.

The wide breadth of the GPP's research helped to move it away from best-practice research and offer a more comprehensive picture of innovation and its transfer. To undertake in-depth critical assessments of government, the GPP selected a large number of cases, but not on the basis of the governments' apparent success in implementing reforms. This allowed a description of the wider context of reform, with a number of innovative governments closely studied by those who seek to learn from them. The finding that the number of governments that have created a PIS is dramatically larger than the number that actively use performance information suggests that laggard governments frequently do not learn the right lessons.

One of the most influential MFR success stories was that of Indianapolis under Mayor Steve Goldsmith, during whose administration (1992–99) the city became known as one of the foremost users of performance information in public decisions. Indianapolis deliberately used its budget as the city's overall strategic plan, stating in their MFR survey that "while other cities may choose to have a formal strategic planning document separate from the budget, we believe that it is optimal to wrap our strategic plan up in our budget. Quite frankly, a city's plan must be able to fit within its financial means." In addition to the budget, monthly performance reports and individual agency multiyear departmental plans guided the planning process in Indianapolis. Planning was driven by a mixture of the mayor's vision for the city and departmental input. The city incorporated into the budget the goals identified in the departmental planning process, as well as a city vision statement. Mission statements, medium- and short-term goals, specific performance measures, discussion of the implementation process, and key external factors from the departmental level were all included in the budget. Departments also identified how their activities linked to the city's high-level goals.

A deliberate effort was made to inform decisions on management capacity, and in turn performance, through regular use of timely data. Indianapolis supplemented performance information in the budget with monthly reports that summarized how departmental performance measured up against objectives. The monthly reports tracked about 150 indicators, such as the number of requests for pothole repairs and the percentage filled within seven days, response times for emergency services, and the number of transportation complaints received. A central overseer examined the data and identified problem areas for management to address. The accountability dimension was ensured by the mayor's involvement, reviews of the reports by senior appointees, and the availability of the reports to the public. In its GPP survey response, Indianapolis stated that an additional purpose of the monthly review is "to provide a teaching mechanism to our departmental and line management staff on using this monthly report as a management tool." The clarity of the goals expressed in these monthly reports facilitated their use in communicating to new staff the city's objectives and its performance measurement process.

Central success factors in Indianapolis included not only the creation of a high-quality PIS but also consistent staff training on performance management and a political demand for performance information. All too frequently, other municipalities seeking to learn from the Indianapolis case simply try to transfer the requirements for performance reporting (although usually without Indianapolis's frequency of reporting or sense of coordination). This ignores the fact that simply producing more performance information did not, in itself, lead to better outcomes for Indianapolis. The information was important, but it could contribute only in the wider context of a top-down demand for performance, along with managerial capacity to understand and use performance information and a clear sense for how the information could be used.

A specific example of learning the right lessons comes from a detailed case study of San Diego County's attempts to mimic the managed competition innovation Indianapolis was known for pioneering and publicizing.[25] San Diego's effort was deemed a failure because litigation undertaken by unions prevented the county from implementing managed competition. However, government officials found that measures of service quality and efficiency improved in the proposed areas of competition, though no actual competition took place.

How did San Diego achieve the overarching goal of improved efficiency and effectiveness even though it did not fully implement the reform? San

Diego learned that by adopting and implementing the key elements of managed competition, impressive gains could occur even without the actual competition. The most straightforward elements were the creation of detailed performance information about the cost of services, improvements in the capacity of elected officials to monitor performance, and provision of better information with which to pursue improvement.

However, San Diego also implemented the less procedural but highly challenging contextual aspects of reform. The city created a competition team that fostered a top-down pressure to perform by highlighting areas of potential improvement, creating targets, and monitoring performance. The city also gave managers increased administrative flexibility in their pursuit of goals. A wider reform of government, resulting in the adoption of a general management system—which San Diego describes as "a comprehensive guideline established in 1998 for implementing, monitoring, and reviewing all functions and processes that affect the delivery of services to county residents"—offered a supportive environment for such changes.

One of the lessons of San Diego's experience is that the informal aspects and context that make up a particular reform are just as important for changing managerial behavior as adoption of the reform's formal procedural aspects. The San Diego case also highlights the misguided tendency of many public managers and public management academics to define success in terms of the adoption of a reform's formal procedures, regardless of whether the reform actually had the desired impact, and to classify other efforts as failures even if they achieve the reform's intended goal.

Challenges for Governments

In many respects, MFR represents an alternative philosophy to public management, one with lofty targets. The focus is on the level of results achieved for a given set of inputs rather than just the inputs themselves. Managing for results calls for traditionally stove-piped, or insular, management systems to work together toward the achievement of these results. The GPP found that governments have been working toward the achievement of these goals, but significant challenges remain.

The trends that emerged in 2000 and 2002 appear to be continuing in the 2005 GPP survey (although MFR is now reclassified as "information," to incorporate a greater emphasis on information technology). Aspects of MFR that can be converted into standard procedures are spreading. Those that require behavioral change on the part of users remain weak, in particular, the issue of performance information use. Performance auditing is spreading and becoming more sophisticated. More states are creating performance information systems than ever before. But in some cases, they are failing to build on past efforts. Instead, a new model of results-based government is presented by successive governors. For instance, the most recent round of GPP analysis credits Governor Bob Riley's efforts to introduce performance budgeting in Alabama. But this effort is the third such performance budgeting reform in the past decade. The previous efforts of Governors Don Siegelman and James Folsom were introduced with fanfare but never seemed to impact agency decision making and died quietly.

A skeptical viewpoint suggests that such an episodic approach to MFR is doomed to a familiar cycle of failure. Lots of time and energy is devoted to creating a PIS that fails to be used by agency officials who assume it will disappear over time and who are proved correct when it is abandoned by a new governor anxious to put his or her own mark on government reform. While Alabama may be an outlier in terms of repeated failures, the 2005 Government Performance Project reports that many states are in the same position: starting to embrace managing for results, in the process of planning, building, or improving a PIS, optimistic about the future of results-based government, and in some cases able to offer examples of how performance information has made a difference. The 2005 GPP report offers numerous examples. Alaska has "positive momentum"; Wyoming's "recent adoption of a results-based accountability model are promising developments"; "although Arkansas does not currently have a statewide strategic plan, there is momentum in the state due to the governor's new performance-based budgeting system"; in Georgia, "the agency strategic planning system appears somewhat fragmented, but new requirements just passed may add value to the process"; planning in both Illinois and Kansas is described as "a work in progress"; "Maryland became engaged in strategic planning in 1997, but has yet to fully implement the process." As for using information, in many states performance information is available to managers, but it is hard to say whether it is being used. Some anecdotal examples of performance information being used in specific agencies can be found, but this does not imply systematic use, and legislators complain of information overload.

For many states, the promise of MFR looms large, and the major gains and benefits of MFR appears just a couple of years away. But at this stage in the development of MFR systems in state government, it is reasonable to expect that more progress might have been made. The lack of use of per-

formance information is perhaps the most serious of a number of challenges facing managing for results. These challenges, discussed below, have
thus far largely defied optimistic assumptions that they are solvable and will
be solved with time. The inescapable question that arises is whether these
challenges can be overcome, or whether progress will remain mired in practical difficulties, conflict with existing systems and practices, and a belief that
the job is already done.

MFR as an Integrating System

The GPP black box placed the MFR system atop other management systems,
reflecting the idea that it was an overarching management system that
would cause other management systems to reorganize. Reorganization, it
was thought, would lead to better coordination and better contribution to
governmental goals. While this also was the intent of many reformers, thus
far it has not come to pass for most governments. Many governments do
indeed create and publicize a set of government-wide goals, but they do not
systematically ask how they can reorganize traditional management systems to facilitate the achievement of these goals.

More often, MFR is prompting the overseers of the individual management systems to think more strategically. They have created plans for their
systems but have not necessarily tried to link these goals with government-
wide plans. Strategic planning and performance measurement have been
adopted to track and improve the capacity of what remain separate systems. Instead of reorienting their management systems outward, toward
government-wide goals, they have applied the language of MFR inward,
to achieve system-specific goals. For instance, strategic planning is common for capital management and information technology systems, and
workforce planning is increasingly common for human resource management.[26] But these plans rarely consider how to achieve broad governmental performance measures.

Implementers of MFR have had difficulty in creating the type of horizontal management integration discussed above. Much of the management
doctrine that underpins MFR claims that improved efficiency can be achieved
only if a focus on results is accompanied by increased managerial authority. If MFR does indeed prompt horizontal coordination between management systems, we should see reform of financial management and human
resource systems that significantly increase authority for line managers.[27]
However, changes in these systems have been modest. Case studies demon-

strate little effort to decentralize managerial authority, and such reforms were the least intensively adopted of the past decade.[28]

Managing for results clearly has influenced other management systems, most likely for the better, but has not as yet brought about the envisaged focus on public sector outcomes or coordination. This difference is illustrated in figure A.1, a further modified version of the black box. Managing for results is presented in the figure as an add-on management system that influences other management systems, rather than as an integrator, but in reality it is interpreted and used according to the priorities of the stewards of each management system.

Using Performance Information

A clear lesson from the GPP is that governments have adopted the language and procedures of managing for results. They set strategic goals, measure performance, and audit and distribute this information. This, in itself, is a major change. However, if the use of performance information is the critical standard for MFR, much remains to be done. Government employees find themselves surrounded with mounds of performance information, but they do not always have a clear idea of its purpose.

The existence of such information always can be justified on the grounds of increased transparency and accountability, but this ignores the fact that adoption of MFR was, and continues to be, justifiable by improved performance. This problem raises the potential for MFR to fall victim to its own popularity. The concept was popularized in terms of its own compelling logic and frequently repeated case studies that demonstrated the real improvements it brought to several governments. As other governments sought to acquire both the appearance of having an MFR system in place and the presumed benefits it would bring, the lessons of these cases frequently were boiled down and packaged in terms of the adoption of procedures—strategic planning, performance measurement, and performance auditing. The conditions for success that were more difficult to transfer—particularly wider organizational changes—either were lost in the translation or have proved difficult to implement in less hospitable environments.

In implementation, the creation of performance information all too frequently is treated as an additional budgetary reporting mandate, not an opportunity to improve performance. At the center of government and at the agency level, financial management staff are usually responsible for ensuring that performance information is reported. Such staff tend to lack training, time, and sufficient interest to consider how performance information can be used to improve performance and instead simply call for continued reporting.

Meeting the Challenges: The Role of Leadership

Managing for results is a tool with which leaders can set out a vision and reshape an organization. It is also the leadership's responsibility to meet the challenges described above. As previously suggested and as illustrated in table 6.1, leadership in MFR usually means executive branch leadership, whether from elected officials, central agency staff, or line agency leaders.

Research at the state level has revealed the importance of leadership to MFR. Data from the GPP state surveys shows that when senior executive branch officials believe MFR is one of the governor's priorities, they are more likely to incorporate performance information into their decisions.[29] However, creating and reforming a management system requires more from leaders than simply choosing and promoting the right reform. It also implies institutionalization and use of the reform. Institutionalization means translating the vision for the system into reality by creating or changing administrative rules and structures. Central agency officials have had primary responsibility for institutionalizing MFR. Their actions can either empower other actors to use information or discourage them completely. In states where central officials sought to dominate the policy agenda by choosing goals and standards, other actors were less inclined to use performance information. In contrast, when central officials supported other actors by providing access to performance information, decision makers were more inclined to use this information.[30]

A final leadership responsibility is to actually use MFR, demonstrating its value and importance to members of the organization and thereby encouraging their use of the system. This remains perhaps the greatest challenge for leaders, and there is clear potential for improvement. Cross-state data and in-depth case studies suggest that senior executive branch officials have demonstrated little active use of MFR and have done little to encourage agency managers to use performance information. However, leadership comes from different levels of government, and evidence also suggests that agency leaders have a stronger influence than governors or legislators on the nature and intensity of MFR use by agency staff.[31]

Elected officials and central agency staff set the framework of a government's MFR system, but the challenge of making the system work ultimately resides with agency leaders. Case study findings are encouraging. Agency leaders search for ways to ensure that MFR is used to add value to their organization. An example is Vermont, where agency leadership in the area of corrections used MFR for a number of purposes: to facilitate a basic questioning of existing policies, to craft an alternative vision of the agency's role, and to communicate this vision to agency stakeholders.[32] This learning process was facilitated by learning forums that encouraged actors to closely examine information, consider its significance, and decide how it will affect future action. Such forums are characterized by structured dialogue, collegiality among a wide range of participants, avoidance of defensive reactions, a willingness to examine entrenched assumptions and practices, and the use of performance data and experiential knowledge to assess whether an agency is achieving success or failure and to increase the possibility of innovation. Learning forums do not occur by themselves, so perhaps the greatest challenge—and opportunity—faced by agency leaders with respect to MFR is to create learning forums that help managers make sense of performance information and seek ways to use it.

APPENDIX

Methodology

Once the GPP had established the conceptual relationship of managing for results with other management systems and a set of criteria that frames MFR as a management system in itself, the next step was to create a methodology to collect data. The simultaneous use of surveys, interviews, and content analysis provided triangulation, the availability of different types of data compensating for the potential shortcomings of any particular type, thereby improving the internal and construct validity of the data collected and the conclusions made. In-depth written surveys were sent to all of the governments assessed during the project—all fifty state governments, thirty-five of the largest cities, and forty of the largest counties (although only thirty-six counties responded).

The pilot survey and initial state assessment surveys relied on open-ended questions that facilitated detailed descriptions about the design and practice of each government's MFR system. The collection of this information allowed future iterations of the survey to incorporate an increasing number of closed-ended questions about specific and better-understood aspects of the MFR system.

After the pilot studies, formal content analysis replaced the practice of simply examining relevant documents. For MFR, researchers examined government-wide budgets, strategic plans, performance reports and a sample of agency strategic plans and performance reports. The data collected enabled objective comparisons of the level and type of performance information governments' produce. Two separate coders coded every document, and a third coder, the codebook designer, helped resolve discrepancies.[33]

The third leg of the MFR methodology was the interviews conducted by reporters from *Governing* magazine with public officials and stakeholders. Together, the various types of data collected provided a comprehensive picture of the procedures and routines in each government's MFR system.

NOTES

1. Patricia W. Ingraham and Donald P. Moynihan, "Evolving Dimensions of Performance from the CSRA to the Present," in *The Future of Merit: Twenty Years after the Civil Service Reform Act*, ed. James P. Pfiffner and Douglas A. Brook (Baltimore: John Hopkins University Press, 2000), pp. 103–26.

2. See, for example, Allen Schick, "Getting Performance Measures to Measure Up," in *Quicker, Better, Cheaper? Managing Performance in American Government*, ed. Dall Forsythe (Albany, NY: Rockefeller Institute Press, 2001), pp. 39–60.

3. Donald P. Moynihan and Patricia W. Ingraham, "Look for the Silver Lining: Managing for Results in State Government," *Journal of Public Administration Research and Theory* 13, no. 4 (2003): 469–90.

4. George W. Downs and Patrick D. Larkey, *The Search for Government Efficiency* (New York: Random House, 1986).

5. Allen Schick, "Budgeting for Results: Recent Developments in Five Industrialized Countries," *Public Administration Review* 50, no. 1 (1990): 26–34.

6. Aaron A. Wildavsky, *Budgeting: A Comparative Theory of Budgeting Processes* (Boston: Little, Brown, 1975).

7. Julia E. Melkers and Katherine Willoughby, "The State of the States: Performance-Based Budgeting Requirements in 47 out of 50," *Public Administration Review* 58, no. 1 (1998): 66–73; Theodore H. Poister and Gregory D. Streib, "Strategic Management in the Public Sector," *Public Productivity and Management* 22, no. 3 (1999): 308–25; Ron Snell and Jennifer Grooters, "Governing-for-Results: Legislation in the States," draft report to the National Council of State Legislatures (1999); Xiaohu Wang, "Performance Measurement in Budgeting: A Study of County Governments," *Public Budgeting and Finance* 20, no. 3 (2000): 102–18.

8. Jeffrey L. Brudney, F. Ted Hebert, and Deil S. Wright, "Reinventing Government in the American States: Measuring and Explaining Administrative Reform," *Public Administration Review* 59, no. 1: 19–30.

9. Patricia Ingraham and Amy Donahue, "Dissecting the Black Box Revisited: Characterizing Government Management Capacity," in *Governance and Performance: New Perspectives*, ed. Carolyn Henrich and Laurence Lynn (Washington, DC: Georgetown University Press), pp. 292–318.

10. William Earle Klay, "Management through Budgetary Incentives," *Public Productivity and Management Review* 41, no. 2 (1987): 59–71.

11. Christopher Foreman, "Reinventing Politics: The NPR Meets Congress," in *Inside the Reinvention Machine: Appraising Governmental Reform*, ed. Donald Kettl and John DiIulio (Washington, DC: Brookings, 1995), pp. 152–69.

12. Snell and Grooters, "Governing-for-Results."

13. Donald F. Kettl, *Reinventing Government: A Fifth-Year Report Card* (Washington DC: Brookings, 1998).

14. For definitions, descriptions, and examples of different types of performance information, see Donald P. Moynihan, *The State of the States in Managing for Results*, Alan K. Campbell Public Affairs Institute Working Paper, 2001, www.maxwell.syr.edu/gpp/pdfs/The_State_of_the_States_In_MFR.pdf.

15. Ibid.

16. Malcolm Holmes and David Shand, "Management Reform: Some Practitioner Perspectives on the Past Ten Years," *Governance* 8, no. 4: 551–78; quotation on p. 551.

17. Carolyn J. Heinrich, "Do Government Bureaucrats Make Effective Use of Performance Management Information?" *Journal of Public Administration and Research Theory* 9, no. 3 (1999): 363–93.

18. Moynihan and Ingraham, "Look for the Silver Lining."

19. Ibid.

20. Paul J. DiMaggio and Walter W. Powell, "The Iron Cage Revisited: Institutional Isomorphism and Collective Rationality in Organizational Fields," *American Sociological Review* 48, no. 4 (1983): 147–60.

21. David E. Osborne and Ted Gaebler, *Reinventing Government: How the Entrepreneurial Government Is Transforming the Public Sector* (New York: Penguin, 1992).

22. U.S. General Accounting Office, *Managing for Results: State Experiences Provide Insights for Federal Management Reforms*, GAO/GGD-95-22 (Washington, DC, 1994).

23. Osborne and Gaebler, *Reinventing Government*.

24. E. S. Overman and K. J. Boyd, "Best Practice Research and Post-bureaucratic Reform," *Journal of Public Administration Research and Theory* 4, no. 1 (1994): 67–84.

25. Matthew Andrews and Donald P. Moynihan, "Why Reforms Don't Always Have to Work to Succeed: A Tale of Two Managed Competition Initiatives," *Public Performance and Management Review* 25, no. 3 (2001): 282–97.

26. B. J. Reed, "Strategic Information Systems Planning in U.S. State Governments: Status and Prospects Indicated by Quantitative Analysis of Year 2000 Government Performance Project Data," Government Performance Project Learning

Paper Series (Syracuse, NY: Alan Campbell Public Affairs Institute, Syracuse University, 2001); Sally C. Selden, Patricia W. Ingraham, and Willow Jacobson, "Human Resources Practices in State Government: Findings from a National Survey," *Public Administration Review* 61, no. 5 (2001): 598–607.

27. Donald P. Moynihan, "Managing for Results in State Government: Evaluating a Decade of Reform," *Public Administration Review* 66, no. 1 (2006): 78–90.

28. Brudney, Hebert, and Wright, "Reinventing Government."

29. Donald P. Moynihan and Patricia W. Ingraham, "Integrative Leadership in the Public Sector: A Model of Performance Information Use," *Administration and Society* 36, no. 4 (2004): 427–53.

30. Ibid.

31. Donald Moynihan, "Pursuing Rationality in Public Management: Managing for Results in U.S. State Governments" (PhD diss., Maxwell School of Citizenship and Public Affairs, Syracuse University, 2002).

32. Donald P. Moynihan, "Goal-based Learning and the Future of Performance Management," *Public Administration Review* 65, no. 2 (2005): 203–16.

33. Intercoder reliability also was calculated for the second round of state analysis and totaled over 83 percent.

CHAPTER 7

Integration of Management Systems in State and Local Government

ORA-ORN POOCHAROEN AND
PATRICIA W. INGRAHAM

Traditionally, government management systems have been adopted singly and incrementally, creating insular sets, each with its own rules, regulations, and perceptions of effective performance. One blatant example is the resulting failure—or inability—to account for public personnel in agency and program budgets. This occurs because personnel are allocated in terms of full-time-equivalent employees. Budgets are allocated in dollars. How many full-time equivalents can be had for each thousand dollars is difficult to determine. Thus, despite the fact that public personnel are often an agency's or program's largest single expense, it is hard to tie that expense to specific budget items. Similarly, it could be assumed that public organizations that make large computer purchases would have comparable capacities and technologies in each of their departments. Not so. Many governments now have computer systems that do not "talk" to one another because computer acquisition has been viewed as an issue for each management system rather than for the organization's overall management.

Analyses of high-performing—or, to paraphrase Garrison Keillor, even "good enough"—organizations suggest that such insularity is a serious barrier to effective organizational communication and performance. Effective organizations do not have stove-piped internal structures; rather, they have crosscutting objectives and systems. In all of the analyses described in this book, integration is one of the qualities assumed to contribute to high capacity in government. This assumption is clearly presented in the analytical model discussed in chapter 1 (also see figure A.1 in appendix A to this volume) and is borne out in the analyses of strong states, such as Virginia and Washington, in which the strength of one well-developed management system builds capacity in other systems. Information sharing through managing for results has improved both communication and integration among systems in other governments, such as the city of Phoenix and the state of Missouri, that have emphasized MFR as a capacity driver.

The analytical model used by the Government Performance Project also assumed a critical role for leadership as a broad integrating influence on effective performance. Leadership—both political and administrative—is important for several reasons. First, leaders give voice and substance to a government's vision. In speeches, strategic planning and budgetary documents, and daily actions intended to effectively mobilize government resources, leaders provide a common value base and clear priorities. In the strategic pursuit of leaders' priorities, the need to bridge horizontally across government agencies and systems is consistently present. The GPP analyses subsequent to active data gathering examined those governments that were graded well across all or most of the management systems and then looked at those whose grades were poor. A readily identifiable leader or team of leaders was consistently present in high-capacity governments and always absent in low-capacity settings.[1] The ability to systematically compare governments in this way permitted broad specification of leadership qualities in diverse settings, and, though the project did not specifically identify a leadership focus in initial analyses, this broad comparative perspective allowed leadership to emerge as a significant factor.

This comparison also permitted the testing of the GPP's implicit assumption that some broad level of leadership is necessary for strategic clarity and priority setting. Two of the systems, financial management and managing for results, demonstrated these properties most readily, and two major sources of information, the surveys and the accompanying document analysis, were most useful in linking the roles of specific leaders or leadership teams with strategic budget and evaluation systems. The leadership activity found in the GPP analysis was not generally that of the rugged individualist leader, but rather a leader or team who set long-term priorities, reinforced and safeguarded strategic priorities, and charted meaningful implementation courses. The GPP analysts termed this "integrative leadership." The leaders and leadership teams identified were notable for spanning political and administrative differences and terms and thus in building capacity for long-term integration and effectiveness.[2]

Horizontal and Vertical Integration

In analyzing both the presence and the creation of integration across management systems, it is important to note that there are two different yet overlapping strategies for achieving those objectives. The first is pursuit of vertical integration. Donald Moynihan's discussion in chapter 6 examines this strategy of integration in some depth, noting that in effective MFR systems the jurisdiction has a comprehensive strategic plan that incorporates vision or mission statements, long- and short-term goals, specific targets, and performance measurements for the entire government. Function-specific management systems, such as human resources, align their strategic plans to the government-wide strategic plan accordingly. The targeted number of personnel, the amount of budget, and the expected outputs and outcomes are linked in overall strategic plans. This vertical integration assures that every function of the jurisdiction is moving in one direction toward the same goals.

The other strategy is horizontal integration. *Horizontal integration* refers to the alignment and coordination of management systems achieved by implementing continuous communication and cooperation across them. Horizontal integration includes the participation of representatives of each management system in the strategic planning process. It also includes open communication and efforts to share performance information among management systems at all levels, from top managers to employees. Maricopa County is one example of success in this regard. Maricopa's four-phase corporate review process is headed by a team made up of the county's deputy administrator, budget manager, human resources director, chief financial officer, performance measurement auditor, and other management representatives. Horizontal integration ensures that each function pursues its own goals in alignment with broader crosscutting governmental objectives.

Measuring Integration

Despite the significance of integration, measuring levels of integration is a challenging issue, requiring close observation of the complex relations among the systems analyzed. Again, the ability to step back from several years' experience with capacity assessment and compare a broad set of governments enhanced the ability to explore the issue. The GPP successfully identified characteristics of management systems based on sets of criteria-based indexes for each system. Numerical scores of the characteristics of each management system from the GPP database permitted us to explore findings quantitatively. In this chapter, we use indirect associational correlations between characteristics of management systems to assess levels of integration (for state and county scores, see appendix C to this volume).

Table 7.1 displays the correlation coefficients of management systems in state and county governments. Missing data from city governments did not permit inclusion of that level.

The correlation coefficients present evidence of positive relationships among the systems analyzed and support the GPP model's assumptions of basic associations. They may suggest that alterations in one system will bring about changes in another. The correlations do not allow us to examine more specific relationships but do suggest that, as predicted, financial management, information technology, and managing for results are the most likely levers of influence.

The coefficients may also be ranked from high to low to observe pairs of management systems with the strongest correlations. Figure 7.1 illustrates the distinct clusters that emerge, and they demonstrate a somewhat different pattern from that in table 7.1. Solid lines in the figure represent correlation coefficients that are significant at the 0.01 levels. Dotted lines represent correlation coefficients that are significant at the 0.05 level. Managing for results, financial management, and capital management systems cluster, for both state and county governments.

While the positive correlations do not demonstrate a causal relationship, the statistically significant correlations between managing for results and other systems provides preliminary support for the hypothesis that an increase in MFR management capacity leads to increased integration of other submanagement systems as well. This supports the GPP assumption that managing for results can be an important integrator.

One obvious observation from figure 7.1 is that overall, correlations are higher at the county level than at the state level. At the state level, information technology lags. Managing-for-results systems appear to link to other systems at both state and county levels, but the linkage is weaker in the states. At both levels, the association between financial management and human resource management is weak. As expected, the association between human resource management systems and capital management systems is not significant for either states or counties. The relationship between financial management and information technology management is also weak at both levels. This is not as expected—or perhaps not as desired—because financial planning is highly data intensive and other systems rely on both the timeliness and accuracy of budget information.

Table 7.1. Correlation of Characteristics of State and County Management Systems

	Managing for results		Financial management		Human resources management		Capital management		Information technology management	
	State	County	State	County	State	County	State	County	State	County
Managing for results	1	1								
Financial management	0.580**	0.466**	1	1						
Human resources management	0.366**	0.470**	0.302*	0.375*	1	1				
Capital management	0.287*	0.542**	0.512**	0.623**	0.227	0.103	1	1		
Information technology management	0.359*	0.504**	0.340*	0.417*	0.356*	0.562**	0.341*	0.479**	1	1

* Correlation is significant at the 0.05 level (2-tailed).
** Correlation is significant at the 0.01 level (2-tailed).

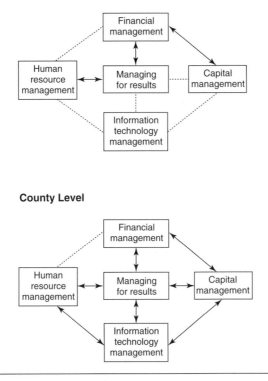

Figure 7.1. Management System Clusters

Montgomery County provides an example of a government overcoming integration obstacles. Montgomery has developed a Web-enabled database that allows department computer systems to exchange information on more than two thousand program measures over time. Maricopa County is another example. Departments in that county are integrated into one standardized MFR system through Web-based strategic plans and monthly Web-based financial reports. Wayne County has demonstrated an integration of human resource management and information technology management through an innovative Web-based personnel performance appraisal system. Despite the challenges, some governments are overcoming them.

We further investigated the relationships among the systems with correlations between the letter grades—the summative measures—of each management system.[3] The results, presented in table 7.2, are as expected, with strong correlations across all of the management systems. The strongest

Table 7.2. Correlation of Grades of State and County Management Systems

	Managing for results		Financial management		Human resources management		Capital management		Information technology management	
	State	County	State	County	State	County	State	County	State	County
Managing for results	1	1								
Financial management	0.649**	0.724**	1	1						
Human resources management	0.537**	0.634**	0.453**	0.606**	1	1				
Capital management	0.612**	0.464**	0.570**	0.648**	0.456**	0.420**	1	1		
Information technology management	0.515**	0.480**	0.442**	0.568**	0.638**	0.545**	0.574**	0.457**	1	1

* Correlation is significant at the 0.05 level (2-tailed).
** Correlation is significant at the 0.01 level (2-tailed).

correlation is between the grades for managing for results and financial management. This is as expected, because budget documents are important platforms for communicating performance information at both state and county levels. In addition, many jurisdictions give authority concerning managing-for-results systems to financial officers instead of having separate MFR departments or offices. The strong association between human resource management grades and information technology grades at the state level is also notable here, although both are clearly influenced by managing for results.

Considering Other Variables

While the population of states in this study was universal, the sample of counties was not. The counties were selected based on total revenue and population. Because these variables alone would have dramatically skewed the county sample toward California and the Southwest, counties were also selected with regional representativeness in mind. It is possible that level of management capacity is associated with the size of the jurisdiction, but since sample selection systematically excluded midsized counties, that comparison is not possible. To explore the issue indirectly, table 7.3 presents correlation coefficients of size of population with individual management systems. The results show that there is no significant correlation, with the exception of human resource management at the county level.

Table 7.3. Correlation of State and County Management Systems with Population, Revenue, and Expenditure

	Population		Revenue		Expenditure	
	State	County	State	County	State	County
Managing for results	0.265	0.136	0.059	0.076	0.044	n.a.
Financial management	0.178	0.059	0.025	0.086	0.025	n.a.
Human resources management	0.155	0.480**	−0.012	0.482**	−0.013	n.a.
Capital management	−0.102	−0.142	−0.179	−0.093	−0.171	n.a.
Information technology management	0.023	0.107	0.099	0.067	0.103	n.a.

* Correlation is significant at the 0.05 level (2-tailed).
** Correlation is significant at the 0.01 level (2-tailed).

The table also explores the correlations of total revenue of each jurisdiction with each management system. The result here is similar to the population correlations. Contrary to expectations that jurisdictions that earn and spend more will have higher capacity, the correlations are low. Although this level of analysis is simple, it is important to note that, from this perspective, improved capacity does not necessarily mean taxing and spending more.

Managing for Results as an Integrator

Managing-for-results systems have attracted increasing attention for the role they are expected to play as integrators of other management systems. Managing for results is expected to positively influence other management systems' capacities and ultimately improve government performance overall.[4] We test these assumptions here, but again, the findings are exploratory in nature. They do, however, generate important questions for both practicing government managers and those who will study these issues in the future.

Managing-for-results capacity is broken down into eight criteria. These criteria fall into two subcategories: strategic capacity and leadership. Table 7.4 displays the results of the correlations at state and county levels for both sets of criteria. (For a list of the criteria of MFR systems, see appendix B to this volume.)

The first important finding is that all the management systems at both the state and county levels are positively correlated with all the MFR criteria, although weakly in some cases. This does not demonstrate a causal relationship, but the large and statistically significant correlations provide preliminary support for the hypothesis that an increase in MFR management capacity can lead to increases in the managing capacities of all other management systems, as well.

At the state level, as predicted, the total MFR score has the strongest correlation with financial management (0.580). Previous research suggests that elements of financial management, such as performance-based budgeting, are strongly related to the concept of performance measures in MFR systems. Furthermore, managing for results and budget reforms are practiced most widely at the state level. The smaller correlation with human resources is also predictable, given the exceptional insularity often built into human resources by stringent civil service laws and regulations that do not mesh easily with strategic planning and change.

Table 7.4. Correlation of MFR Criteria with Other State and County Management Systems

	Financial management		Human resource management		Capital management		Information technology management	
	State	County	State	County	State	County	State	County
Overall managing for results	0.580**	0.466**	0.366**	0.470**	0.287*	0.542**	0.359*	0.504**
Strategic capacity criterion								
MFR 1C: Government plans are responsive to input from citizens and other stakeholders, including employees.	0.297*	0.300	0.309*	0.481**	0.141	0.361*	0.359*	0.558**
MFR 1D: Department plans are coordinated with central government plans.	0.123	0.274	0.222	0.378*	−0.001	0.394*	0.052	0.397*
MFR 2A: Government develops indicators and evaluative data that can measure progress	0.456**	0.413*	0.211	0.267	0.224	0.476**	0.201	0.347*
MFR 2B: Government can ensure that data is valid and accurate	0.281	0.433**	0.060	0.156	0.133	0.415*	0.183	0.155
MFR 4: Government clearly communicates the results of its activities to stakeholders.	0.478**	0.520**	0.278	0.353*	0.275	0.501**	0.266	0.260
Leadership criterion								
MFR 1A: Strategic objectives are identified and provide a clear purpose.	0.513**	0.185	0.385**	0.213	0.307*	0.377*	0.265	0.384*
MFR 1B: Government leadership effectively communicates the strategic objectives to all employees.	0.346*	0.468**	0.182	0.546**	0.211	0.420*	0.313*	0.562**
MFR 3: Leaders and managers use results data for policy making, management, and evaluation of progress.	0.441**	0.372*	0.089	0.515**	0.205	0.466**	0.253	0.594**

* Correlation is significant at the 0.05 level (2-tailed).
** Correlation is significant at the 0.01 level (2-tailed).

The findings are different at the county level. In the counties, the MFR scores are all significantly correlated with other systems, with correlations ranging from 0.542 to 0.466. In general, MFR criteria have higher correlations with the other management systems at the county level than at the state level. It is possible that these broader integrating relationships are related to the more limited scope of responsibilities and functions of counties.

Leadership

The lower panel of table 7.4 shows the results for leadership criteria. Analyzing each criterion reveals other differences between relationships at the state and county levels in terms of the role leadership plays in effective integration. Criterion 1A, "Strategic objectives are identified and provide a clear purpose," is significantly correlated with human resource management and financial management at the state level—0.385 and 0.513, respectively—but not at the county level. This criterion considers the presence of formal MFR systems, formal strategic plans, and departmental strategic plans as well as the frequency of the plans' revisions. Again, the difference in state and county structures may explain this discrepancy. States are generally more centralized than counties. They may use formal strategic plans as vehicles to align goals and performance measures in other management areas, specifically, financial management and human resource management. For counties, which are smaller and generally more decentralized, formal countywide strategic plans may be less influential. Analysis of the documents counties submitted with their GPP surveys suggests that many counties rely on budgets as strategic planning devices and structure their MFR systems around them rather than around countywide strategic plans. This does not deny the presence of integration, but it clearly suggests that governments can use different mechanisms and take different paths to achieve it. The findings also demonstrate the budget's strategic significance in both states and counties.

Criterion 1B, "Government leadership effectively communicates the strategic objectives to all employees," is significantly correlated with all management systems at the county level, but at the state level it is significantly correlated only with financial management and information technology management. County leaders are closer to their subordinates than state leaders are, so this finding supports the GPP's underlying assumption that leadership plays a vital role in enhancing management capacity.

While the findings prove this is true at both the state and county levels of government, the relationship is stronger at the county level. This finding also underlines the importance of communication and the opportunity to communicate. Effective communication of government goals and objectives between managers and employees is vital to effective integration of management systems; future analyses should pursue the question of how size and scope of government effectively support or inhibit a leader's ability to communicate clearly.

As discussed in greater detail in chapter 6, the most critical key to creating high capacity in government is the actual use of performance information by leaders and managers in planning and decision making. Criterion 3, "Leaders and managers use results data for policy making, management, and evaluation of progress," is significantly correlated with every other management system at the county level, demonstrating again the potential for direct leadership in county governments. At the state level, the criterion is strongly correlated only with financial management. This reinforces the earlier point that budgets are frequently the most obvious and most direct strategic planning mechanism available to leaders at the state level, who must rely on less direct but clearly enforceable strategies. Although not reported in this chapter, there is some evidence from the GPP city data that elected officials in cities also use budgets as informal strategic statements.[5]

Throughout the discussion of the systems analyzed in this chapter, as well as in the other chapters of the book, leadership has emerged as a critical but rather amorphous factor. Moynihan observes, for example, that

> without knowing what the government is intending to achieve in the future or what it actually achieved in the past, it is difficult to understand how management contributes to the production process.... Leadership in MFR usually means executive branch leadership, whether from elected officials, central agency staff, or line agency leaders.... When senior executive branch officials believe MFR is one of the governor's priorities, they are more likely to incorporate performance information into their decisions.

Similarly, B. J. Reed, Lyn Holley, and Donna Dufner note in chapter 5 that the plethora of stakeholders involved in IT acquisition and decisions on use requires clear objectives and authority if capacity is to be effectively built. In chapter 2, Yilin Hou describes the need to set the boundaries for oversight and establish a balance for flexibility opportunities within an appropriate set of controls. The states provide clear examples of leadership teams using the budget not only as a strategic document but also an excellent financial management system as the driver for excellence in other systems. All of these suggest a central role for leadership in providing long-term vision, supporting and guiding the definition of central values, and providing the framework for decentralized activities. The relationships indicated in table 7.4 further support these conclusions.

In all of these cases, there are indications that the attributes of leadership are synonymous with the conditions that need to be present for capacity to develop. The most striking evidence of the presence of leadership, however, occurs in the analysis of the high- and low-capacity governments studied by the GPP. Because grades were the summary measure of capacity development, those governments with the highest grades were assumed to have achieved the highest levels of capacity for performance. In these governments, at all levels, a leader or team of leaders was immediately evident. In those governments at the lowest end of the grading, the absence of leaders or leadership was equally striking. Respondents and documents from low-capacity governments referred to "lack of direction," lack of clear authority, unwillingness of persons in top positions to take responsibility, and a seemingly scattershot approach to governmental activity. High-capacity governments were characterized by specific references to leaders or leader teams, clarity about the job to be done and how it fit into overall priorities, clear references to goals and missions of departments and agencies, and a specific sense of how each activity mattered. Of course, this was not nirvana; we found dissatisfaction even in some of the highest-capacity governments. Nonetheless, the broad distinctions were clear.

When and why elected and career leaders make the choice to use management systems as capacity builders, however, remains a question for future in-depth and case analysis. Patterns are discernible in our work, but the ability to draw generalizable lessons is limited by the nature of the analysis. Despite these limitations, the role and influence of what we have called integrative leadership is evident in many of the systems we studied and, most clearly, in those governments determined to be high-capacity governments.

Conclusion

The findings presented in this chapter demonstrate that, while managing for results may be an important integrator for linking up government systems, when observed closely and assessed by criterion, relationships to other management systems, and levels of government, its effects are varied. Therefore, while MFR systems are a good tool, caution is well advised when considering its utility in different settings. It is not a panacea. The chapter's findings also point again to the central role that budget systems and documents play in effective managing for results. The strategic planning elements of MFR and financial management systems prove more compatible with each other than with the more restrictive strategic elements found in systems such as human resource management.

The findings lend additional substance to earlier GPP findings related to leadership. Those analyses identified effective leadership as one critical characteristic of high-capacity government. The findings presented in this chapter support that conclusion. Communication of vision and priorities through written strategic documents and budgets is an important tool that government leaders can and do use. In fact, GPP research demonstrates that the most effective leaders make maximum use of these tools.

Finally, the work reported in this chapter points to many questions that remain in the government performance arena. Broadly, the level of government affects how systems are used and how they can be linked to create capacity. Whether one system drives the others, and when, is not so clear. Managing for results as a separate system is one path to performance. Many governments have shown, however, that other management systems (such as financial management) can be used to implement MFR principles just as successfully. Examination of more than one management system has proved beneficial in understanding this dimension of capacity. The significance of this approach is deepened by the failure to find a relationship between taxing and spending and the ability to build capacity. "Smart" governments have apparently chosen systems they can afford and strategies for building them that fall well within their means.

Although many other dimensions remain unexplored, leadership emerges as fundamental in choosing a clear path for building capacity, for building and using available tools and systems effectively, and for communicating purpose and performance objectives clearly and well. Leadership is a difficult phenomenon to capture, measure, and describe. The clarity with which it presents itself in this research mandates further exploration of this critical characteristic of capacity and performance.

Overall, the Government Performance Project improved the understanding of government management, but as with any understanding, it also deepened awareness of the questions that remain. Those questions are further explored in the concluding chapter of this book.

APPENDIX

Management System Evaluation Criteria and Scores

Table 7.A.1. Managing-for-Results Evaluation Criteria

Number	Criterion
MFR1	Government engages in results-oriented strategic planning.
MFR1A	Strategic objectives are identified and provide a clear purpose.
MFR1B	Government leadership effectively communicates the strategic objectives to all employees.
MFR1C	Government plans are responsive to input from citizens and other stakeholders, including employees.
MFR1D	Department plans are coordinated with central government plans.
MFR2A	Government develops indicators and evaluative data that can measure progress toward results and accomplishments.
MFR2B	Government can ensure that data is valid and accurate.
MFR3	Leaders and managers use results data for policymaking, management, and evaluation of progress.
MFR4	Government clearly communicates the results of its activities to stakeholders.

Table 7.A.2. Scores of State Management Systems (*N* = 40)

	Minimum	Maximum	Mean	SD
Managing for results				
1A	0.17	1.00	0.758	0.2194
1B	0	0.80	0.478	0.2003
1C	0	0.61	0.396	0.1377
1D	0	1.00	0.714	0.3228
2A	0	0.86	0.529	0.2331
2B	0	0.88	0.448	0.2125
3	0.02	0.73	0.553	0.1219
4	0	0.81	0.384	0.1566
Total				
Managing for results	8.59	69.29	53.26	12.0192
Financial management	0.43	0.82	0.67	0.0780
Human resource management	32.59	71.31	50.72	10.0300
Capital management	0.30	0.86	0.62	0.1290
Information technology management	29.00	55.00	43.75	6.6300

Table 7.A.3. Scores of County Management Systems (*N* = 35)

	Minimum	Maximum	Mean	SD
Managing for results				
1A	0.04	0.96	0.5651	0.2967
1B	0.09	1.00	0.6020	0.2276
1C	0.10	0.51	0.2969	0.1047
1D	0	0.75	0.3766	0.2439
2A	0.06	0.90	0.5317	0.1887
2B	0	0.81	0.4797	0.1965
3	0.29	0.97	0.7049	0.1629
4	0	0.88	0.5609	0.2061
Total				
Managing for results	9.69	79.84	51.4640	15.8896
Financial management	30.66	80.61	64.6581	9.9437
Human resource 1 management	111.45	349.65	217.5579	54.334
Capital management	21.00	104.00	72.0000	19.0100
Information technology management	1.62	3.68	2.7963	0.5525

NOTES

1. Patricia W. Ingraham, Jessica Sowa, and Donald P. Moynihan, "Public Sector Integrative Leadership: Linking Leadership to Performance in Public Organizations," in *The Art of Governance,* ed. Patricia W. Ingraham and Laurence E. Lynn Jr. (Washington, DC: Georgetown University Press, 2004), pp. 152–70.

2. Patricia W. Ingraham and Donald P. Moynihan, "Beyond Measurement: Managing for Results in State Government," in *Quicker, Better, Cheaper? Managing Performance in American Government,* ed. Dall W. Forsythe (Albany, NY: Rockefeller Institute Press, 2001), pp. 309–335.

3. The summative measures or letter grades derive from the characteristics of the management systems, adjusted after considering results of interviews and qualitative data.

4. In the GPP, *management capacity* is defined as "government's intrinsic ability to marshal, develop, direct, and control its human, physical, and information capital to support the discharge of its policy directions"; Patricia W. Ingraham and Amy Kneedler Donahue, "Dissecting the Black Box Revisited: Characterizing Government Management Capacity," in *Governance and Performance: New Perspectives,* ed. Carolyn J. Heinrich and Laurence E. Lynn Jr. (Washington, DC:

Georgetown University Press, 2000), pp. 292–318. The authors also speak of "an interactive relationship between the management subsystems and the managing-for-results system."

5. Patricia W. Ingraham, Philip G. Joyce, and Amy K. Donahue, *Government Performance: Why Management Matters* (Baltimore: Johns Hopkins University Press, 2003).

CHAPTER 8

Learning to Build Capacity

Applying the GPP Model to Other Governments

DALE JONES AND DANA MICHAEL HARSELL

The Government Performance Project offered public officials an academic perspective on capacity building with practical applications. Originally, the GPP was designed to leave the most prevalent bodies of government—municipalities and townships—unaddressed owing to constraints on staffing, finances, and time. But these groups encompass critical—and numerous—governments. The U.S. Census Bureau identifies 35,937 municipality- and township-level government entities in the United States.[1] These government entities are often the first point of access for citizens and are responsible for coordinating most of the public services with which citizens are familiar.

In 2000 the GPP city grades caught the attention of New Jersey governor Christine Todd Whitman and New Jersey commissioner of community affairs Jane Kenny. The two asked the GPP to consider evaluating New Jersey municipalities. As a result, the GPP expanded its focus to municipalities and townships.

A new iteration of the GPP became known as the New Jersey Initiative, (NJI). This study of New Jersey municipalities provided GPP researchers a number of opportunities, not the least of which was to advance management practices throughout the state of New Jersey. The initiative also afforded the GPP opportunities to fill a gap in its own research and to assess the transportability of its methodology. A full explanation of the NJI's background, methodology, and findings are available in *The New Jersey Initiative: Building Management Capacity in New Jersey Municipalities.*[2] This chapter provides an overview of the final report and, more important, contributes to the GPP legacy by reflecting on the application of the framework to municipality-level governments.[3] The experiences and lessons learned from the NJI can serve as both a management tool for leaders in municipal governments and a learning and assessment tool for researchers.

Context of the New Jersey Initiative

The New Jersey Initiative applied the GPP model and its methodologies to analyze seven urban and suburban municipalities and their management capacities. After careful deliberation among the NJI researchers at Syracuse University's Maxwell School of Citizenship and Public Affairs, their partners at the Eagleton Institute of Politics at Rutgers University, the NJI advisory committee, and officials in the New Jersey Department of Community Affairs, Maxwell researchers invited leaders in ten municipal governments to participate. Leaders of seven voluntarily agreed to participate: the townships of Brick, Franklin, Irvington, and Old Bridge and the cities of Elizabeth, Paterson, and Trenton. These municipalities are among the twenty-five largest in population of all municipalities in New Jersey. Three of them are suburban and four are urban. Three of the four urban municipalities are categorized as fiscally distressed, according to the New Jersey Department of Community Affairs (see table 8.1). Thus the NJI included a variety of cities and townships in the study.

Researchers conducted criteria-based assessments to analyze the management capacity of the same five central management system areas as the GPP: financial management, capital management, human resource management, information technology management, and managing for results. Although the New Jersey Initiative operated under the same theoretical management capacity framework as the GPP, its data collection procedures were modified to fit the realities of municipality-level management. For

Table 8.1. Characteristics of Municipalities in the New Jersey Initiative, 2000

Municipality	County	Population	Density[a]	Descriptor
Brick Township	Ocean	76,119	2,902	Developing suburban
Elizabeth City	Union	120,568	9,866	Urban
Franklin Township	Somerset	50,903	1,088	Mature suburban
Irvington Township	Essex	60,695	20,528	Urban distressed
Old Bridge Township	Middlesex	60,456	1,587	Mature suburba
Paterson City	Passaic	149,222	17,675	Urban distressed
Trenton City	Mercer	85,403	11,154	Urban distressed

Sources: U.S. Census Bureau, 2000 Census; *2001 New Jersey Legislative District Data Book,* Center for Government Services, Edward J. Bloustein School of Planning and Public Policy, Rutgers, State University of New Jersey; New Jersey Department of Community Affairs.
[a]Persons per square mile

instance, feedback from GPP states and cities demonstrated the enormous commitment of human capital required to complete GPP questionnaires and fulfill requests for supporting public documents. In the early stages of the NJI project, researchers became aware that these municipal governments lacked the staffing and resources to accommodate such large-scale requests. Therefore, three of the five survey instruments were reduced in scope and modified to better assess management capacity in local government. For the financial management, capital management, and managing for results areas, survey instruments were replaced by questionnaires with in-depth, open-ended, semistructured questions. However, all five management teams also conducted in-depth interviews with municipal officials.

In many ways, the NJI process relied on building partnerships between researchers and municipal leaders. The yearlong study included three seminars to keep municipalities informed and to maintain a dialogue between NJI researchers and municipal officials. Researchers also responded to municipal officials' many concerns during these seminars, which helped to abate reservations and skepticism about the intense data collection process. Furthermore, the NJI did not grade the municipalities, as the GPP had done. This allowed researchers to provide a more in-depth assessment of management capacity for each of the seven municipalities. For a comprehensive outline of the NJI criteria and findings, see the appendix to this chapter.

The NJI modifications to the original GPP framework offer insight into the unique challenges students and scholars of local government may face when conducting research at the local level. Arguably, the political process at the municipal and township levels differs considerably from its city, county, and state counterparts. Many of these differences exist because the rules of the political game are different at this level of government.[4]

Certain characteristics of municipal governance can partly explain these differences. For instance, the proximity of municipal governance to its constituents places an emphasis on quality-of-life issues, which can be divisive and are not readily amenable to compromise.[5] Additionally, municipal governments have fewer financial resources at their disposal and their management capacities are generally less sophisticated than their state- and federal-level counterparts.[6]

Municipal governments are also more proximate to political participation than other levels of government, and citizen-initiated contacts with local government officials represent a significant form of participation within the municipal government context.[7] These contacts create an ethic of governance on demand at the municipal level.[8] As a consequence, citizens are more likely to contact municipal officials directly regarding parochial concerns, which can place a significant burden on municipal bureaucracies.

Constraints on Municipal Management

All democratic governments operate within a set of constraints, and local governments are no exception. Particularly because these governments receive—or in some cases, do not receive—funding from the state and county, the municipal agenda is often mandated by a higher power. Although there is a definite indication that municipal officials support and try to foster many of the best practices linked to the five management areas, NJI municipal officials expressed frustration over a number of constraints that impede their ability to carry out the necessary reforms to make improvements and build capacity in the five management areas.

Scarcity of Resources

The most frequently reported constraints were lack of financial and human capital resources. Municipal officials believed that the lack of available resources and the torrent of citizen-initiated contacts diverted attention from proper municipal management toward simply meeting daily needs. One municipal official characterized this daily routine as "management by crisis," and another as "constantly putting out fires." Their responses describe a common problem in government: accommodating excessive short-term constituent demands produces long-term government inefficiencies. One municipal official commented that this management style shifted the role of his administration from stewardship of the public trust to mere delegation.

The scarcity of resources also affected human resource management. For instance, municipal officials noted that the inability to hire "expertise" hinders planning or grant seeking for internal infrastructure upgrades. Municipalities simply cannot afford the level of expertise required to oversee long-term operations or maintenance of upgrades. Indeed, much of the managing-for-results strategic planning systems require intensive initial investments of labor for training and information systems upgrades. Additionally, the expertise needed to upgrade information technology infrastructure is often obtained by contracting. Although contracting out may realize short-term monetary savings for these municipal governments, it does so at the expense of long-term internal capacity building and human capital investment.

Turf Wars

The predominant type of local government home rule in New Jersey is the council-mayor form, which contributes to a weak central administrative function with decentralized operating departments. The business administrator serves at the pleasure of the mayor and oversees central administrative functions, but he or she may have limited central authority to fully manage departments. Consequently, business administrators have difficulty establishing accountability or setting municipality-wide priorities.[9]

Thus municipal officials are often caught in the middle of turf wars between the mayor and the council, which often frustrate long-term municipal planning. Indeed, many municipal officials reported that turf wars hinder efforts to build capacity in these five management areas, since the mayor, department heads, and members of the council often disagree on the most appropriate goals for municipal policy direction.

Turf wars proved especially problematic in the context of the managing-for-results management subsystem, with its emphasis on performance measurement. Developing performance metrics and determining which outputs and outcomes to measure can be particularly divisive in municipal governments, where financial and human capital are already in scarce supply, particularly since the benefits of gathering performance data may not be fully realized for many budget cycles. Turf wars also affect capacity building in capital and financial management, since the allocation of resources within the budgetary process is so politicized. Indeed, municipal officials spoke of epic battles between the mayor and the council and provided accounts of department heads' breaking ranks by dealing with the council directly regarding their programs.

Labor Unions and Organized Interests

Municipal officials characterized labor unions and other interests as a constraint on reforming municipal management. The seven municipal governments assessed by the New Jersey Initiative are highly unionized. At the time of our study, the number of union contracts ranged from five in Brick to fourteen in Elizabeth, and the proportion of the workforce that was unionized ranged from 80 percent in Old Bridge to 96 percent in Franklin. One municipal official noted that new mayoral administrations often inherit strict union contracts and that the frequency of negotiating union contracts made long-term planning difficult, especially with budgetary matters. In one positive step, Trenton now aggressively negotiates long-term union contracts—up to five years in some cases. Municipal officials from Trenton felt that this gave them a better understanding of Trenton's long-term fiscal situation and may better facilitate efforts toward long-term strategic planning.

Civil Service Rules

Of the seven municipalities studied, five participate in the state merit system (Title 11A). The human resource management team found that strict state civil service rules and regulations hinder management capacity building by constraining the ability of municipal officials to place employees they deem qualified into the most appropriate job title and pay category. One municipal official also noted that the testing requirement and non-competitive salary ranges discourage many experienced individuals in the private sector from applying for municipal positions. Additionally, municipalities that operate under the state civil service system find it difficult to creatively enhance the selection process.[10] Although civil service–related constraints were most salient in the area of human resource management, they also inhibit the hiring of expertise needed to build capacity in the other four management areas.

Relations with External Government Entities

Finally, municipal officials characterized municipalities' relationships with other government entities as a constraint, especially in the areas of financial management and capital management. Political constraints from external governments reflect the sort of intergovernmental relations issues that are so prevalent in municipal politics, especially where state and federal monetary assistance is concerned. For instance, the governments of the three municipalities in the NJI identified as fiscally distressed must comply with many more state mandates and have less fiscal maneuverability than other New Jersey municipalities. Additionally, these municipalities must seek state approval for many of their vital hiring and program functions.

Constraints from external government entities were most pronounced in the areas of financial and capital management. Indeed, the state exerts a high degree of control over capital and financial management in municipal governments. The capital and financial management teams found that New Jersey has an elaborate body of local finance law—especially in municipal budget approval procedures, investment guidelines, and reporting and auditing procedures. While these controls were set up to purge corruption in municipal governments, municipal officials assert that these controls contribute to a highly regulated and rigid environment that values and emphasizes procedural compliance over efficient and effective financial or capital management. Although state officials may not consider these regulations to be excessively invasive or demanding, municipal officials felt that the many regulatory constraints greatly inhibit both financial and capital expenditure decision making.[11]

Application of the New Jersey Initiative to the Government Performance Project

The experience of the New Jersey Initiative afforded the GPP an opportunity to reflect on its framework and analytic methods. Overall, four major findings emerged through the study of the Garden State municipalities from across all management areas.

- State regulatory and procedural restraints impede local government management innovation.
- In its regulatory management oversight role, the state does not sufficiently differentiate among municipalities in terms of their characteristics and performance.
- Municipalities lack formalized, centralized, and long-term management planning activities.
- Municipalities do not sufficiently exercise the management prerogatives available to them.

Although the NJI final report speaks directly to the relationship between the state of New Jersey and its municipalities, some aspects studied may serve as a microcosm for the kinds of issues that municipalities and townships are confronting across the country. If studies similar to the NJI were replicated in other municipalities and townships, the findings would most likely reveal distinctions and commonalities between state and municipal governments. In the context of this book, though, the more useful question to ask is not what recommendations can be made to the state and the municipalities but rather what recommendations can be made to academics and researchers as they study these government entities. Beyond the NJI findings and recommendations, there exists a broader picture of what can be learned from conducting a study that uses a framework similar to that of the GPP.

One overarching theme encapsulates the lessons learned from the NJI: Comprehensive assessment of management capacity is more challenging in highly politicized and regulated environments. While it is true that politics occurs at all levels of government, politics tends to be more pervasive at the local level. New Jersey Initiative researchers discovered that the line between politics and administration was more blurred in municipal governments than in state, county, and large city governments.

This finding was anticipated; thus adjustments were made accordingly to the original GPP methodology. Candidate municipalities attended an introductory seminar to gain full understanding of the research process and expectations. This initial step was not conducted for other GPP studies but was important for the NJI in order to foster trust and build relationships between the NJI researchers and government officials. Project leaders kept the participating municipalities informed of their progress through memoranda and a series of seminars. Throughout the project, researchers made decisions and communicated in ways that were intended to allay municipality concerns. For example, during the early stages of the project, NJI leaders decided that a narrative report would provide a more constructive way of communicating results than assigning traditional letter grades. Additionally, researchers were keenly aware of the intense political environment in which NJI participants worked, and research teams made every effort to protect and maintain the confidentiality of NJI participants.

Despite these early attempts to abate municipalities' concerns, officials expressed political concerns during the entire life of the project. One mayor chose to opt out of the project, partly because he was facing reelection during the period of study and did not want to take the chance that the project's findings might affect his reelection. Among those municipalities in the project, it was common for business administrators and chief financial officers to make statements reflecting a desire to "protect" their mayors and council members from any negative fallout from the project. A third example illustrates how municipalities were cautious participants, why they were reluctant to submit data, and their concerns about political matters. At the interim seminar midway through the project, more than one municipal official articulated significant reservations about the identification of municipalities in the final report. Participants made it clear that they did not want the names of their municipal governments to appear if management capacity was judged to be poor in any of the five management system areas. Researchers resolved this concern by guaranteeing their earlier policy of confidentiality to municipal officials. Furthermore, researchers maintained that it was also important to highlight municipal governments that performed well or demonstrated innovation in any of these management areas. Therefore, researchers wrote the final report in ways that exemplified municipalities when results were positive and used relative anonymity when results were not good.

Given the highly politicized environment, it is not surprising that municipalities were cautious participants in the project. Researchers worked to build trust with the municipalities and practiced open communication. Nevertheless, even after the municipalities agreed to participate in the study, they were cautious in terms of interacting with the project. For example, among the original set of invitees, one mayor was confident that his municipality would participate. However, after attending the introductory seminar, that mayor did not return telephone calls to officially commit as a project participant. In another case, the business administrator in one municipality did most of the talking during the financial management interview, even though the chief financial officer was present. Municipal officials even expressed concern about how the interview transcripts would be used. Fortunately, after receiving assurances from researchers that information would be treated confidentially, most interviewees were forthcoming during the interviews. Although a few state, county, and large city governments in the GPP also displayed some degree of cautiousness, the smaller municipal governments tended to be more guarded.

Throughout the process of conducting the study, researchers observed an ongoing tension between municipal officials and state government officials. To a large extent, state financial management and civil service legal requirements drive this tension. The existence of an "us versus them" attitude does not typically give rise to good governance. This may be partly a reflection of the state's higher level of oversight of those municipalities in the Distressed Cities Program. Another contributing factor may be that the higher-performing municipalities feel frustrated by the state's "one size fits all" oversight approach. Regardless of the reasons, researchers noticed disagreements over policy, mistrust, disdainful comments, and an arms-length relationship between the municipalities and the state. However, at all times both parties maintained a professional demeanor.

In this highly politicized setting, with municipal officials guarded about their involvement, it is not surprising that municipalities provided less data than researchers requested. Since they were apprehensive about providing "inside information" and somewhat nervous about how that information might be used, officials were generally slow in submitting documents and completing surveys and questionnaires. It was noted at the introductory seminar that some of the municipalities felt overwhelmed by the size of the financial management and human resource management surveys. Consequently, the capital management, information technology management, and managing-for-results teams modified their data collection efforts, relying on questionnaires and interviews. Unfortunately, in some cases, the surveys and questionnaires were answered briefly or not at all. This poor reporting of information appeared to reflect a shortage of personnel and a reluctance to assign limited human resources to the task of responding to surveys and questionnaires. Although researchers were often told of large quantities of performance data that were compiled and distributed to council members in some municipalities, efforts to obtain examples of these documents were unsuccessful.

It was also unclear to what extent, if at all, these documents were publicly available. In one municipal government, two researchers were given permission to remove public documents from the premises to photocopy, but only after explaining the NJI project to a municipal employee. The researchers were told that it was typical to charge fifty cents a page for photocopies of public documents—a cost that could be prohibitive for citizens interested in obtaining any large public documents. Of course, minimal staff in some municipalities also may have contributed to some of these problems. Although acquiring sufficient data was a matter of concern in a few cases for the Government Performance Project (and it can be a challenge in any study), the problem was more pronounced for the New Jersey Initiative.

Finally, the NJI learned that having a project partner within the state is highly beneficial for project success. In dealing with the conditions explained above—excessive political concerns, cautious participation, constant tensions, and insufficient data flow—the NJI grantee institution benefited from having a partner institution located in the same state as the municipalities in the study. The Eagleton Institute of Politics at Rutgers University proved to be a critical asset to the Maxwell School of Syracuse University. The Eagleton Institute contributed its expertise on New

Jersey politics and government, established the New Jersey Initiative Advisory Committee and recruited its members, developed a positive relationship with the municipalities and the state, helped to build trust and cooperation from the municipalities, served as a liaison between municipal officials and Maxwell School researchers, and hosted project meetings and municipality seminars. The teamwork between Maxwell and Eagleton permitted successful completion of the project.

It should be noted, however, that occasionally other interests would surface from the Eagleton Institute Advisory Committee members, and even state officials in the New Jersey Department of Community Affairs. At times, these entities attempted to influence the "spin" of the final report. Although Maxwell School researchers invited, welcomed, and used some constructive feedback from these groups on the draft final report, they retained final editorial privilege. The lesson learned is that while project partners provide valuable assistance, an investment of time and energy is required to manage the relationships among partners.

Conclusions from the New Jersey Initiative Study

As is often true, hindsight provided great clarity in considering the application of the GPP framework to these municipal settings. Themes familiar to the GPP state, county, and city studies emerged in the New Jersey study. However, many challenges of local governments are more pronounced, since they are subject to the constraints of the county, state, and federal governments and operate on a level that is much closer to its citizens. The municipal government perspectives offered through the NJI are indicative of the many challenges facing local governments nationwide. With a greater understanding of these challenges, creative and comprehensive solutions can be developed to enhance management practices at the municipal and township level.

In terms of the Government Performance Project itself, the NJI provided an opportunity to reexamine the analytical framework. We found that a process that was successfully applied to states, counties, and cities needed to be modified to better fit the municipality context. This is likely to occur in other small settings, as well. The NJI experience, with methodological modification and reduction, can serve as an important guide here. Knowing these differences, can it be said that the GPP methodology is transportable to municipal government settings? Based on the findings of this pilot study of municipality-level governments, the answer is yes, for both its analysis of municipality-level governments and the practical application of its findings and recommendations. But it is transportable only insofar as researchers are able to solicit cooperation and enter partnerships with government officials during the analysis, and to the extent that municipal officials are committed to building management capacity—and have the authority to do so—at that level of government.

To what extent the municipal governments analyzed in New Jersey followed the recommendations of the NJI final report—or were able to—is unclear. The governments lacked the central authority to make many of the recommended changes on their own and needed to actively partner with the state to build management systems and capacity. At the same time, the relationship between the municipalities and the state through the course of the NJI study was generally less than positive. The local governments have little flexibility to operate in innovative ways and are heavily constrained by the pervasive political and regulatory environment that exists in the state of New Jersey. The politics of local government can also inhibit the development of management capacity.

Therefore, it was the conclusion of the NJI researchers that municipality-level capacity building in such a context can best be accomplished through a series of reforms and actions intended to increase collaboration between municipal governments and the state. Chief among these reforms for municipal governments are regulatory relief, innovative actions, implementation of best practices from other locales, and prudent risk taking. Paradoxically, some level of fundamental capacity must exist in local governments for these additional capacity-building steps to occur. It may well be that this initial step will require dramatic movement away from the status quo, with more gradual changes taking place once basic capacity has been created.

APPENDIX

Criteria and Findings of the New Jersey Initiative

Financial Management Results

Criterion 1: Municipality has a multiyear perspective on budgeting.
Finding 1a: There is an absence of a long-term perspective and planning for budgeting.
Finding 1b: Budgets are prepared for the current year only.

Criterion 2: Municipality has mechanisms that preserve stability and fiscal health.
Finding 2a: Some municipalities have excessively outdated property valuations that cause inequity in taxation and result in reduced financial resources.
Finding 2b: Tax collection rates in some urban municipalities are far too low, at approximately 85 percent.
Finding 2c: Municipalities have inadequate cash management because they are prohibited from making long-term investments and are constrained in short-term investment options.

Criterion 3: Sufficient financial information is available to policy makers, managers, and citizens.
Finding 3a: Most municipalities submit their audited annual financial statements after the mandated six-month time frame.
Finding 3b: Budgets are often adopted late.

Criterion 4: Municipality has appropriate control over financial operations.
Finding 4a: The municipal debt limit set by the state hinders municipal flexibility, and municipalities are circumventing current debt limitations.
Finding 4b: The expenditure cap law for municipalities impedes their flexibility in satisfying taxpayers' service demands, particularly in fast-growing municipalities.

Capital Management Results

Criterion 1: Municipality conducts a thorough capital planning process.
Finding 1a: Municipalities complete a six-year capital improvements plan; however, the plans do not include detailed project descriptions and justifications, descriptions of the planning process, overall summaries of the plan, or glossaries of terms that would make them informative, user-friendly documents for the public.
Finding 1b: There is little or no formal opportunity for citizen input on capital plans.

Criterion 2: Municipality monitors and evaluates projects throughout the implementation process.
Finding 2: The municipalities vary with regard to whether they monitor projects and whether they prepare and distribute regular tracking reports.

Criterion 3: Municipality ensures the adequate and appropriate maintenance of capital assets.
Finding 3a: Generally, useful data for asset maintenance are not available in the municipalities.
Finding 3b: Municipalities use fixed asset inventories for accounting purposes, but they do not use them for maintenance purposes.
Finding 3c: Municipalities do not perform regular condition assessments, nor do they keep or report ongoing records of asset condition outside the responsible departments.

Human Resource Management Results

Criterion 1: Municipality conducts strategic analysis of present and future human resources needs.

Finding 1a: Municipalities focus little systemic, centralized effort on planning for future workforce needs and labor availability.

Finding 1b: The availability of data and an infrastructure to support data access and analysis are severely limited in the municipalities.

Criterion 2: Municipality is able to obtain the employees it needs.

Finding 2a: Clear distinctions in the selection process emerged between civil service and non–civil service municipalities. Civil service municipalities appoint employees provisionally and use more testing.

Finding 2b: Most selection processes are centralized, with responsibility being granted to the state, municipal administration, or central human resources staff.

Finding 2c: Residency requirements constrain the selection process.

Finding 2d: Recruiting efforts and innovations are limited.

Finding 2e: Perceptions of the quality of hires do not vary between civil service and non–civil service municipalities.

Criterion 3: Municipality is able to maintain an appropriately skilled workforce.

Finding 3a: Career opportunities are typically limited to an employee's current department.

Finding 3b: Training opportunities beyond those required for state certification are limited.

Finding 3c: State government most often provides supervisory and management training, and the central human resource management division most often provides computer training and orientation.

Finding 3d: Municipalities offer education incentives, including tuition reimbursements and increased pay.

Finding 3e: Turnover is low.

Finding 3f: Disciplinary processes are labor intensive and inflexible.

Criterion 4: Municipality is able to motivate employees to perform effectively in support of the municipality's goals.

Finding 4a: There is little formal opportunity to provide performance-related feedback to employees and little effort to solicit feedback from employees.

Finding 4b: There is no effort to link performance and rewards.

Finding 4c: Reward systems encourage employee longevity.

Finding 4d: There is little use of nonmonetary rewards to recognize outstanding performers.

Finding 4e: Municipalities offer excellent benefits.

Criterion 5: Municipality has a human resource management structure that supports its ability to achieve its workforce goals.

Finding 5a: The classification systems are a source of frustration.

Finding 5b: Labor-management partnerships are starting to be used.

Information Technology Management Results

Criterion 1: Municipality conducts strategic analysis of present and future information technology needs (planning capacity).

Finding 1a: All municipalities have at least some minimal IT planning embedded in their budget processes.

Finding 1b: Three municipalities have no formal IT planning process. One municipality had used formal planning to prepare and implement a large-scale capital upgrade to its network, but it currently ties planning to the annual budget process. One municipality characterizes its planning process as top-down, based on general directions coming from the business administrator but developed through a team effort. One municipality claims to have a five-year plan that is revised annually, but its implementation remains tied to the budget process. One municipality identified the use of a multiyear plan implemented through monthly committee meetings. One municipality indicated it has two planning processes—one to manage plans for public safety and the other to manage plans for the general public.

Finding 1c: Few of the municipalities have long-term planning capacity oriented toward the next major cycle of infrastructure updating.

Criterion 2: Municipality obtains IT infrastructure as needed (capital procurement and maintenance capacity).

Finding 2a: Municipalities use three distinct strategies for large-scale capital purchases such as upgrading networks: capital bonds, grants from the federal and state governments, and internal funding of one-time operating budget expenditures.

Finding 2b: Upgrading the core infrastructure remains problematical for all the municipalities.

Finding 2c: Management of the hardware replacement process generally occurs through the budget process, with IT management oversight. However, functional department managers, with the exception of public safety, often do not make IT a priority.

Criterion 3: Municipality obtains software applications as needed (application development or procurement capacity).

Finding 3a: Only three municipalities maintain significant internal capacity to generate their own software applications, and they use the capacity to augment their application development.

Finding 3b: Municipalities mostly rely on vendors to provide software applications.

Criterion 4: Municipality adequately stores and retrieves data (data management capacity).

Finding 4a: In all the municipalities, the main orientation to data management is to establish applications for specific uses and users.

Finding 4b: In most of the municipalities, geographic information systems are the favored approach for creating integration across multiple applications; however, the governments are at the early stage of pursuing this technology.

Criterion 5: Municipality obtains and retains adequate IT human resources (IT human resource management capacity).
Finding 5a: The almost complete diffusion of office automation tools in the municipalities generates a large demand for training.
Finding 5b: In municipalities where IT applications are developed internally, both the IT departments and the functional departments that use the applications have training responsibilities.
Finding 5c: Vendors are used heavily in the provision of training both for municipalities that rely exclusively on vendor-provided software and for municipalities that develop applications internally but also buy software from vendors.

Criterion 6: Municipality reliably operates and maintains IT systems (systems management and maintenance capacity).
Finding 6a: The three basic models for operations found in the municipalities are client server systems, departmental computing, and contracted services. To some extent, all the municipalities use both client server approaches and departmental systems approaches.
Finding 6b: Two municipalities contract out for central data-processing and maintenance activities, although they also have their own wide-area network for office automation.
Finding 6c: There is a strong correlation between those municipalities with strong IT leadership (most commonly from business administrators or financial directors) and those with internal application development capacity (including the capacity to operate and maintain the locally developed IT applications).

Managing for Results

Criterion 1: Municipality engages in results-oriented strategic planning.
Finding 1a: Leadership vision exists in all the municipalities.
Finding 1b: None of the municipalities has a formal, unified, stand-alone, comprehensive, municipality-wide strategic plan.
Finding 1c: Department-level strategic plans are rare. The city of Trenton is the only municipality that requires its departments to have strategic plans.

Criterion 2: Municipality develops indicators and evaluative data that can measure progress toward results and accomplishments.
Finding 2: Performance measures are basic.

Criterion 3: Municipality leaders and managers use results data for policy making, management, and evaluation of progress.
Finding 3: Use of performance data is minimal.

Criterion 4: Municipality clearly communicates the results of its activities to stakeholders.
Finding 4: Communication with stakeholders occurs through a number of means, but municipalities generally do not communicate results information.

NOTES

1. U.S. Census Bureau, Bureau of the Census, *U.S. Census of Governments: Government Units in 2002,* GC02-1 (P), 2002, www.census.gov/govs/cog/2002 COGprelim_report.pdf.

2. New Jersey Initiative, *The New Jersey Initiative: Building Management Capacity in New Jersey Municipalities* (Syracuse, NY: Alan K. Campbell Public Affairs Institute, 2002).

3. This chapter includes New Jersey Initiative project results from research conducted by faculty experts Stuart Bretschneider (information technology management), Amy Kneedler Donahue (public management), Carol Ebdon (capital management), Yilin Hou (financial management), Dale Jones (managing for results), and Sally Coleman Selden (human resource management); capital management project consultants Connie Bawcum, Max Bohnstedt, and Suzette Denslow, from the National Academy of Public Administration; and research associates Dana Michael Harsell (managing for results), Willow Jacobson (human resource management), Ora-orn Poocharoen (managing for results), and Yonghong Wu (financial management). Faculty experts and research associates are associated with the Maxwell School of Citizenship and Public Affairs at Syracuse University. The National Academy of Public Administration provided financial support and the expertise of its capital management team.

4. Lawrence J. R. Herson and John M. Bollard, *The Urban Web: Politics, Policy, and Theory* (Chicago: Nelson-Hall, 1998).

5. Ibid.

6. See Theodore H. Poister and Gregory Streib, "Performance Measurement in Municipal Government: Assessing the State of the Practice," *Public Administration Review* 59, no. 4 (1999): 325–35.

7. Michael W. Hirlinger, "Citizen-Initiated Contacting of Local Government Officials: A Multivariate Explanation," *Journal of Politics* 54, no. 2 (1992): 553–64.

8. Ibid.

9. For more information, see *The New Jersey Initiative: Building Management Capacity in New Jersey Municipalities,* chap. 3.

10. For more information, see ibid., chap. 4.

11. For more information, see ibid., chaps. 2 and 3.

CHAPTER 9

Counting the Ways Management Matters to Performance

PATRICIA W. INGRAHAM AND DONALD P. MOYNIHAN

Understanding state and local government management practices is a complex undertaking. Putting those practices in the context of government performance is even more difficult. For elected officials, citizens, and students of government, it may be hard to see the links between better management and better trash service, for example. Increasingly, however, both research and practical experience point to the multidimensional nature of performance in government—and to the importance of management capability in many elements of performance. As the chapters in this book demonstrate, the complexity of management in state and local government adds to the difficulty of establishing clear links between management and performance.

Over the past twenty years, state and local governments were catapulted from the good times of the technology boom and strong economies to the more harsh realities of the dot-com bust and post-9/11 difficulties. Problems of looming deficits and program limitations forced more intense consideration of program results and of better ways of managing resources. As noted in chapter 6, governments that had turned away from managing for results and other evaluation efforts turned back to them.

Even when resource constraints became less pronounced, demands for service continued to increase, and meeting citizen expectations continued to be difficult. Public managers and elected officials searched for tools and policy instruments that were not only within their control but also held promise of leading to better results. Management systems were one likely candidate. The criteria-based approach used by the Government Performance Project, analyses of state and local government service delivery, and other assessment activities contributed to a growing agreement about what good management is and how it is practiced.

The Many Paths to Performance

The preceding chapters present the management choices state and local governments make in rich detail. They contain lessons about levels of government, about the management systems studied, and about linking management capacity to broader issues of performance. There are also lessons about the Government Performance Project itself and the methodologies it employed to study state and local governments. Underpinning these common lessons, however, is extensive variation both across and within governments. The governments studied here chose a variety of paths to what they considered to be effective management. Some governments pursuing higher levels of effectiveness believed that strength in several systems provided the best path. The better-managed governments described in this book focused on three or more of the management systems studied; only the very best focused on all five.

It is important to note, however, that state and local governments were pursuing similar objectives, albeit in different ways. Some of the cities we analyzed, for example, did not emphasize strategic planning and assessment in their management plans and activities, but they focused on strategic goal setting through careful budgets and budgetary processes. Some governments devised specific plans for soliciting citizen input about goals and priorities and for communicating results to citizens. Others relied only on speeches by public officials, but attempted therein to convey the same information contained in the more elaborate plans. All the governments studied coped with the common problem of limited planning horizons implicit in the short election and budget cycles that frame the work of elected and appointed officials. This deficit is noted by every author in this volume and for every system studied.

Management Systems and Performance

In the state and local governments studied by the GPP, all but the lowest-capacity governments were cognizant of and committed to the idea of good management as a link to performance. For the most well managed cities, counties, and states, this was evident in the overall design of their management systems. Accountability standards were clear; specific goals and objectives had been established. When problems existed, there was a strategy for moving toward a remedy. For governments that did not do so well, efforts to deal with consistently recurring problems were a notable drain on time and resources. In these cases, the most fundamental steps—assembling better information about infrastructure assets, future workforce needs, or better ways of using information technology—had not been taken. The governments that did very well in GPP analyses—Yilin Hou cites Utah in chapter 2, for example—engaged in consistent searches for better ways of doing business. In fact, the governments with the highest grades were among the most avid consumers of information about how other governments pursued good management. Only the governments that fell in the lowest grade range were stagnant in this regard.

The experience of the governments that fell into the large middle category of the governments studied here—those that had B grades from the GPP—also provided important strategic lessons about priorities among management systems. Each of these governments did a very good job in one or more of the systems studied. But for various reasons, many had chosen to emphasize one or two but not all of the systems. Hou's analysis demonstrates that financial management systems were most often given the highest priority. They were also the management systems in which most governments did best. In cases such as Virginia, financial management systems were the driver for excellence in other management activities. They were viewed as the foundation upon which other excellent systems could be based. In other settings, budgets became de facto strategic planning mechanisms and communications tools. In still others, both officials and citizens viewed the budgetary process as a key means of informing citizens about government activities and inviting their participation in setting future priorities.

The governments that received a grade of C or lower also provide important lessons, but these lessons are most often about the extent to which environmental or legal constraints have an impact on government's ability to build capacity in management. Overhead controls created by state civil service systems (discussed in chapter 4), for example, seriously limit governments' capacity to tailor workforce abilities to emergent needs. The absence of clear purpose and leadership in lower-graded governments was also a frequent characteristic. "No one," lamented a manager in one of these governments, "is willing to take responsibility."

In some rare instances, new leaders of low-capacity governments drew attention to management failures to call for future change. The results were mixed. In Washington, D.C., the "reformer" mayor, Anthony Washington, sought to build management systems that valued performance, customer service, and participation but encountered both political and managerial problems in implementation.[1] Other governments struggled to overcome entrenched traditions as well as unfavorable environmental influences. In Alabama, efforts to introduce performance budgeting and results-based management floundered on the cynicism arising from the failures of similar reforms in the past and on Alabama's inadequate and confusing resource allocation system.[2] On the other hand, some newly elected officials in counties and other local governments that did not do well publicly committed themselves to continued efforts to improve, and, as Donald Moynihan notes in chapter 6, many management reforms continue to surface regularly if they do not take hold the first time. The benefit of trying again is demonstrated by Hou's observation in chapter 2: a government that is able to accurately forecast revenues and expenditures, and to use good economic times to prepare for bad, is much more likely to have policy and program choices in the future. Officials and managers who plan are more likely to be able to steer the ship of state. That outcome is hard to ignore for both citizens and elected officials and is an incentive to try again.

The findings in the preceding chapters also point to the impact of environmental and political conditions. Again, financial management provides a relevant example. Quite aside from the fact that the budget is a profoundly political document, state and local budgets are significantly affected by decisions made at other levels of government and by the courts. Unfunded mandates for social services and other activities are likely to destabilize state and local budgets for years. The tobacco money windfall—at first too good to be true, then a readily available crutch to survive economic downturns, then possibly not there at all—provides another example of the ease with which even a solid financial management system can be derailed. More recent analyses of state revenue growth also document the swings that budgets encounter. The Rockefeller Institute reported that state revenue growth for the first part of 2005 was the strongest since 1991, growing 11.7 percent. That success followed abruptly on the sharp downturns that occurred after September 11, 2001.[3]

The analyses in the preceding chapters also demonstrate great variation in the ability of governments to change in order to create capacity. A common view of bureaucratic organizations, governmental or not, is that they resist change, or are at least very slow to change. The pace of change in managing-for-results systems is generally slow, as chapter 6 notes. Managing for results has gone through numerous iterations in many settings and continues to do so, but in some states, it seems not to have passed stage one:

systems are "on the books" but show little evidence of actual implementation. Carol Ebdon, in chapter 3, strikes the same note in terms of capital management systems. She observes that, with time frames of five to ten years, these systems exhibit even less nimble behavior than other systems and in most cases change very slowly.

Information technology and human resource management systems, however, can tell a different story. For IT, the perception that the new century would stimulate a crisis caused most organizations to pay specific attention to the qualities and capacities of information technology. In chapter 5, B. J. Reed, Lyn Holley, and Donna Dufner argue that "Y2K riveted the attention of elected officials everywhere to the need to prepare legacy systems for the turn of the century." Governments took new notice of the role that IT played in ongoing operations and used the opportunity to upgrade, integrate, and more carefully coordinate their systems. Y2K created a deadline and a sense that any failure to act would be costly—perhaps catastrophic. Governments met the deadline and moved ahead. One outcome was a proliferation of chief information officers, whose presence is intended to allow governments to be better prepared for IT crises in the future. Chapter 5 also demonstrates, however, that as the crisis passed, so did priority attention to information technology. As a result, a great deal of work remains to be done in building IT capacity in state and local government.

Oddly, human resource management provides lessons about both slow and swift change. Many state civil service systems are grounded in statute, complex history, and the omnipresent shadow of political patronage. States have designed a disparate set of systems, from highly decentralized to central hierarchies. The latter, especially, are sharply defined by bureaucratic constructs and control and change slowly and incrementally. There are instances of dramatic change, however. Two states—Georgia and Florida—were so dissatisfied with the performance of their state civil service systems that they abolished them and created a fundamentally different design for managing state personnel. In both states, the change was rapid. Also in both cases, there was strong external impetus for the change that occurred: in the case of Georgia, gubernatorial dissatisfaction with the existing system led to speedy consideration of alternatives and rapid adoption of major change. In the case of Florida, while the governor's dissatisfaction was also a factor, intensive lobbying by an elite group of businessmen was a catalytic force. In both cases, improved public performance was the anticipated outcome. When the Pew Centers conducted a new round of GPP analysis in 2005, Georgia was rated among the top-capacity governments for human resource management.

Lessons about centralization and decentralization also differ from system to system in state and local government, but human resource management continues to provide a useful example. In chapter 4, Sally Coleman Selden and Willow Jacobson document an initial "reform" move in state governments from highly centralized systems toward highly decentralized systems but then a move back to a more strategic balance. This balance is characterized by clear central guiding principles and objectives but also substantial flexibility and discretion for departments and agencies. The information technology story, at least to this point in history, is one of movement from great decentralization to a more centralized set of activities, most often characterized by the presence of a chief information officer to oversee procurement and future development.

There is no clear answer to whether centralized or decentralized systems work best. When Georgia created the new human resources system noted above, for example, it consciously chose a decentralized design. All the chapters in this book point to a similar, if rather ambivalent, conclusion about the benefits of centralization versus decentralization in developing effective management strategies: Some level of centralized information gathering is essential to good decision making and effective evaluation. Both efforts are also aided by a clear central or overarching purpose and set of principles. Beyond that, the choices that state and local governments make are very much guided by need and political setting. Most states reforming human resource management, for example, have moved away from the strongly centralized systems that civil service commissions represented. Most state and local governments reforming information technology, on the other hand, have moved toward centralization in terms of planning and acquisition. As in much else about government, it depends on the context.

Most of these lessons draw on two years' data from state governments, and we have referred repeatedly to state government examples throughout this chapter. There are also important lessons to be learned from exploring the comparative experience of county and city government, however, and we devote the next two sections specifically to these levels of government. These descriptions rely on only one year's data and lessons drawn from them.

The Counties: 2001

The results of the assessment of county management systems reveal that counties, though providing an array of critical core public services to citizens, often lack the power and authority to appropriately address a full range of problems. This is most notable in areas such as social welfare and mental health, where higher-level policy changes and mandated service requirements have had a particularly harsh effect. Even counties that fared well in the GPP analysis, such as Fairfax County, Virginia, suffer from significant revenue-raising and allocation constraints and consequent policy limitations.

The county average grade of C+ was slightly lower than the average grades for cities and states. The leading counties in the GPP evaluation were Maricopa and Fairfax, both with an average grade of A−. Fairfax was the only county to receive an A or A− in every category. It is worth noting that both Fairfax and Maricopa (which surrounds Phoenix) are "reformed" counties with professional county managers who report to elected officials. Other counties that did relatively well, however, have other governmental forms, including elected county executives, and counties that fell to the bottom of the overall group also represent different management structures. In other words, not all "professionally managed" governments did well in the analysis, and not all "politically managed" governments did poorly. Some of both fell into both categories, though the highest-capacity city and county governments were reformed structures in which professional managers worked with elected officials.

Counties showed modest strength in financial management, with an average grade of B−. All but one county received the Government Finance Officers Association Certificate of Achievement for Excellence in Financial Reporting. On the other hand, only 15 percent of the counties had a legally required rainy-day fund, and nearly half did not take advantage of the bull market of the 1990s by pursuing long-term investments. Many noted that they did not do so because it was impossible to find an appropriate budget "cushion" for such investments (see chapter 2).

Human resource management was generally troublesome for counties; the average grade was C+. The absence of a unified county personnel system hampered the human resources efforts of many counties and often forced internal competition for potential employees. The tight job market of the 1990s caused many counties to reexamine their recruitment and merit pay policies, but overall, these governments lag behind others in creating change and greater flexibility in the area of human resource management, despite the centrality of their personnel in the actual delivery of critical services—social welfare and health, for example.

Many counties are making efforts to move toward greater coordination in programs and organizational structures, but the extremely decentralized nature of many county governments makes it difficult to implement unifying systems such as information technology. As in most other governments, different county offices or other levels of government use different IT systems that are not compatible with one another. In those counties that had the highest IT capacity, the analysis found technology-coordinating committees, strategic IT plans, frequent assessment of problems and potential solutions, and integrated procurement. Even in these cases, however, there was sometimes difficulty with databases that could not be accessed across agencies. Despite these difficulties, as Reed, Holley, and Dufner note in chapter 5, "the level of systems integration within functions . . . is higher in counties than at the state level."

Strategic planning, in the face of the decentralized functional arrangements often found in counties, faces many obstacles in county government. This is reflected somewhat in the average GPP managing-for-results grade of C+. Only 25 percent of the counties evaluated had formal countywide strategic plans at the time the GPP analysis was conducted. Budgets tend to be the primary vehicle for communicating county goals and results.

The Cities: 1999

The results for the thirty-five largest cities show a different set of patterns. Analysis of these cities underlines the profound variation present in city management—from the A of Phoenix, commonly recognized as one of the best-managed cities in the world, to the F of New Orleans, about which little else need be said. The difficulties of that city in responding to the demands of Hurricane Katrina demonstrate the very real impact that such lack of capacity can have. Many of the cities analyzed used Y2K as an opportunity to integrate information technology with other management systems and to align IT capacity with real decision needs. Furthermore, many cities are using Web sites and other interactive technology to communicate with citizens and to improve service delivery in significant ways.

Managing for results has a long history in large cities and also demonstrates innovations in strategic planning and in linking planning to results and measurement. Some cities are revitalizing older systems to refocus on performance. Others, such as Indianapolis, are applying MFR practices and measures to most city services and linking the results to budget consequences. Phoenix, San Antonio, and Austin have linked broad strategic objectives to budgets, agencies, and programs and have created clear measures for managing for results.

Human resource management is system in which some cities showed substantial strength, while many others demonstrated serious weakness. Eight of the thirty-five cities received a grade of B or higher for their human resources systems, reflecting both innovative approaches and a streamlining of civil service systems. High-capacity cities such as Austin, Phoenix, Minneapolis, and Denver have strong workforce planning strategies and flexible hiring practices. There are strong but balanced procedures for dismissing employees who are not performing well. At the same time, many cities, like counties, continue to be burdened by outdated laws, rules, and regulations, many of which are—again—determined by state law or by federal mandates.

Financial and capital management results were also mixed for the large cities. While most engaged in some form of long-term fiscal planning and forecasting (three to five years), the accuracy of the forecasts varied. There are many reasons for this: economic up and down turns, mandated expenses, and new collective bargaining agreements all have significant impacts on local budgets. Collective bargaining agreements for police, fire, and health care professionals were particularly troublesome in terms of budgetary strains. The combination of these fixed costs, coupled with necessary unfunded mandate spending, seriously limit options for other critical choices.

In financial management, cost accounting and contract management were the two major problem areas. Virtually all of the cities surveyed acknowledged the difficulties posed for both management and performance evaluation by burgeoning contracting-out activities and by collective bargaining agreements. For capital management, the overriding issue was the mismatch between maintenance needs and funds available for maintenance. Even in strong economic times, years of deferred expenses continued to take a toll. The impact of the choices made—and the cities that made them—can be shocking. Los Angeles, for example, so heavily dependent on roads and bridges for every aspect of daily life, estimated that they deferred as much as 70 percent of necessary road maintenance costs and had no plan for catching up.

At the same time, city governments are home to some of the most dramatic changes and efforts to change while also confronting enormous challenges. New York, Washington, and Detroit are leading examples. Washington and Detroit were both well behind the good management curve in the mid-1990s, and efforts to create and implement new systems have had mixed results. New York City is legendary for bouncing back again and again—most recently, after September 11, 2001—but each new bounce also encounters new challenges. In chapter 8 of this volume, Dale Jones and Dana Michael Harsell document the profound effects that constant change can have on the ability of local governments to get back on their feet and move ahead. As a result, management systems in some cities demonstrate patterns of frequent testing and change, the result of struggling to recover from dire circumstances. In Phoenix, on the other hand, changes occur most often in response to learning from other good governments and systems. The "we can do always do better" approach is a positive incentive for change in Phoenix and in other top-capacity governments.

Strong management capacity in the nation's largest cities is also linked to strong leadership. Effective management is unquestionably linked to the clear mission and vision for performance that effective leadership provides. Strong mayoral and professional leadership played an important role in each of the governments that received high grades for management. Mayoral leadership was also clearly evident in the cities trying hardest to turn themselves around. The absence of effective leadership was one of the clearest characteristics of cities that did not do well. The same is true of other levels of government. Overall, leadership emerged as a strongly consistent influence on high capacity across systems and across governments. This finding emerged despite the earlier decision, based on cautionary advice from experts and leading managers, to not specifically focus on leadership in the study. As noted in chapters 1 and 7, subsequent analysis of high- and low-capacity governments provided solid evidence of leadership's role, as did further content analysis of strategic documents and interviews.[4]

Analysis of the GPP data did not find consistent regional variations, political variations, or structural variations that appeared to be linked to the presence of high capacity, but leadership and a strategic vision or sense of purpose were always present in high-capacity governments. The absence of leadership was a consistent factor in the lowest-capacity governments at all levels and was evident in interviews, documentary analysis, and other external assessments.

Linking Capacity to Performance: The Black Box Revisited

At the end of this book, we return to one of the premises that prompted the analyses presented in it. To a great degree, the field of public administration is based on the assumption that the quality of public management is related to the performance of an organization. The appeal of the "management matters" adage, however, has masked a dearth of actual empirical evidence. This is in part because of the ambiguity of what public performance actually means and the challenge of quantifying its many dimensions. More troubling from a public perspective, the ambiguity has masked the difficulty of determining the overall effectiveness of government.

The GPP undertook the task of defining management capacity in some detail and collecting usable data about it, with the goal of prompting empirical examination of the theory that capacity leads to performance. Capacity was viewed as contributing to the potential for performance but not as performance itself—not, that is, as improved measures of service delivery or improved citizen satisfaction with government. A basic assumption in the conceptual model (see figure A.1 in appendix A to this volume) underpinning the criteria and analysis was that absent capacity, such performance was not likely to occur. Clearly, management is not the only component of government capacity necessary for performance. Just as clearly, however, basic common sense tells us that even in the best of other conditions, bad management will not be a positive influence on performance.

The simplicity of the proposed theory and the model was not intended to overlook environmental factors—politics, level of economic development, and demography—often the focus of books about state and local government. Researchers were aware of the real influence of such factors but saw the need to focus emphasis on the neglected management capacity variable. Unless this variable could be unpacked, the remainder of the endeavor was impossible. To rely on the black-box terminology common in evaluation and policy analysis, there would be nothing in the middle to serve as translator of resources to services.

Traditionally, the metaphor of the black box has assumed a neutral relationship of management to both policy choices and policy outcomes. The Government Performance Project fundamentally argued that what happened within the management components of government was not neutral and, further, that variations inside management systems could be unpacked and analyzed. The strategy of examining common management systems had the added advantage of enabling the use of standardized research tools and producing comparable results. The data collected, GPP analysts reasoned, could then be included in other analyses that assessed the impact of capacity on a variety of measures of performance, while controlling for appropriate environmental variables.

The GPP did not attempt to directly measure or grade integration of management systems, but it did make a further assumption that systems that "talked" to one another would be more effective than those that operated in isolation. The analysis looked for secondary evidence of this concept in interactions between the systems studied. However, in analyses conducted after the primary data collection had ended, analysts did not find strong evidence of either intention or practice in integrating human resource management systems with, for example, financial management or information technology systems, except at the county level. On the other hand, as chapter 7 demonstrates, there is limited support for the assumption. Some states showed associations between financial management and managing for results. The best-performing counties demonstrated patterns of integrating for purposes of tracking performance on a variety of measures; several also demonstrated a common-sense—but not universally present—pattern of integrating budget and financial management system information with other management systems. City data were not analyzed in relation to integration because of data deficiencies, so the pattern there is unknown.

Although the GPP did not directly measure leadership, in the analyses that followed data gathering, leadership—identified as an activity, not necessarily as personified in a single individual—emerged as a significant characteristic of those governments that were able to build high capacity in their management systems. While the GPP did not model data collection techniques to collect information on leadership from the three primary sources of data—the surveys, the document analyses, and the journalists' interviews—information about the role of leadership at all levels of government emerged from all three as well as from subsequent content analysis. The information came up most often in analyses of what the governments thought they needed to do and how they needed to do it. This was most frequently contained in budgetary documents and related information but was found as well in specific references in the surveys, strategic planning documents, and interviews.

Interestingly, however, in some of the cases in which leadership was most often mentioned by agency and department heads and by others, the leaders or leadership teams did not rely on formal strategic planning documentation. In Indianapolis, Milwaukee, Phoenix, Fairfax County, and other locations, there was an emphasis on strategic planning as a team-building and information-collecting process, not as preparing "credenza ware," as one staff member from Phoenix put it. As substantial evidence now emerging about the nature of collaboration reveals, early consensus about an organization's purposes and goals has an emphatic impact on the ability to actually achieve them. The "integrative leadership" described in chapter 7 and elsewhere in this book achieves that purpose through team building and consistent and focused communication.

As the above discussion implies, integrative leadership is team-based leadership. In each of the high-capacity cases, the "obvious" leader—most often, the top elected or appointed official—consistently referred to the other team members and relied heavily on them. Because electoral cycles rarely match implementation cycles, a leadership team was central to long-term implementation plans. The provision of such continuity came from another set of potential leaders, however—central agency officials. Central agency officials can shepherd management improvement proposals from one administration to the next, particularly when reforms are seen as bipartisan good government efforts or technical management exercises. The importance of central agencies as leaders increases where discontinuity of executive branch leadership is the norm. Governors in Virginia, limited to a single term, have come to depend on the Department of Planning and Budget, for example, as such a linking mechanism.

Getting the right mix of leaders and actions is important. Leadership is about both who is involved and how they act. Leaders frequently used managing for results as a system to reform government, arguing that decision makers should seek to use performance data. An analysis of these efforts found that different groups of leaders were important in different ways. The involvement of the governor in leading an MFR system encouraged other senior officials to take performance information seriously in making decisions. Active leadership by agency leaders was more important for encouraging agency-level managers to use performance information. Central agency officials could either encourage or discourage the use of managing for results. If they sought to use MFR as a means to control the policy agenda, senior officials were less likely to use performance information. If central agencies adopted the role of enablers of MFR, focusing on ensuring greater access to performance information, managers were more likely to use this data.[5]

The vision or purpose component of integrative leadership was also key. The high-capacity governments were focused governments. They did not try to do a little bit of everything but had clear strategic purposes and objectives and a clear plan for attaining them. Resources were carefully targeted, and evaluation information about the success of expenditures was monitored. The leaders or leadership teams were critical, because they enforced the boundaries set by the strategic statements. The tendency for mission and goals to expand with time, so common in many government programs and activities, was limited whenever possible so that both activities and resources stayed on target. This is obviously a political activity, and elected leaders in this group clearly believed, as did Harry Truman, that the buck stopped with them.

Again, we did not find political, income, or regional explanations or variations in capacity development. To be sure, two of the top city governments examined were city manager structures, but the GPP also found strong performance in governments with strong mayors and in commission structures such as that found in Minneapolis. Some of the governments found to be high capacity existed in relatively prosperous environments—Phoenix and Austin are examples, as, at the time of the analysis, were the states of Washington and Virginia—but resources alone did not allow these governments to solve problems or to address them strategically. They had used the resources available to them to create strategic management capacity, knowing that it would have to be used to address a broad variety of problems.

Research Products and Findings on Capacity and Performance

The GPP model and assumptions underpinning it were consistently reexamined by both the academic analysts and the participating governments—the latter at annual learning conferences. Still others used the data (and supplemental information) to examine both the linkages within the model and those between management capacity and other elements of policy choice and performance. That activity is ongoing, but a short summary of the relevant literature is presented in the following section.

While each area of government has prompted academic analysis and publication, the state level has been most frequently analyzed. In part, this is because it provides a manageable sample size that represents the entire universe of that level of government (although a sample of fifty places a strong limit on degrees of freedom in quantitative analysis). In contrast, data from city and county government samples suffered problems of representativeness, because these governments were chosen for geographic diversity as well as for dimensions of population and budget size.

The first set of studies related not to the actual data collected but to the theory and methods that underpinned the data collection. These studies are useful not only in directing our thinking about state and local government but also in informing additional thinking about management systems as targets of policy choice. Early publications focused on the underlying theory, the concept of management capacity, and the research methods by which this concept could be assessed. As noted previously, the revised black-box model addressed a critical void in public management theory. Explanation and exploration of the various dimensions has been a topic of some concern.[6] Explaining how these concepts could be used has also been a focus of ongoing analysis. Several authors have examined other potential measures of management.[7]

Data from the GPP and state governments as units of analysis have also been increasingly employed in theory development and testing. This work has sought to demonstrate the connections between capacity and performance and to show how capacity can be developed. At the broadest levels, political scientists have sought to explain what accounts for the overall capacity of governments, using GPP grades to examine how socioeconomic, political, and citizen preferences create government capacity across states.[8] Stephen Knack finds that more populous and more diverse states tend to have higher overall GPP grades.[9] At the level of citizen preferences and interests, research conducted by Knack and by David King, Richard Zeckhauser, and Mark Kim—drawing on Robert Putnam's hypothesis that social capital improves government—tests the effect of social capital.[10] The authors report a positive and significant relationship for the overall state grade—that is, for government's ability to manage its programs well.

Public management scholars have also used the data for more narrow analyses of capacity in specific management areas. The logic of this approach is to identify findings that not only engage in theory testing but also point to practical levers for capacity building and performance improvement. In some cases these analyses focus on how capacity in a particular management area was established. For example, Ed Kellough and Sally Coleman Selden note that states with more professional legislatures were likely to reform civil service systems, whereas more unionized states resisted such changes.[11] Jacobson, Rubin, and Selden identify the patterns associated with the development of training in states.[12] Other scholars have examined whether capacity had the intended effects on administrative measures of performance. For instance, Selden and Moynihan find that family-friendly policies have had a significant effect on one goal of most human resource management systems, reducing involuntary turnover among employees.[13] Hou, Moynihan, and Ingraham demonstrate that the creation of institutional rules has a positive impact on states' ability to maintain fiscal stabilization funds to counter economic downturns.[14]

The use of administrative measures of performance is clearly of interest to public management scholars, but the ultimate goal remains that of linking capacity to performance. This has proved difficult, in part, because there is a dearth of government performance measures collected in the same way across different governments. In fact, the absence of such measures has caused some scholars to use GPP grades as a proxy for government performance.[15] In addition, policy analysts have begun to tie state government capacity to measures of policy choices. Jerrell Coggburn and Saundra Schneider find that states with higher capacity tend to favor collective over specialized benefits in allocating resources.[16]

The ongoing research has also highlighted areas that warrant further attention, prompting case studies into topics such as reform implementation and citizen participation.[17] For multiple-case comparisons, grades provide a useful method for more systematic case sampling, where the different practices of high and low performers can be compared to assess distinct managerial practices.[18] Kenneth Meier and Laurence O'Toole have made good progress in linking other characteristics of management to specific performance measures (test scores) in school districts.[19]

Looking Forward: Questions for the Future

There are a number of items on future state and local research agendas. The thorny problem of successfully specifying a link between management capacity and performance is the obvious mountain in the path to greater clarity in determining precisely how, when, and why management matters. As noted above, the level of activity and organization at which the links might be made is not yet clear, nor is the extent to which capacity must be developed before an impact can be seen. At the same time, the research agenda around these questions is one of the richest in public management and public policy literature.[20]

The analyses presented in this book demonstrate that capacity can be developed in a variety of political and economic circumstances—and as chapter 8 notes, cannot be in others—but also illustrates the difficulties confronted even by high-capacity governments in feeding performance information back into critical decision-making loops. The grading analyses discussed in earlier chapters did not measure the external environmental influences that necessarily affect management capacity. However, some of the empirical analyses that have used GPP data have included control measures for the external environment. These reflect political conditions and institutions as well as socioeconomic factors. Other researchers have sought to measure these influences on capacity and performance as separate variables, further increasing knowledge in this area.[21] For example, Sanjay Pandey, David Coursey, and Donald Moynihan apply the black-box model to red-tape theory by examining the impact of delay in specific management systems on performance.[22] They find that red-tape in human resource management and information systems has a negative impact on employee-based performance measures, and they argue for including culture (that is, level of red tape) as an additional integrative factor to an amended future model.

Indeed, the role of administrative and management variables in broader governance frameworks is now the focus of a growing body of research.[23] A common purpose of this empirical study of governance is to identify and separate administrative capacity variables while controlling for other environmental influences. Just as the GPP has examined the concept of capacity in different management systems, Carolyn Heinrich, Laurence Lynn, and Carolyn Hill specify organizational treatments, structures, and managerial roles and actions as factors that shape performance. How such variables are defined and measured may vary slightly depending on the definition of performance employed, but there is a clear intent among such research efforts to identify broad theoretical constructs of management that can be applied in a variety of contexts.

Conclusion

The overall lesson of this book is that good management is fundamental to good government in states and municipalities across the United States. Elected and career officials in these governments recognize management's importance and increasingly are viewing management systems as policy tools to be used in the pursuit of better performance. The malleability of the systems and the willingness of state and local governments to tailor them to specific needs and purposes clearly point to the need to better understand how and when the link between management and performance is forged. The findings in this book demonstrate that there are multiple paths to building capacity in government; there will ultimately be many ways to examine the links between that capacity and better performance. At a time when demands on governments are becoming increasingly complex and difficult to meet, the constantly expanding role of state and local governments is ever more important. Understanding these governments and their policy options for managing their affairs is also increasing in importance.

State and local governments are not only laboratories of democracy, they are also incubators for ideas about alternative policy choices. As more and more policy responsibility devolves to them, the management and policy lessons to be learned have not been adequately gathered and examined. Furthermore, the U.S. federal government has not focused on developing the capacity of these critical lower levels of government. Consequently, the nation is behind the curve in learning from state and local experience. To close the gap, lessons such as those presented in this book will be critical. State and local governments and their many experiences with alternative management strategies and approaches are rich sources for learning about both success and failure in efforts to improve government performance and accountability. The analyses included here can be an important component of that learning process.

NOTES

1. Donald P. Moynihan, "Normative and Instrumental Perspectives on Public Participation: Citizen Summits in Washington, D.C.," *American Review of Public Administration* 33, no. 2 (2003): 164–88.

2. Donald P. Moynihan, "Managing for Results in an Impossible Job: Solution or Symbol?" *International Journal of Public Administration* 28, no. 3 (2005): 213–33.

3. Rockefeller Fiscal Service, "State Revenue Growth Continues in Most States," SRR 61, September 9, 2005, http://rfs.rockinst.org/pub/revenue (accessed March 4, 2006).

4. Patricia W. Ingraham, Jessica Sowa, and Donald P. Moynihan, "Linking Dimensions of Public Sector Leadership to Performance," in *The Art of Governance: Analyzing Management and Administration,* ed. Patricia W. Ingraham and Laurence E. Lynn Jr. (Washington, DC: Georgetown University Press, 2004), pp. 152–70.

5. Donald P. Moynihan and Patricia W. Ingraham, "Integrative Leadership in the Public Sector: A Model of Performance Information Use," *Administration and Society* 36, no. 4 (2004): 427–53.

6. Patricia W. Ingraham and Amy Kneedler Donahue, "Dissecting the Black Box Revisited: Characterizing Government Management Capacity," in *Government and Performance: New Perspectives*, ed. Carolyn J. Heinrich and Laurence E. Lynn Jr. (Washington, DC: Georgetown University Press, 2000), pp. 292–319.

7. See, for example, Kenneth Meier and Laurence O'Toole, "Public Management and Organizational Performance: The Impact of Managerial Quality," *Journal of Policy Analysis and Management* 21, no. 4 (2002): 629–43; and Rhys Andrews, George Boyne, and Richard Walker, "Strategy Content and Organizational Performance: An Empirical Analysis," *Public Administration Review* 66, no. 1 (2006): 52–63.

8. Steven Knack, "Social Capital and the Quality of Government: Evidence from the U.S. States," *American Journal of Political Science* 46, no. 4 (2002): 772–85; David C. King, Richard C. Zeckhauser, and Mark T. Kim, "The Management Performance of the U.S. States," 2002, http://ksghome.harvard.edu/~.dking.academic.ksg/Grading_States_v1.PDF.

9. Stephen Knack, "Aid Dependence and the Quality of Governance: A Cross-Country Empirical Analysis," Policy Research Working Paper (Washington, DC: World Bank, 2000).

10. King, Zeckhauser, and Kim, "Management Performance"; Robert Putnam, *Making Democracy Work: Civic Traditions in Modern Italy* (Princeton, NJ: Princeton University Press, 1993).

11. Ed Kellough and Sally Coleman Selden, "The Reinvention of Public Personnel Administration: An Analysis of the Diffusion of Personnel Management Reforms in the States," *Public Administration Review* 63, no. 2 (2003): 165–76.

12. Willow Jacobson, Ellen Rubin, and Sally Coleman Selden, "Examining Training in Large Municipalities: Linking Individual and Organizational Training Needs," *Public Personnel Management* 31, no. 4 (2002): 485–506.

13. Sally C. Selden and Donald P. Moynihan, "A Model of Voluntary Turnover in State Government," *Review of Public Personnel Administration* 20, no. 2 (2000): 63–75.

14. Yilin Hou, Donald P. Moynihan, and Patricia W. Ingraham, "Capacity, Management, and Performance: Exploring the Links," *American Review of Public Administration* 33, no. 3 (2003): 295–315.

15. King, Zeckhauser, and Kim, "Management Performance."

16. Jerrell D. Coggburn and Saundra Schneider, "The Quality of Management and Government Performance: An Empirical Analysis of the American States," *Public Administration Review* 63, no. 2 (2003): 206–13.

17. Matthew Andrews and Donald P. Moynihan, "Why Reforms Don't Always Have to Work to Succeed: A Tale of Two Managed Competition Initiatives," *Public Performance and Management Review* 25, no. 3 (2002): 282–97; Donald P.

Moynihan, "Normative and Instrumental Perspectives on Public Participation: Citizen Summits in Washington D.C.," *American Review of Public Administration* 33, no. 2 (2003): 164–88.

18. Donald P. Moynihan and Patricia W. Ingraham, "Look for the Silver Lining: When Performance-Based Accountability Systems Work," *Journal of Public Administration Research and Theory* 13, no. 4 (2003): 469–90.

19. Kenneth Meier and Laurence J. O'Toole Jr., "Public Management in Intergovernmental Networks: Matching Structural and Behavioral Networks," *Journal of Public Administration Research and Theory* 14, no. 4 (2004): 469–94.

20. Hal G. Rainey and Jay E. Ryu, "Framing High Performance and Innovativeness in Government: A Review and Assessment of Research," in *The Art of Governance: Analyzing Management and Administration,* ed. Patricia W. Ingraham and Laurence E. Lynn Jr. (Washington, DC: Georgetown University Press, 2004), pp. 20–45.

21. Amy K. Donahue, "The Influence of Management on the Cost of Fire Protection," *Journal of Policy Analysis and Management* 23, no. 1 (2004): 71–92; Yilin Hou, "Subnational Counter-Cyclical Fiscal Policies: Testing the Effects of Budget Stabilization Funds and General Fund Surpluses on State Expenditures" (PhD diss., Maxwell School of Citizenship and Public Affairs, Syracuse University, 2002); Knack, "Social Capital"; Kenneth Meier, Laurence J. O' Toole Jr., and Sean Nicholson-Crotty, "Multilevel Governance and Organizational Performance: Investigating the Political Bureaucratic Myth," *Journal of Policy Analysis and Management* 23, no. 1 (2004): 34–47.

22. Sanjay K. Pandey, David Coursey, and Donald P. Moynihan, "Management Capacity and Organizational Performance: Can Organizational Culture Trump Bureaucratic Red Tape?" paper presented at Determinants of Performance in Public Organizations seminar, Cardiff, Wales, May 6–8, 2005.

23. Carolyn J. Heinrich, Lawrence E. Lynn Jr., and Carolyn J. Hill, *Improving Governance: A New Logic for Empirical Research* (Washington, DC: Georgetown University Press, 2001); Ingraham and Lynn, *Art of Governance.*

The Analytical Model for the GPP

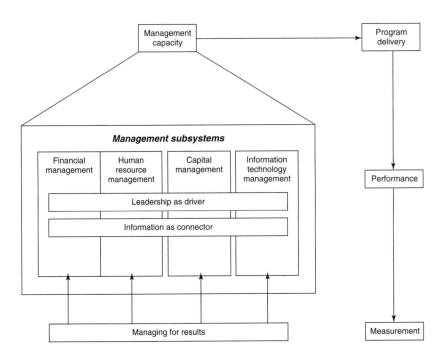

Criteria Used by GPP Analysts

The Government Performance Project conducted criteria-based assessments in the five areas of government management: financial management, human resource management, information technology management, capital management, and managing for results. Senior advisory panels consisting of academics and practitioners developed the criteria, which were later refined based on direct feedback from governments evaluated by the project. Following are descriptions of the five management areas and the criteria on which their assessments were based.

Financial management focuses on budget allocation, forecasting, budget execution, accounting, financial reporting, debt management, and investment. The criteria for financial management are as follows:

- Government has a multiyear perspective on budgeting.
- Government has mechanisms that preserve stability and fiscal health.
- Sufficient financial information is available to policy makers, managers, and citizens.
- Government has appropriate control over financial operations.

Human resource management focuses on workforce planning, hiring, retention, reward and discipline, and training. The criteria for human resource management are as follows:

- Government conducts strategic analysis of present and future human resource needs.
- Government is able to obtain the employees it needs.
- Government is able to maintain an appropriately skilled workforce.
- Government is able to motivate employees to perform effectively in support of its goals.
- Government has a civil service structure that supports its ability to achieve its workforce goals.

Information technology management focuses on uses of IT systems in management: hardware and software performance, integration with other management systems, training, cost, and reporting capability. The criteria for IT management are as follows:

- Government-wide and agency-level IT systems provide information that adequately supports managers' needs and strategic goals.
- Government's IT systems form a coherent architecture.
- Government conducts meaningful, multiyear IT planning.
- IT training is adequate.
- Government can evaluate and validate the extent to which IT system benefits justify investment.
- Government can procure the IT systems needed in a timely manner.
- IT systems support the government's ability to communicate with and provide services to its citizens.

Capital management focuses on long-term planning, initial construction or purchasing justification, capital and operating budget interaction, and maintenance. The criteria for capital management are as follows:

- Government conducts thorough analysis of future needs.
- Government monitors and evaluates projects throughout their implementation.
- Government conducts appropriate maintenance of capital assets.

Managing for results focuses on strategic planning, performance measurement, and the implementation of performance information. The criteria for managing for results are as follows:

- Government engages in results-oriented strategic planning.
- Government develops indicators and evaluative data that can measure progress toward results and accomplishments.
- Leaders and managers use results data for policy making, management, and evaluation of progress.
- Government clearly communicates the results of its activities to stakeholders.

Governments Evaluated by the GPP

Table C.1. Cities and Grades

City	Average grade	Financial management	Human resources management	Information technology management	Capital management	Managing for results
Anchorage	C	C+	C	C	B−	C−
Atlanta	C+	B−	B−	D+	C	B−
Austin	A−	A	A−	B	A−	A−
Baltimore	B−	B+	C+	C	B	B
Boston	B−	B−	C−	B	B+	C+
Buffalo	C−	C	D	C	C−	D+
Chicago	B−	B	C−	B−	B+	C+
Cleveland	C	B−	C−	C−	B−	C
Columbus	C	B−	C−	D+	B−	D
Dallas	C+	B+	C	D+	B−	B
Denver	B−	B+	B−	C+	B−	B−
Detroit	B−	B−	B−	B−	C	B−
Honolulu	B	B−	C	B+	A−	B
Houston	C+	B+	C	C−	B−	B−
Indianapolis	B+	B	A−	B	B+	A−
Jacksonville	B−	B	C+	C	B	B
Kansas City	B−	B+	B	C	B+	B−
Long Beach	B	A−	C	B	B	B−
Los Angeles	C	B−	C−	C−	C+	C−
Memphis	C+	B	D	C	B	B−
Milwaukee	B	B+	C+	B−	B+	A−
Minneapolis	B+	A−	B	A−	B+	B−
Nashville	C+	B	B	D+	C+	C−
New Orleans	C−	C−	F	B−	B−	D+
New York	B	B	B−	B	B+	B
Philadelphia	B	B−	B−	B+	B−	B
Phoenix	A	A	A	A−	A	A
Richmond	C+	B	C	C	C−	C+
San Antonio	B	B+	B+	B−	B	B+
San Diego	B	B+	C	C	B+	A−
San Francisco	C+	B	C	C+	C+	C
San Jose	B−	B+	C	C	A−	C+
Seattle	B	B+	B	B	B+	B
Virginia Beach	B+	A−	B	B	A−	B
Washington	C+	B−	B−	C+	C	C+

Table C.2. Counties and Grades

County	Average grade	Financial management	Human resources management	Information technology management	Capital management	Managing for results
Alameda, CA	C+	C+	D+	B	B−	C
Allegheny, PA	D	C−	D−	D	D+	D
Anne Arundel, MD	C	C+	C	B	C−	D+
Baltimore, MD	B+	A−	B−	A−	A−	B
Broward, FL	B−	B+	B+	C+	C+	B
Clark, NV	C+	B+	C−	C	C+	B
Contra Costa, CA	B−	B−	B−	B−	B−	C−
Cook, IL	C+	B−	D	B−	C+	B−
Cuyahoga, OH	C	B	C−	D+	C−	B−
Dallas, TX	B	B+	B+	B−	B−	B
Erie, NY	C+	B−	C−	B	C+	C
Fairfax, VA	A−	A−	A−	A	A−	A−
Franklin, OH	B	B	B−	C+	B+	B
Fulton, GA	C	B−	C	C−	C	C
Hamilton, OH	B	B	B	C+	B+	B+
Harris, TX	C+	B−	C+	C+	B−	C+
Hennepin, MN	B	B+	B−	B+	B+	B
Hillsborough, FL	C	B	D	C−	C	C+
King, WA	C	B−	D+	C−	B	C
Los Angeles, CA	C	B−	B−	C−	D+	C+
Maricopa, AZ	A−	A−	B+	A	B+	A−
Mecklenburg, NC	B	B−	B	B	C+	B+
Miami-Dade, FL	C+	B−	B−	D+	C	B−
Milwaukee, WI	B−	C+	C+	B−	C+	B
Monroe, NY	C	C	C−	D	B	C
Montgomery, AL	B	B+	B+	B−	C	B+
Nassau, NY	D−	F	D	D+	D−	F
Oakland, MI	B	B	B	A−	B−	C
Orange, CA	B	B	B−	A−	B	C+
Palm Beach, FL	C+	B	C	C−	B	B−
Prince George's, MD	B−	B+	B−	B+	C	C+

(continued)

Table C.2. Counties and Grades (*continued*)

County	Average grade	Financial management	Human resources management	Information technology management	Capital management	Managing for results
Riverside, CA	C+	B−	B	C	C−	C
Sacramento, CA	C+	B−	C	C+	C−	B−
San Bernardino, CA	C−	C	C−	D+	C−	D
San Diego, CA	B+	A−	B−	B+	A−	A−
Santa Clara, CA	C+	B	C+	D+	B−	C−
Shelby, TN	B	B	B	B−	B	B−
Suffolk, NY	C−	B−	C−	C	B−	F
Wayne, MI	B−	B−	B−	B−	B−	C+
Westchester, NY	C+	B	D+	B−	A−	D+

Table C.3. States and Grades

County	Average grade	Financial management	Human resources management	Information technology management	Capital management	Managing for results
Alameda, CA	C+	C+	D+	B	B−	C
Alabama	D / C−	D+ / C+	C− / D+	D / C−	D− / D+	F / D+
Alaska	C / C	C / C	C− / C	C− / B	C+ / C	C− / C−
Arizona	C / C+	B− / C	C+ / C	D+ / B−	D+ / C+	B− / C+
Arkansas	C−	B− / B−	C+ / C	D / C−	C / C	D / C−
California	C− / C+	C− / B−	C− / C	C+ / B−	C− / C+	C− / C−
Colorado	C+ / C+	C / C+	B / B−	C / C	C / B	C / C+
Connecticut	C− / C	C− / C	C− / C	D+ / C+	C+ / B−	D+C−
Delaware	B / B+	A− / A−	B / B	B / B	B / B+	B / B
Florida	C+ / B−	B / B	C+ / B−	C− / C+	C / B−	B / B+
Georgia	C+ / B−	C+ / B−	B− / B−	C / C+	C / B−	C+ / B−
Hawaii	C− / C	C− / C	C− / C	F / C−	B− / B	C− / C
Idaho	C / B−	B− / C+	C / B	D+ / B	B− / B−	C− / C−
Illinois	B− / B	B+ / B+	B / B	D+ / C+	B− / B	C / B−
Indiana	C+ / B−	B / B−	C+ / B	C / B−	C / B−	C / B−
Iowa	B / B+	A− / A−	B+ / B+	C+ / B	B− / B+	B+ / A−
Kansas	B− / B	B− / B−	B+ / B+	C+ / A−	B / B	C / C+
Kentucky	B / B+	B+ / A−	B / B+	C+ / B+	A− / B+	B / B+
Louisiana	B− / B−	B− / C	C+ / B	C− / B−	B / B	B / B+
Oklahoma	C / C	B− / C+	C− / C−	C− / B−	C / C	D+ / D+
Oregon	B− / C+	B / B−	C+ / C	C+ / C	B− / B−	B+ / B
Pennsylvania	B / B+	A− / A−	B / B+	B / B+	B / B	B− / B
Rhode Island	C− / C	B− / B−	F / C−	D / D	C+ / C+	C / C
South Carolina	B / B+	B+ / A−	A− / A	B / B	B− / C+	B− / B
South Dakota	B− / C+	B+ / B−	C+ / B−	B / B	B / B−	D / D
Tennessee	B− / B−	B / C	C+ / B−	B+ / B+	B− / C	C / B−
Texas	B / B	B / B+	B / B	B / B−	C / B	B+ / A−
Utah	A− / A−	A / A	B+ / B−	B+ / A	A / A−	B+ / B+
Vermont	B− / B−	B / B	B− / C	C / C+	B / B−	B− / B
Virginia	A− / B+	A / B+	B / B+	A− / A−	A / B+	A− / A−
Washington	A− / A−	A− / B+	B+ / A−	A / A	A / A−	B+ / A−
West Virginia	C+ / C	B / B−	C+ / C+	C / C−	C+ / C	C / C
Wisconsin	B / B−	C+ / C+	B+ / A−	B / B−	A− / B+	C / C
Wyoming	C / C	C+ / B−	B− / C+	D+ / C−	C+ / D	C / C+

Note: Grades based on the 1998 evaluation are listed first. Grades after the 2000 evaluation are given second.

Contributors

Donna Dufner is an associate professor of the College of Information Science and Technology at the University of Nebraska, Omaha. She holds a PhD in management (computer and information science) from Rutgers University; an MS in computer and information science from the New Jersey Institute of Technology; and an MBA from the University of Chicago. She has published in a wide variety of journals, including *Journal of Group Decision and Negotiation, Journal of Organizational Computing, Communications of the Association of Information Systems (CAIS)*, and *Public Productivity and Management Review.* Dr. Dufner's research interests are asynchronous group support systems, asynchronous learning networks, project management, and service learning.

Carol Ebdon is an associate professor in the School of Public Administration at the University of Nebraska, Omaha. Her research interests are in the areas of state and local budgeting and finance. Recent publications include studies on citizen participation in the budget process, local government revenue diversification, tax structures, and capital management practices. Dr. Ebdon's most recent article, "Searching for a Role for Citizens in the Budget Process," was published in 2004 in *Public Budgeting and Finance.*

Dana Michael Harsell is an assistant professor of political science and public administration at the University of North Dakota in Grand Forks. He teaches courses in American government, public administration, and public management. His research interests include administrative reform, government performance, and public management. Dr. Harsell holds a BA in political science and psychology and an MA in political science, both from the University of Montana, and a PhD in political science from Syracuse University.

Lyn Meridew Holley is an assistant professor at the University of Nebraska, Omaha. Dr. Holley has published articles in several journals, including *Public Performance Management Review* and *Communications of the Association of Information Systems (CAIS)*, as well as chapters in *Leadership for America: Rebuilding Public Service, New Strategies for Public Pay,* and the Marcel Dekker *Encyclopedia of Public Administration.* Research in progress relates to the policy and management dimensions of the delivery of services to the elderly, public management of human resources, and the special challenges of serving minority and ethnic elders.

Yilin Hou holds a PhD from the Maxwell School of Citizenship and Public Affairs, Syracuse University. He is an associate professor in the Department of Public Administration and Policy, School of Public and International Affairs, University of Georgia. He conducts research in public finance and budgeting and in strategic management. His recent publications, focusing on fiscal and budgetary stabilization and fiscal policy at the state level, have appeared in *Public Budgeting and Finance, Public Administration Review, American Review of Public Administration,* and *Encyclopedia of Public Administration and Public Policy.*

Patricia W. Ingraham is founding dean of the College of Community and Public Affairs, Binghamton University. Her most recent book is *The Art of Governance: Analyzing Management and Administration* (edited with Laurence E. Lynn Jr.). She is the author or editor of ten other books. She has published extensively on issues related to civil service systems, administrative reform, and performance in public organizations. Her current research focuses on leadership and organizational effectiveness. Dr. Ingraham has been recognized for distinguished contributions to the joint tradition of political science and public administration by the American Political Science Association (the 2004 John Gaus award), the American Society for Public Administration (the Dwight Waldo and the Paul Von Riper awards), and Syracuse University (the Chancellor's Distinguished Research award).

Willow S. Jacobson is an assistant professor in the School of Government at the University of North Carolina, Chapel Hill. She specializes in human resource management, organizational theory, and public management. Dr. Jacobson's research has appeared in *Public Administration Review* and *Public Personnel Management.*

Dale Jones is an associate professor of public administration in the L. Douglas Wilder School of Government and Public Affairs at Virginia Commonwealth University, where he is also director of the National Homeland Security Project. Dr. Jones's research focuses on homeland security, collaboration among agencies, and leadership and management of public sector organizations. He has published in *Public Administration Review* and *American Review of Public Administration* and is the author of the book, *Downsizing the Federal Government: The Management of Public Sector Workforce Reductions.* He earned a PhD in public administration from Syracuse University, an MA in public policy from George Washington University, an MBA in management from Wright State University, and a BS in aeronautical engineering from the U.S. Air Force Academy.

Donald P. Moynihan is an assistant professor at the LaFollette Institute at the University of Wisconsin, Madison. He studies public management reforms, especially in the areas of performance management, homeland security, and citizen participation. He has published in a number of edited volumes and journals, including *Public Administration Review, Journal of Public Administration Research and Theory, Administration and Society,* and *American Review of Public Administration.* In 2002 he won the award for best journal article from the Public and Nonprofit Division of the Academy of Management. He received his PhD in public administration from the Maxwell School at Syracuse University.

Ora-orn Poocharoen is on the Faculty of Political Science at Chulalongkorn University, Thailand. She earned bachelor of law and master of law degrees from Hitotsubashi University and the University of Tokyo in Japan, respectively. She received her PhD in public administration at the Maxwell School of Citizenship and Public Affairs, Syracuse University. Her current fields of interest are public management, public sector reforms, comparative public administration, and development administration. She has presented papers at international conferences on topics including new public management, managing for results, and human resource management.

B. J. Reed has been on the faculty of the University of Nebraska, Omaha, since 1982. He served as chairman of the department from 1985 to 2000 and as dean of the College of Public Affairs and Community Service since the fall of 2000. He has published in numerous journals, including *Public Administration Review, American Review of Public Administration, Inter-*

national Journal of Public Administration, Public Productivity and Management Review, and *Public Budgeting and Finance.* He is the author of several books on diverse topics, including economic development, strategic planning, financial administration, and intergovernmental management. He served as president of the National Council of the National Association of Schools of Public Affairs and Administration in 2003–4 and was inducted into the National Academy of Public Administration in 2005.

Sally Coleman Selden is an associate professor of management at Lynchburg College. Dr. Selden's articles have appeared in *American Journal of Political Science, Administration and Society, American Review of Public Administration, Review of Public Personnel Administration, Journal of Public Administration Education, Public Administration Review,* and *Journal of Public Administration Research and Theory.*

Index

Page numbers followed by *b* refer to boxes, by *f* refer to figures, and by *t* refer to tables.